Education and Class

Education and Class

The Irrelevance of IQ Genetic Studies

Michel Schiff
CNRS and INSERM

Richard Lewontin
Harvard University

with contributions from
A. Dumaret, M. Duyme, J. Feingold, J. Schulz, and S. Tomkiewicz

CLARENDON PRESS · OXFORD
1986

Oxford University Press, Walton Street, Oxford OX2 6DP
Oxford New York Toronto
Delhi Bombay Calcutta Madras Karachi
Petaling Jaya Singapore Hong Kong Tokyo
Nairobi Dar Es Salaam Cape Town
Melbourne Auckland
and associated companies in
Beirut Berlin Ibadan Nicosia

Oxford is a trade mark of Oxford University Press

Published in the United States
by Oxford University Press, New York

British Library Cataloguing in Publication Data
Schiff, Michel
Education and class: the irrelevance of
IQ genetic studies.
1. Intellect — Genetic aspects
2. Nature and nurture
I. Title II. Lewontin, Richard C.
153.9'2 BF431
ISBN 0–19–857599–8

Library of Congress Cataloging in Publication Data
Michel, Schiff.
Education and class.
Bibliography: p.
Includes index.
1. Intellect—Genetic aspects. 2. Intelligence
levels—Social aspects. 3. Nature and nurture.
I. Lewontin, Richard C., 1929– . II. Title.
BF431.M46 1986 153.9'2 86–2563
ISBN 0–19–857599–8

Set by
Promenade Graphics Ltd, Cheltenham
Printed in Great Britain by
J. W. Arrowsmith Ltd, Bristol

Foreword

by A. H. Halsey

Professor Social and Administrative Studies, University of Oxford

I believe this book to be an important contribution to the nature–nurture controversy. That the controversy itself is important will not be denied – for it underlies our conceptions of what human achievements are possible and how mankind can attain its best possible self. What can be denied is the utility of repeating either old dogma or contested theory. The formula for a worthwhile contribution is to produce crucial new empirical evidence to test a precise theoretical proposition. The ideological implications can, under those conditions, be properly expounded. Michel Schiff and Richard Lewontin seem to me to have followed the formula triumphantly.

Those who are unfamiliar with the field might immediately question the need for any reference to ideology in a book about a problem in natural or social science. Unhappily such reference is indispensable. The science of human affairs may, and does, aspire to value-free objectivity. How far that idea of human science is attainable is too complex a subject to be satisfactorily answered in a foreword: but three relevant points can be made. First, all the great masters of the human sciences – Weber, Marx, Durkheim, Freud *et al* – have been motivated by passionate concern with the political, social or cultural issues of their day. The choice of problem is legitimately so made. Objectivity in that sense is a methodological ideal. Secondly, as a matter of historical fact, theories of human differences (between individuals, races, classes, or sexes) have been generated and almost as often vitiated by prejudice which has intruded not only into the posing of questions but, fatally, into the methods of obtaining answers.

Thirdly and therefore, the book is welcome in that the authors steadfastly and indeed belligerently declare their ideological bias to environmentalism, proceed to produce a clear, empirically-based answer to a central theoretical question; and they go further to discuss methodological and conceptual issues in such a way as to demonstrate that their ideological preconceptions are both separate from and a source of illumination of the difficulties of concept and method.

The structure of the book is well designed to bring out the characteristics I have praised. Personal interests are announced in the introduction. In Part I the announced engagement is elaborated into an argued view of the history and present state of the literature on inequality, its biological and social origins, and the nature of intelligence testing. In Part II there is an account of Schiff's remarkable enquiry into children of blue-collar origin

v

adopted into upper-middle-class families, and an analysis of the degree to
which universities are meritocratic in the sense of accessible to talent irres
pective of its social origin. Then, in Part III, the reader is led into illuminat-
ing technical discussion of theory and measurement of genetics, social
structure, and the IQ scores.

The book as a whole is accordingly a refreshing experience – a balanced
exposition of values and investigations. It will refresh the reader by happy
contrast with the recent exposure of Sir Cyril Burt as a dominating figure
who slid from obsession through pseudo-science into outright fraud. Schiff
and Lewontin have restored our confidence that passion can ascend
through meticulous science to genuine theoretical advance.

The first of their investigated questions in Part II is a direct and contrary
answer to the problem posed by Professor Jensen in his controversial
article 'How much could we boost IQ and scholastic achievement?'. The
second is highly relevant to the current virtually world-wide debate about
the expansion or contraction of universities and the social openness of
access to them. With respect to the second study, some will say that the
issue of individual differences in intelligence is not important because what
really matters is social efficiency. Our power over our lives is immensely
greater than that of our ancestors, not because we are genetically different
from them, but because we have found ways of storing and using inven-
tions. Cultural evolution has made us more able to live longer, and to
dominate our world much more than our forbears. We are much more
clever, though our mental capacity has not changed.

In another sense, however, individual differences concern us because in
the modern world people are given educational opportunities and jobs on
the basis of tests which predict their competence to use the opportunities or
to do the jobs well. People are then rewarded differentially with unequal
incomes and unequal prestige or status. On this view, it follows that the
explanation of differences in capacity – perhaps especially mental capacity
– is crucially important.

Some of the argument is highly technical so it may be helpful if I define
what is meant by the heritability of IQ. First IQ (or intelligence quotient) is
essentially a score on answers to questions requiring the exercise of reasoning, whether verbal or non-verbal. IQ tests are conventionally standardized so that for the population as a whole the average person scores 100,
and the proportion of all people scoring higher or lower falls at each step
away from the average. The question is what causes variations in IQ – the
genes or the environment?

Heritability is the proportion of the total variance which is attributable
to genetic factors in the population at that time. If all variance in IQ scores
was due to genetic variation, then the heritability of IQ would be one. If
environmental factors accounted for all IQ score differences, heritability

would be zero. No one, to my knowledge, believes in a heritability of one, and very few believe in a figure of nought. But the figure of 0.7 or 0.8 – that is, 70 per cent or 80 per cent determination of IQ by genes – can be found in many psychology textbooks.

Strictly speaking such an assertion is meaningless untill a time and population are specified. Let me explain why. Suppose, however implausibly, a group of people all came from repeated division of the same fertilized egg. They would all have exactly the same genetic make-up. Hence any differences between them in IQ would be environmentally caused. Heritability would be zero. Now, suppose that the population has genetic variety, but all children are brought up in an exactly uniform environment. Then all IQ differences would come from genetic differences. Heritability would be one. So putting the two extreme hypothetical examples together, the heritability of IQ – or indeed of any other trait – is a function of the amount of variation, genetic and environmental, in the population. If either changes, so does the heritability of IQ.

So much for the vocabulary of the debate. In a recent radio conversation I discussed all this with Professor Jensen asking him first to review the evidence from studies of separated identical twins. He quickly dismissed Burt: 'The most famous study of separated identical twins was that of Sir Cyril Burt which has since been discredited. Some of the data are probably fictitious, and since we don't know just which part is fictitious, we have to throw out all of it'. Jensen confirmed that the elimination of Burt reduced the number of separated identical twin cases from 120 to 67, but stressed the meticulous method of a current study at the University of Minnesota which like three other such studies, yields a heritability measure of 0.70. He believes in this estimate: 'Most of the correlation would have to be due to their having common genes rather than to common environment because they were reared in disparate environments'.

I challenged this assumption. Critics of separated twin studies have hinged their argument largely on the question of how disparate the environments of separated twins really have been. In previous studies there was not a random allocation of the separated twins over all social conditions so that the correlation that was shown could be attributed just as plausibly to restricted environmental variance as to genetic differences. But Jensen did not entirely concede the point.

Although these twins have been reared in environments that are probably correlated to some extent – more so than environments picked at random from the population – the correlation is still much higher than that of unrelated children who are reared together in the same home, or of ordinary siblings or fraternal twins (who have half of their genes in common) who are reared together. The correlation for ordinary siblings and fraternal twins is about 0.5, and I don't think anyone could argue that their environments are less similar than the environments of twins who were separated.

We then moved to the evidence on children moved at or near birth to a different environment – the studies of adopted children. Jensen again maintained that the evidence supported the notion that intelligence is substantially inherited. In this connection I referred particularly to the study by Michel Schiff and his colleagues of children born to mothers in unskilled jobs and adopted before six months by upper-middle-class families. Schiff's work, I insisted, was remarkable for its painstaking avoidance of interfering with the lives of those in this 'natural laboratory'. The mothers were not directly contacted, and the adopted children were always tested with at least two others from their school class to avoid labelling them as special cases. These adopted children, by being catapulted into professional families, had their IQs raised 14 points, and were thoroughly assimilated to upper-middle-class norms of educational achievement.

Jensen, while still sticking to the view that within the more or less uniformly good environment of an upper-middle-class home, 'a very large part of the variation among persons is due to genetic factors', also observed that a good environment will have favourable effects on IQ. His emphasis, however, shifted:

if the environment is already quite adequate – a good humane environment where the child has plenty of freedom to explore the physical environment, to interact with his social environment, and to attend normal school, and so forth – any other kinds of interventions that we presently know how to do will not have any dramatic effects on the child's IQ.

This point is of great importance for social policy. I reminded Professor Jensen of the notoriety he attracted in his *Harvard Educational Review* article of 1969 in which he asked how far IQs could be boosted by schooling, and in which he gave gloomy answers derived from his genetic views. The Headstart programmes were declared a failure, but both the debate and attempts at positive discrimination went on. But an American consortium of studies led by Lazar and Darlington brought critically revised evidence in 1980, establishing the existence of lasting effects from preschooling in four main ways. First, they show that the beneficiaries are less likely to be assigned later to special or remedial classes. This effect of preschooling was shown to be there for children of the same initial IQ, sex, ethnicity, and family background. It persisted even when the comparison was controlled for IQ scores at age six.

Secondly, there has been the same lasting effect with respect to drop-out from school, and what the Americans call 'retention in grade', i.e. being held back to repeat a year's work because of poor performance. According to the evidence of the eight projects which had collected the relevant data, early educational experience protects against these failures. The protection holds for all poor children regardless of sex, ethnic backgrounds, early IQ, and family circumstances.

Thirdly, achievement in mathematics at age 10 (fourth grade) is significantly improved by pre-schooling. The evidence also suggests a trend to better scores on reading tests at the same age.

Fourthly, children from poor families who went to pre-school programmes scored higher than the 'control' children on the Stanford Binet IQ test for up to three years afterwards. In some projects, this superiority was maintained, but not among those who were aged 13 or over.

Jensen's reply showed some hope of agreement between us. He thought that Headstart programmes had had beneficial effects but not on intelligence and attainment so much as attitudes to school and behavioural problems.

Yet, I asked, had subsequent evidence really changed his 1969 view about group differences, particularly racial differences, in intelligence? And we were again at odds. Jensen was 'more firmly convinced' than in 1969 that 'it is a reasonable hypothesis that genetic factors are implicated in Black/White IQ differences ', although 'it is still a question about which we have to remain scientifically agnostic because in the years since 1969 no definitive evidence has come forth that would settle this question'.

I am convinced that the evidence produced here by Schiff and Lewontin marks a crucial step forward in the weight of evidence in favour of those who insist on the importance of environmental, and especially class, influence on intellectual development.

Those who adhere to more heriditarian views will not necessarily be convinced. But those among them who, like Jensen, are scientists first and ideologues second may well accept the implications of this book for social policy. In my conversation with Jensen I offered the conclusion that scientific resources should be concentrated on demonstrating the best method of redressing the unfairness of group differences in educational attainment, and Jensen concurred 'absolutely, absolutely. Any forms of racial discrimination, based simply on a person's racial ancestry, should be rooted out wherever we find it. I have no argument with that and, in fact, I've advocated that all my life'.

We thus established a crucially important island of agreement in a sea of disagreement. Racial differences, I added, whether genetic or not, are not as large as individual differences within any racial group, so there is no reason why anyone should have to be treated on the basis of his race. Race is a poor clue to any important human traits. It is a scientific fact, with a strong political implication, that individual differences on either view are more important than almost any group differences which might form the basis for political organization. And we can go further and say that differences between individual people in their capacity to do jobs, do not tell us clearly and unequivocally how differently people should be rewarded for what they do. So a good deal of the sting can be taken out of the scientific controversy by making it clear that there are not straightforward policy implications from any particular scientific view. It is perfectly possible for readers in either Jensen's or Schiff's and Lewontin's position to be strongly opposed to social discriminations of any kind against any social group.

Preface

Personal introduction: Michel Schiff

After ten years of research in high energy nuclear physics, I decided to change fields and eventually ended up in a field which is at the frontier between genetics and psychology: human behaviour genetics. As I was making this switch, a geneticist told me that if I was interested in behaviour genetics, I should work with rats rather than with people. Since I was interested in people rather than in rats, I stuck to my original project. Except for some theoretical work on genetics and schizophrenia, I have concentrated my efforts on IQ and school achievement.

In 1970, I happened to read the second edition of Stern's textbook of human genetics. At the time, I knew virtually nothing about IQ and the genetic studies of IQ scores. However, I had a strong environmental bias, so what I read in this textbook appeared very strange to me. As I decided to look into this issue more deeply, I had no idea that I would stay with it for so long.

One of the first papers I read was Jensen's article entitled, 'How much can we boost IQ and scholastic achievement?' There again, Jensen's implicit answer (not much) was contrary to my intuitive conviction. In 1913, an English author named Richardson had posed a related question: what would happen if 'offspring of poor parents' were reared from birth by 'well-to-do and well-educated families'? It became gradually clear to me that, in spite of the fact that Richardson's question lay behind the whole nature-–nurture controversy concerning IQ, nobody had attempted to answer it directly. The adoption study designed to answer this question was performed between 1972 and 1977, and its main result appeared in *Science* in 1978.

In 1937, three authors, reporting on the first study of separated twins, made the following comment concerning the evolution of their thinking on the nature–nurture issue (Newman *et al. 1937*):

If, at the inception of this research project over ten years ago, the authors entertained any hope of reaching a definitive solution of the general nature–nurture problem or even of any large section of the subordinate problems involved, in terms of a simple formula, they were destined to be rather disillusioned.

Thirteen years after initiating the study of working-class children adopted early into upper-middle-class families, I could express my conclusion about *the* nature–nurture issue in similar terms. Even more important, I now realize that questions concerning genetic effects are essentially irrelevant to social issues I care about like access to education.

Before attempting to answer any apparently factual question, we should take a serious look at the question itself: Why is the question formulated in this particular manner? what could alternate answers be? what would each of these alternate answers mean? what is the best empirical way of distinguishing in an unambiguous way between the possible alternatives? This sort of preliminary inquiry is, of course, needed for any scientific question, but nowhere has it been so necessary and so conspicuously lacking as in the IQ controversy. I hope that this book will make the point clear.

Personal introduction: Richard Lewontin

The problem of inequality consumes our social consciousness. In a society whose foundation is said to rest on principles of liberty, equality, and fraternity, the persistence of gross inequalities of status, wealth, and power is a particularly unsettling source of anguish. One explanation of inequality has been that family and social environment are unequal, producing groups of 'disadvantaged' people: blacks, women, members of the working class. Since, 200 years after the American and French Revolutions, immense social inequalities remain, any theory of the social origin of inequality carries with it the serious possibility that there are deep structural defects in our social organization. A more generally accepted theory has been that inequalities are a manifestation of inherent and unalterable biological differences between people. Such a biological determinist theory, then, both explains as natural and justifies as inevitable the social inequalities of which we are a part.

As a biologist, and a geneticist in particular, I have, of course, a professional interest in any theory that attempts to explain social relations by recourse to claims about biology. Moreover, the particular biological issues raised are directly relevant to my own scientific development and expertise. My first research, as a PhD student, concerned the way in which genetic differences between organisms were manifested in different environments. That work, and everything I have learned since, has taught me that the organism is not determined by its genes, although its different traits are undoubtedly influenced to varying degrees by its genetic constitution. Most of my mature research life has been devoted to the other biological question raised by theories of inherent inequality: the problem of how much genetic variation actually exists between individuals within a species. The chief lesson of that work has been the extreme difficulty of measuring genetic variation in anatomical and behavioural traits, even in experimental organisms, and its near impossibility in human beings. Thus, my work as a biologist has led me to be extremely sceptical of claims that one or another intellectual or temperamental ability is a fixed, inherited property that differentiates one person from another.

Just as theories of innate differences arise from political issues, so my own interest in those theories arises not merely from their biological content but from political considerations as well. As I was growing up, Fascism was spreading in Europe, and with it theories of racial superiority. The impact of the Nazi use of biological arguments to justify mass murders and sterilization was enormous on my generation of high school students. The political misuses of science, and particularly of biology, were uppermost in our consciousness as we studied genetics, evolution, and race. That consciousness has never left me, and it has daily sources of refreshment as I see, over and over again, claims of the biological superiority of one race, one sex, one class, one nation. I have a strong sense of the historical continuity of biological determinist arguments at the same time that my professional research experience has shown me how poorly they are grounded in the nature of the physical world. I have had no choice, then, but to examine with the greatest possible care questions of what role, if any, biology plays in the structure of social inequality.

Introducing the book

As its title indicates, the main goal of the book is *not* to provide the latest information concerning the genetic analysis of IQ scores or the latest word in mental testing. On the contrary, we try to show that, as far as education is concerned, most genetic studies are not only unsound but are also irrelevant.

Another goal is to caution the reader against the illusion of objectivity in certain areas of academic research. Our second focus, then, is neither the genetics of IQ scores nor social discrimination in education; it is the functioning of academia, within a certain field.

In February of 1969, A. R. Jensen published a long article in the *Harvard Educational Review* entitled, 'How much can we boost IQ and scholastic achievement?' Using a simplified genetic model to analyse the correlation between IQ scores of various types of relatives, the author drew two conclusions:

(*a*) The mean scholastic and psychometric differences usually observed between black and white children probably have a broad genetic base.

(*b*) While he did not give any quantitative or explicit answer to the question posed in the title of his article, Jensen strongly implied that the answer was 'not much'.

Even if, for the sake of argument, one accepted the existence of a quantity such as the 'heritability of IQ' and even if one accepted Jensen's high estimate of this hypothetical quantity, this estimate would lead to neither of the two conclusions outlined above. This has been known for over half a century, so that specialists might wonder why we decided to add to the information pollution created by the controversy over the genetics of IQ scores.

We believe that this book will be useful to graduate students and to research workers in the human sciences who have been mystified by highly technical writings, particularly in the field of human behaviour genetics. The facts presented in the central part of the book stem from original research; what is more important, they have a relevance to the issue of social heredity which most of the studies usually quoted do not have. On the theoretical side, we have endeavoured to clarify both the technical aspects concerning genetics and IQ and the crucial issue of the social relevance or lack of relevance of these technical questions.

In the human sciences, the argument of authority often consists in resorting to a needlessly complex mathematical formalism. We hope to help the reader to become more aware of the distinction between 'facts' and computer outputs. More generally, we hope to contribute to a healthly distrust of expert authority.

Montrouge, France
Cambridge, Mass.   M.S.
December, 1985   R.L.

Acknowledgments

The Grant Foundation and INSERM jointly financed the adoption study described in Chapter 3. They also contributed substantially to the making of this book. Their long-standing support is gratefully acknowledged.

Several colleagues provided both encouragement and useful criticism: we are specially indebted to A. Jacquard, L. Kamin, and B. Mackenzie.

Permission to reprint the following material is gratefully acknowledged:

Figure 1.1 from R. K. Adair, *Concepts in Physics*, (New York, Academic Press, 1969). Reprinted by permission of Academic Press.

Chart 2a from B. S. Bloom, *Stability and change in human characteristics* (New York, Wiley and Sons, 1964). Reprinted by permission of the author.

Figure 15 from H. J. Eysenck, *Race, intelligence and education* (London, Temple Smith, 1971). Reprinted by permission of Temple Smith.

Tables 1A and 1B, from H. Munsinger, 'Children's resemblance to their biological and adoptive parents in two ethnic groups', *Behavior Genetics*, **5**, 1975. Reprinted by permission of Plenum Publishing Corporation.

Figure 1, R. Plomin and J. C. de Fries, 'Genetics and intelligence: recent data', *Intelligence*, **4**, 1980. Reprinted by permission of Ablex Publishing Corporation.

Table 4, W. H. Sewell and V. P. Shah, 'Socioeconomic status, intelligence and the attainment of higher education', *Sociology of Education*, **40**, 1967. Reprinted by permission of the American Sociological Association.

Contents

Contents

List of figures

List of tables

Part I

Genetics, IQ, and social class

1. Historical origins

1. Biological determinism in past centuries

The idea that differences between people in temperament and ability are based on innate physical differences that are 'in the blood' is a very old one. Plato, in Book Two of *The republic*, urged rulers who wanted to legitimate their dominance to spread the story that they belonged to a different race, created by the gods from gold, while the run of men were descended from a race of brass and iron. European folk-tale is filled with the importance of blood as a determiner of character. In *Cinderella*, the ugly and wicked women were the *step*-sisters of the beautiful and virtuous heroine, not her biological sibs. The chief legitimation of social power, before the European and American revolutions of the seventeenth and eighteenth centuries, however, was not blood but grace. Kings ruled by the 'Grace of God' and offered Divine Right as their source of justification. Blood certainly had a role to play in this scheme of justification, and illegitimacy was an absolute bar to inheritance of noble privilege. Thus, Richard, Duke of Gloucester, in the last step of his plot to take the English throne, instructs his co-conspirator Buckingham to 'infer the bastardy of Edward's children'. Blood, however, played a secondary role to grace, a grace that could be conferred or lifted by God, irrespective of any claim to biological inheritance. Cromwell said that God's grace had been removed from Charles I and offered the King's severed head to prove it.

The revolutions of the seventeenth and eighteenth centuries that finally overthrew the autocratic and feudal European order and replaced it with the rule of money necessarily denied the old sources of legitimacy. Merchants, bankers, entrepreneurs of every sort had to be free to rise in the scale of social power; peasants had to be 'free' to be removed from the land to which they had historically been bound by feudal ties. A mobile labour force, responsive to the demands of capital, empowered to bargain on the labour market for the sale of its labour power, was a prerequisite for the rapid expansion of industrial production. All of these pressures conspired to replace the ideology of a society fixed by Divine Right with an ideology of freedom and equality. According to the Founding Fathers of the American Republic, 'all men are created equal', although, of course they did not mean *all* men since they continued to hold slaves. To make their challenge to the ruling classes of the eighteenth century, the revolutionaries had to appeal to universal principles of freedom and equality, whatever their own reservations may have been. A slogan of 'Liberty and equality for some' would not have been very convincing. Unfortunately, the ideal of universal

equality came into immediate contradiction with the facts of social existence. The American and French Revolutions did not create societies of
equality, but simply replaced one lower class by another. The inequality in
economic conditions in the industrial centres of Britain in the mid-
nineteenth century was not significantly less than it was 200 years earlier if
we can judge from Gregory King's famous compilation of health taxes in
1688. No one who reads Mayhew's contemporary accounts of the conditions of the working poor in London in 1849 can suppose that the victory
of parliamentary democracy in the seventeenth century really promoted
either economic or social equality. And so it continues to the present day:
there are rich and poor; those with high status and those with low; those
with power over their own lives and the lives of others and those who are
totally without the power to control their own conditions of work and life.
How is all this inequality to be reconciled with the legitimating ideal on
which our society is built?

There have been two main forms of explanation for continuing
inequality. The first, 'environmentalist', mode traces the inequality among
individuals to inequalities in opportunity. Poor education, social prejudice,
racism, and bad luck cause some people to be 'deprived' or 'disadvantaged'. These disadvantages, acquired early in life, cannot be easily overcome, if at all, so a permanent lack of skill and intellectual ability and
defects of temperament doom the person to a life of relative poverty and
powerlessness. To this theory, Oscar Lewis has added the notion that cultural deprivation is self-perpetuating in families, deprived parents depriv-
ing their children, to produce a self-sustaining and trans-generational
'culture of poverty'. The problem with the cultural theory of inequality is
that it does not provide an explanation either for the origin of the environmental variation or for its continuance in the face of a claimed social com-
mitment to equality. If people are simply the products of social
circumstances, and if we all agree that freedom and equality are our ideals
of social construction, then why have we failed to abolish privilege and
poverty? Without a deeper analysis, the cultural explanation of inequality
is simply a description and not a causal story. Such a deeper analysis, however, soon challenges the basic assumption that our society is indeed
devoted to equality and ends by prescribing revolutionary social reorgani-
zation, a result not widely welcomed.

The second mode of explanation begins with the assumption that the
social structure does indeed promote equality, so that persistent differences in status, wealth, and power must be the consequences of internally
generated differences between individual human beings. Some people
have what it takes, while others do not. In Cassius's words, 'The fault, dear
Brutus, is not in our stars, But in ourselves that we are underlings'. This
explanation for persistent differences of status, wealth, and power between

individuals, classes, races, and the sexes has been offered all through the nineteenth and twentieth centuries, in literature as in science. The precise mechanism claimed for individual differentiation has changed as ideas about human biology have altered, but the underlying theory has remained: the source of social inequality is the inequality in ability and temperament among individual human beings that arises from causes *internal* to the person. The power of such an explanation to excuse and justify the manifest inequalities in our social existence was explicitly recognized by the greatest biologist of the nineteenth century, Charles Darwin, when he wrote in *The voyage of the Beagle*:

If the misery of our poor be caused not by the laws of nature, but by our institutions, great is our sin.

Within the tradition of blaming individual persons for their own state, there have been both accidental and causal theories. Accidental theories simply assign differential success to arbitrary differences in temperament whose source is left unspecified. Some people just try harder than others; some are lazy; some have reached the conclusion that society owes them a living, have fallen in with bad companions and been insufficiently strong minded to resist their blandishments. Mayhew, that most sympathetic of the nineteenth-century commentators on the poor, divided them into three separate groups, 'according as they *will* work, they *can't* work, and they *won't* work'. Such accidental theories, although still current in popular consciousness, have passed out of favour as the modern ideology of natural science has taken over intellectual and political life. As the nineteenth century progressed, mechanical and causal explanations of phenomena displaced unanalysed results as a sufficient description. Accidental theories of temperament really haled back to the idea of grace, conferred on some but not others with no humanly decipherable reason. Instead, the entire universe of phenomena, including human psychic and social activity, was drawn into the sphere of mechanical explanation. So, in the last century, theories of the importance of innate biological differences between people became the dominant mode of explanation of social inequalities and have remained extremely important up to the present. Emile Zola spoke in the spirit of the nineteenth-century intellectuals, when he wrote, about the causes of temperament and social success, that 'Heredity has its laws, just as gravitation does', although it would, in fact, be 30 years before Mendel's laws were rediscovered.

Zola was not alone among novelists of his time in the belief that blood governed personality. The novels of Dickens and George Eliot depended repeatedly on the final triumph of heredity over environment for the resolution of their plots. Oliver Twist, although he was brought up, from birth, among the dregs of Victorian society in a parish work house and then was apprenticed to a gang of professional criminals, retained that nobility of form and mind that was a consequence of his birth to middle-class parents. Eliot's Daniel Deronda, although raised as an English gentleman, reverts to the Judaism of his biological ancestry. It remained for Zola, however, to devote an entire cycle of novels, the Rougon-Macquart series, to a working out of the consequences of heredity and its laws. The Rougons and the Macquarts are the two halves of a family descended from Adelaide Fouqué, whose first, lawful, husband was Rougon, a solid hard-working peasant, while her later lover, Macquart, was a violent and unstable criminal. From these two sires arose the successful, ambitious, entrepreneurial Rougons and the depraved, alcoholic, criminal Macquart line.

Zola was influenced by developments in continental anthroplogy that were particularly relevant to interpreting differences in temperament and ability. Paul Broca, the founder of the Anthropological Society of Paris and editor of the *Anthropological Review*, was a strong proponent of craniometry, the measurement of the dimensions of the skull, as an indicator of intellectual ability. The triumphant mechanical materialism of the time, having rejected dualistic notions of the mind as separate from the body, yet lacking any real sophistication about the complexities of the central nervous system, made the simplest kind of equation of the mental and the physical. Great minds must have been the manifestation of large brains which, in turn, must be contained in large heads. At the same time, there was a growing certainty, and no little evidence, that physical characteristics like size were heritable, although the rules of inheritance remained obscure. It then followed that mental ability would also be heritable since it was only a manifestation of brain size. Earlier, at the turn of the century, a more detailed equation between brain size and function had been developed by the Austrian Franz Joseph Gall, in his theory of phrenology. If the brain were really the organ of temperament and thought, then it seemed only sensible to suppose that different psychic functions resided in different parts of the brain. There was already evidence that localized brain injuries impaired some but not all functions. Indeed, Paul Broca is now best remembered for his localization of the speech function to a part of the frontal lobe. Then, given the supposed association between function and size, it seemed obvious that persons with different aspects of their temperaments or abilities more highly developed would have the appropriate regions of their brains enlarged, and this enlargement would, in turn, be reflected in swellings of the skull to accommodate the brain region underneath. Thus, stock brokers and merchants would have enlarged 'bumps of acquisitiveness' while great scholars would be known by the 'bump of knowledge' and Casanova by his 'amatory bump'.

A rather later development of the same general character was the creation by Cesare Lombroso in Italy of criminal anthropology around 1900. Part of the intellectual inheritance from the pre-reductionist science of the Renaissance was the notion of organic unity. One would not expect the brain and skull to develop independently of the rest of the body. One ought to expect other bodily features, especially facial expressions and the dimensions of the various parts of the head as a whole, to reflect the same underlying sources of development as the brain. A criminal brain would be housed in a criminal head. Lombroso, using measurements and photographs of convicted criminals, established a system of classification of chins, noses, ears, mouths, and eyes that revealed the murderer, the thief, the psychopath, and the forgerer. Using Lombroso's system, detectives could spot a criminal at a glance, just by the length of his ear lobes.

As extraordinary as the theories of phrenology, craniometry, and criminal anthropology may seem, they are not, on the face of it, absurd but only wrong. As it turns out, there is no correlation at all between the size of an adult's brain and his or her ability to perform intellectually. Indeed, within the so-called normal range of behaviour, there is nothing at all about brain structure that has yet been found to be related to intellect or character. Both Lenin's and Einstein's brains have been examined minutely with no positive result, and the French writer Anatole France had one of the smallest brains on record. Nor is it the case that special abilities or the hypertrophy of personality traits have any detectable relationship to the size of different regions of the brain. Indeed, 'acquisitiveness' and 'amative tendencies' are not localized at all, which is hardly to be wondered at since they are not unitary things but descriptions of complex social relations. Moreover, the external shape of the skull does not accommodate itself in detail to the shape of the brain. Finally, it is simply not the case that there is any organic relation between the shape of the nose and any characteristic of the brain. All of these supposed physical relations do not exist, but in a simpler world they might have. They simply represent a naïve application of a general mechanistic reductionist approach to understanding mental function and social relations in the absence of any real knowledge. Such a naïve approach is still apparent in some novels by Agatha Christie and in the popular mind.

2. Early history of mental tests

As sophistication about the relation between the physical and mental increased somewhat around the turn of the present century, the vain hope that mental performance could be predicted from anatomical measurements gave way to the idea of measuring mental performance itself. 'The child is father of the man', so the child's mental attributes ought to be indicators of the future adult's performance. While the measurement changed, the theory did not. Human mental attributes are seen as manifestations of properties that are already immanent at birth. The development of the adult is regarded as an unfolding of a pre-set pattern, so that measurements at an earlier stage can predict the outcome at a later stage. All that is required is to devise an instrument that will detect and measure that intrinsic property of which performance at every stage is only the outward manifestation. It is in this theoretical framework that the mental testing movement has grown.

The historical irony of mental testing is that it began with a totally different theoretical basis. Between 1905 and 1911, Alfred Binet and Theodore Simon, two French psychologists, devised a series of tests of children's mental performance designed to aid schools in more effective teaching. The idea was to identify children who might be expected to have difficulty in learning with the standard educational methods, and to induce teachers to work with such children to bring them to the same standard as others. There was no implication that such children were destined to be stupid adults because they lacked some intrinsic ability necessary to success. Binet, on the contrary, was explicit in his rejection of any theory of fixed mental abilities. He spoke against the 'brutal pessimism' of the idea of stupidity.

The tests devised by Binet and Simon were soon put to a different use. Imported into the United States and reworked by Lewis Terman at Stanford University in 1916, an instrument originally designed to help teachers help students became transformed into a device to label the unteachable. Beginning with Terman and continuing up to the present day, mental testing has been regarded as a technique for revealing intrinsic differences between people in the capacity for learning and reasoning. Those with low intrinsic capacities, in this theory, *cannot be taught* and are destined for social failure. While their brains may be of equal size, they are of lower quality and can absorb less. The tests then became screening devices to see which children are worth spending educational effort on, and which are destined to be underlings to the more intelligent Caesars. *Intelligence* is then turned from a description of manifest behaviour into an unseen intrinsic property, measurable by intelligence tests, independent of the superficial effects of experience and training.

The mental testing movement in the United States received two major forward impulses in the first quarter of this century. The first was the World War of 1914–18. The entry of the United States into the war in 1917 resulted in the institution of universal male conscription and the necessity of training men of varied cultural and educational experiences to become a homogeneous, disciplined military force. Robert Yerkes, one of the American developers of the IQ tests and President of the American Psychological Association, convinced the army to administer intelligence tests – the

Alpha for literate men and the Beta for those not literate in English – to about two million men (Yoakum and Yerkes 1920). It is not clear to what extent the results of the classification tests were put into actual practice in assigning men to various activities, but what is certain is that mental testing became accepted and legitimized as a mass practice. Also, for the first time, the same intelligence test could be standardized on an immense population sample.

The second historical phenomenon that gave an impetus to mental testing was the large migration of foreign-born into the United States after the turn of the century. Between 1900 and 1930, 18 million immigrants entered the United States, more than in all the previous 100 years of censused history. In 1920, 13 per cent of the population of the United States was foreign-born. Most immigrants were poor and illiterate in English or, indeed, in any language. They came predominantly from southern and eastern Europe and were mostly Catholics and Jews entering a Protestant country. They were perceived as mentally and temperamentally inferior, and mental tests given at Ellis Island, the immigrant receiving station, beginning in 1912, confirmed the prejudice. On the basis of these tests, Henry Goddard, who administered them, was able to state that: 'One can hardly escape the conviction that the intelligence of the average "third class" immigrant is low, perhaps of moron grade . . . we may still question whether we cannot use moron laborers if we are wise enough to train them properly' (Goddard 1917). When it was pointed out that the scores on the Army Alpha test increased as the number of years of residence in the United States increased, so that English literacy and acculturation were important factors, the mental testers disagreed, asserting that the tests were totally free of linguistic competence and culture. Rather, they said, earlier immigrants came from the better stock of northern Europe while later immigrants came from the inferior southern and eastern countries. There was no question that the early mental testers regarded the inferiority of immigrants as inherent, and they called up again the notions of Lombroso. In 1924 the American Congress passed an immigration restriction act that severely limited the numbers of immigrants from southern and eastern Europe, setting quotas proportional to the ethnic representation of the United States in 1890, when most American families came from Britain, Germany, and Scandinavia. While the testimony of the mental testers on the racial inferiority of immigrant groups was not responsible for the restricted immigration laws, it lent an air of scientific objectivity and legitimacy to what otherwise would have appeared merely a blind prejudice and economic self-interest. The consequence of the immigration act was that immigration dropped from 4.1 million in 1920–30 to a mere half million in the 1930s.

3. Genetics, race, and class

Beginning in the 1930s, the emphasis of mental testing shifted away from the immigration problem in the United States and concentrated more on race and class, which had been early preoccupations of IQ testers. In Britain, as in the United States, tests proliferated and became a standard procedure in schools where they were an important instrument in legitimizing discrimination against working-class children and non-Whites. As early as 1916, Terman had written that a low level of intelligence,

> . . . is very, very common among Spanish–Indian and Mexican families of the Southwest and also among negroes. Their dullness seems to be racial, or at least inherent in the family stocks from which they come . . . The writer predicts that . . . there will be discovered enormously significant racial differences in general intelligence, differences which cannot be wiped out by any scheme of mental culture . . . There is no possibility at present of convincing society that they should not be allowed to reproduce, although from a eugenic point of view they constitute a grave problem because of their unusually prolific breeding. (Quoted by Kamin 1974)

One of the major results of the Army Alpha Test Program was to show that American Blacks scored lower than Whites, and a special point was made of this by Yerkes (1921). Even earlier, in 1909, Cyril Burt had given crude mental tests to children of working-class and professional families with the inevitable result.

The concentration on race and class beginning in the 1930s and continuing up until the present day was accompanied by a considerable effort to show that IQ performance is innate and inheritable. On the one hand, there was a continuing documentation of the poorer performance of blacks and working-class children on IQ tests, and, on the other, a variety of statistical studies on relatives meant to show that IQ was inherited, using, albeit rather defectively, the developing science of quantitative genetics. At the same time, the world eugenics movement was growing, and fears that the genetically mentally inferior were outbreeding the better classes were repeatedly raised. All of these strains came together in the person of Sir Ronald Fisher. He was the inventor, in the 1920s, of most of the statistical methods now used in biological research, especially the *analysis of variance* by which different weights are assigned to different interacting causes, as for example between heredity and environment in influencing a trait. Simultaneously he was the inventor of the modern theory of quantitative genetics that shows how Mendel's laws can be used to generate the observed similarity between relatives in continuously varying traits like height, weight, and IQ scores. In his most influential work, *The genetical theory of natural selection*, in 1930, Fisher outlined a complete genetical theory of evolution while at the same time calling for a eugenic programme to prevent the deterioration of the species. He claimed that the lower classes were outbreeding the upper, and that, as a consequence, there was a negative correlation between fertility and mental ability. Through his mathematical formulation, Fisher had apparently given a rational basis to the eugenic fears of his predecessors. Actually, if childless individuals are taken into account instead of being omitted, the negative correlation between IQ and fertility disappears (Higgins *et al.* 1962; Bajema 1963). It is interesting to note that Fisher's erroneous prediction was followed by a large number of publications about the predicted decline of intelligence (Bradford 1937; Cattell 1937; Roberts *et al.* 1938, 1941; Moshinsky 1939; O'Hanlon 1940; Burt 1946; Thomson 1946; Carter 1954; Papavassiliou 1954; Scott and Nisbet 1955). These publications represented updated versions of the fear of the 'Yellow Peril'. The fact that sophisticated authors, including Fisher, the founder of modern statistics, should let an elementary error of logic go undetected for so long illustrates how logic can sometimes be distorted by prejudice.

In Britain, the leading advocate of the theory of inherited class differences in IQ was Cyril (later Sir Cyril) Burt, who devoted a career of 60 years to the claim that class differences were determined by differences in innate intelligence. His work contributed to the institution, just after the Second World War, of the 11-plus examination which tracked school students either into a university preparatory course or into a terminal certificate that denied them entry into all professions and administrative posts. Burt supported his contention that IQ was intrinsic and inherited in a series of papers, of which he was a co-author, on the IQ testing of twins. According to Burt, the correlation between identical twins, who had been reared apart in separate households from earliest childhood, was 0.771 (for twins reared together, Bust reported a correlation of 0.944). Thus, even when twins were raised in families that had, as he asserted, no similarity in socio-economic background, twins were remarkably alike in IQ performance. These reports were widely regarded as definitive proof for a large effect of genes in determining mental ability. Then the roof caved in. In 1973, Leon Kamin discovered indications of fraud in Burt's data. For example, successive papers adding more and more twin pairs nevertheless continued to give the correlations of 0.944 and 0.771 to the third decimal place. No trace could be found of the original data. No details were given of the tests administered and none about the children themselves. After Kamin had challenged Burt's data in 1973, Jensen (1974) rushed to disavow them (Hirsch 1981). It is now widely agreed that 'there now seems no reasonable doubt that Sir Cyril Burt perpetrated a fraud in that he fabricated data' (Connolly 1980).

Burt's reports were not the only work on the inheritance of IQ by any means, although they were the largest reported study on identical twins raised apart and the only one to claim no environmental correlation between the adopting families. By 1967, there were some 50 studies of various degrees of relationship including three studies of identical twins raised apart. In general, authors agreed that IQ was heritable, although the intensity of heritability estimated varied widely. A thorough analysis of the studies and their deficiencies has been made by Kamin (1974), and all suffer in some degree from serious methodological problems. The consensus among the researchers in the field, nevertheless, was clearly on the side of a substantial heritability of IQ performance.

In the United States from the very inception of IQ testing, as we have seen, but especially after the First World War, the relationship of race to IQ became an important issue. Many studies showed a lower Black performance on IQ tests, and these were brought together in Audrey Shuey's *The testing of Negro intelligence* (1958), which presented a hereditarian explanation of the observed differences. Blacks, it was claimed, were genetically inferior to Whites in intelligence, a claim that echoes Terman's claim made 40 years before. This opinion was by no means unanimous among IQ testers, however. (An interesting light on these opinions is shed by the fact that there is a correlation of 0.55 between the socio-economic characteristics of the *investigators* and the strength of their hereditarian views [Sherwood and Nataupsky 1968].) In fact, the official policy of the United States government had already become, by the time of the publication of the Coleman Report in 1966, that IQ differences between Blacks and Whites were a consequence of differential education and family experience, and that a concerted effort should be made to improve the education of Black children. Compensatory education programmes, such as Head Start, had been in place since the early 1960s in an attempt to redress the differences.

In 1969, the hereditarian view of racial differences in IQ became, almost overnight, a powerful force again, precipitated by the publication in 1969 of Arthur Jensen's famous article 'How much can we boost IQ and scholastic achievement?' Jensen argued that compensatory education had been tried and had failed. His explanation was that IQ was highly heritable and that, as a consequence, the differences in average IQ performance between Blacks and Whites were largely genetic and therefore unchangeable. His prescription for social action was to provide a kind of vocational training for Blacks, who were ill-suited to tasks demanding high cognitive skills, and a relaxation of the pressure to place Blacks proportionately to their numbers in professional schools, positions of administrative authority, and other places of social power. It was not discrimination, but lower intrinsic ability, that was the cause of Blacks' lack of social power. Jensen's argument for the biological fixity of racial differences in status was soon followed by a renewal of the claim that class differences were also heritable and unchangeable. The argument, most clearly put by Richard Herrnstein, was that

1. Social and economic success demands cognitive ability;
2. IQ tests measure cognitive ability;
3. IQ is highly heritable;
4. therefore, social and economic power are biologically heritable.
5. What is heritable is unchangeable;
6. therefore, class position necessarily runs in families because it runs in the genes.

The political implications of that theory of the origin of social class differences were also clearly drawn by Herrnstein (1971):

. . . the privileged classes of the past were probably not much superior biologically to the downtrodden, which is why revolutions had a fair chance of success. By removing arbitrary barriers between classes, society has encouraged the creation of biological barriers. When people can freely take their natural level in society, the upper classes will, virtually by definition, have greater capacity than the lower.

This is precisely the opinion expressed 50 years before by Henry Goddard (1920), when he claimed that:

As for an equal distribution of the wealth of the world that is equally absurd . . . These facts are appreciated. But it is not so fully appreciated that the cause is to be found in the fixed character of mental levels. In our ignorance we have said let us give these people one more chance – always one more chance. (Quoted by Kamin 1974)

Here we have laid out explicitly the theory of meritocracy. Before the revolutions of the eighteenth century, artificial privilege ruled society. But now, in a society of mobility and freedom, it is the natural inequalities that are responsible for unequal success. Since these differences are innate, they are unchangeable, so society is unchangeable. We have reached the state of maximum social entropy, the highest degree of equality of which our species is capable.

The immediate consequence of the rejuvenation of biological theories of race and class differences was an intense debate that, among other things, led to the discoveries about the Cyril Burt fraud and to a careful re-examination of the methodology and concepts of IQ research. The issue has become a wider one, however, than simply the question of IQ. A new broad emphasis on innate causes of human behaviour has arisen, including sociobiological theories of human nature. Both in the general scientific literature and in popular consciousness, genes have tended to become dominant as determiners of sickness and health, suffering and welfare, peace and war. There has been a renewed emphasis on biological differences between men and women as determiners of their differential social position. For everything that is human, whether individual or social, there are genes postulated, and fixity implied. At the same time, an opposition has formed, pointing out the ideological origins of biological determinism, the factual and conceptual errors of its claims, and the political nature of its activities. This book is part of that opposition. It, and the studies on which it is based, are direct attempts to oppose the errors of biological theory of social class, and to present competing evidence that class is a *social* phenomenon, *created* by the structure of social relations, and not dictated by our genes.

2. IQ scores, school achievement, and social class of origin

This chapter deals with social heredity, specifically with the correlation of the social class of parents with IQ scores of children and with their school status. We first present some facts about social heredity and conflicting views about that heredity. We then discuss the confusion between IQ scores and intellectual processes, and attempt to clarify some of the technical confusions about IQ scores.

1. Some facts about social heredity

In this first section, we present some information concerning social heredity. The term 'social heredity' is an unusual combination of words. This is because heredity has become associated with *biological* transmission, while the word social is associated with *environmental influences*. Social heredity is the tendency of children to resemble their parents in terms of social status.

That, *on the average*, children of upper-middle-class parents are given higher scores than children of working-class parents was already known to Binet, the French inventor of IQ tests. From a comparison of international data, we have estimated standardized mean IQ scores to be 96 and 109 for children of 'low' and 'high' social groups respectively (see Chapter 4). These numerical values are misleading, however, unless the following facts are kept in mind.

The first fact is the statistical nature of the relationship between the social status of the parents and various characteristics of their children. The characteristics of parents do not *determine* the characteristics of their children, be it by biological, psychological, or social transmission. In the particular case of IQ scores, the variability within a group of children of a given social class is almost as large as the variability within the whole population. There exists a large overlap between the distribution of scores of children of contrasted social groups. The variance of IQ scores of children of a given social class is about 80 per cent of the total variance in the population. (This number 80 per cent bears no direct relation to the alleged heritability of 0.8). About 15 per cent of the children of lower-class origin score *above* the mean of the upper-middle-class group.

The second fact will be examined later, specially in Chapter 4: the degree to which the social class of parents correlates with the educational and social status of an individual depends both on the nature of the variable used to measure that status and on the particular metric used to represent that variable. For instance, the social class of the parents only accounts for 20 per cent of the variance of IQ scores. Yet, the probability of being classified as mentally retarded or the probability of entering graduate school varies by a factor larger than 10, depending on the social class of the parents. Much of the confusion about social heredity stems from a lack of awareness of this second fact.

The social class of parents correlates both with IQ scores and with school achievement of their children. A comparison is presented below between the two types of correlations. To make this comparison, we need to express IQ scores and school achievements on comparable scales. We shall therefore transform the usual scale of IQ scores. Basically, one compares the distribution of ranks obtained by a group of children on one scale (the IQ scale) with the distribution of ranks on another scale (performance in primary school). The following comparison between the social heredity of IQ scores and the social heredity of educational status is drawn from French educational statistics.

In a national sample studied by the French Ministry of Education (Ministère de l'Education) (1976), 28 per cent of all schoolchildren were at least one year behind as they entered sixth grade; this situation can be considered as mild school failure. In addition to these 28 per cent, 18 per cent of all schoolchildren had been placed in remedial classes or in classes for 'slow learners'; this situation can be considered as a serious failure. Adding the two types of failure, one obtains a total rate of failure of 46 per cent: almost half of all schoolchildren met with some kind of educational 'accident' during primary school. Meeting with such an accident is just as probable as having an IQ score lower than 100. The probability of failure, however, depends strongly on the social class of the parents, varying from 13 per cent for children of senior executives and professionals to 67 per cent for children of unskilled workers.

What was relatively unique in the French educational system was the fact that repeating a grade and being put in a special track were extremely common. Hence social discrimination in school was rather visible (see Fig. 2.1). This visibility is now decreasing, as it has been in other countries. However, we shall see in Chapter 4 that the amount of social discrimination and of social waste is approximately the same in all OECD countries, except for the fact that the 'failure' is usually replaced by a less visible form of tracking. The effects of social discrimination then become visible only at the level of secondary school or even at the college level.

Let us now consider IQ scores. We are so mystified by the apparent metric properties built into IQ scales that we tend to forget the way in which IQ scores are really defined. These scores are conventional numbers with an arbitrary correspondence to the *rank* assigned to an individual within his age cohort. If the test places an individual at the 50th percentile, he is given the conventional score of 100; if the performance of the individual is surpassed only by 16 per cent of his age cohort, he is given a score of 115; if only 16 per cent of the children of the same age have lower performances, the individual is given the conventional score of 85. In other words, the distribution of IQ scores is made to be normally distributed, with a mean value of 100 and a standard deviation of 15.

In order to make IQ scores comparable to school failure, we shall define two types of threshold. The first threshold is defined by analogy with school failure; it corresponds to the median value defined during the standardization of the test. By definition of the median score, half of the scores correspond to this type of failure. The threshold for serious failure is here defined as being one standard deviation below the threshold for mild failure. For tests defined in the conventional way, the thresholds defined above correspond to scores of 100 and 85 respectively. It is not surprising that this type of metric corresponds better to social reality than the usual one because the original Binet scale and all scales derived from it are ordinal scales related to school performance in primary grades.

With the above procedure, we have defined a scholastic scale and a test scale in such a way that for the general population these two scales practically coincide. We can now make a quantitative comparison of the correlation of social origin with the two types of scales. The results of this comparison are presented in Fig. 2.1.

This graph shows that the social class of the parents correlates with IQ scores and with achievement in primary school in the same way. The near equivalence between the rate of school failure and the rate of psychometric failure is observed for all social groups. For serious failures, which are socially more significant, school appears even more socially discriminating than IQ tests. Similar findings of additional discrimination were reported in the United States in the case of ethnic groups (McCartin *et al.* 1966).

Conflicting views of the social heredity of IQ scores

Discussions of social heredity are often presented in the context of *the* nature–nurture debate. In this debate, some authors stress the importance of biological differences between children of contrasted social groups, while others stress the importance of family environment. As we shall see, the nature–nurture debate is actually a smokescreen for a debate over the interaction between individual differences and social structure. Among contemporary writers, the most explicit advocates of a theory of social heredity based on the quantitative genetics of IQ scores have been Gottesman (1968), Herrnstein (1973), and Eysenck (1973). In a chapter entitled 'The biogenetics of race and class', Gottesman wrote:

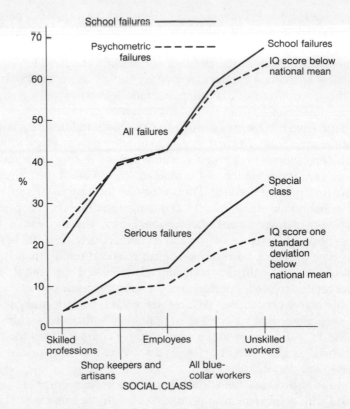

Fig. 2.1 Comparison of the correlation of social class of origin with IQ scores and with school achievement.
Three levels of achievement have been defined: (1) When a child achieves at or above the national norm, he is said to succeed; (2) below that norm, he is said to fail; (3) when the performance is more than one standard deviation below the norm, we speak of serious failure. This graph shows that the influence of the social class of the parents is the same for school failure as it is for psychometric failure. (From Schiff *et al.* 1982) (Source of raw data: INED–INOP, 1973; Ministère de l'Education 1976)

The existence of class barriers, however permeable, fosters relative reproductive isolation; yet social mobility permits a constant winnowing for achievement and learning ability. Migration to an appropriate social ecological niche follows. The net result of an open class system with equality of opportunity and assortative mating is to make genetic factors no less important for an understanding of human society than they are for other mammalian species.

Actually, the conditions of validity of quantitative genetic analysis can sometimes be met in agriculture or in experimental animal populations but

are never met in the analysis of human behaviours that are socially significant. The point we wish to make, however, is that the real issue is elsewhere, namely in the manner in which social classes and social structure
are being considered, or neglected.

The crucial distinction then is not between heredity and environment but
between individual and social descriptions of social inequality. From the
point of view of a grade school teacher faced with the failure of working-
class children, it does not make much difference whether he or she links
this failure to 'poor genes' or to 'poor family environment'. In both cases,
failure will seem inevitable, and in both cases, one will be 'blaming the victim' (Ryan 1971).

The reluctance to look at social class

In the scientific literature, quantitative data on social heredity are relatively rare. In his book on inequality (1972), Jencks made the following
comment:

Considering the vast sums that have been spent testing millions of American
students, reliable data on the relationship between test scores and economic status
is remarkably hard to find.

The handful of studies on the class differential of IQ scores that used
representative samples can be compared to other types of studies using
IQ scores. Under the heading 'Intelligence tests', the yearbooks of mental measurements by Buros up to 1978 list 6000 references. Every con-
ceivable 'factor' has been correlated to IQ scores, including the season
of birth, so that social class of origin appears as one among many variables.

One way to demonstrate the reluctance of authors to face the reality
of social class is to analyse the terms used to designate that reality in
titles of scientific articles. In a list of 24 references on the effect of parental social class on the intellectual development of children (Wright
1969, p. 197), one finds 17 different ways of designating social class, and
yet the word 'class' itself appears only once out of 24 times (see Table
2.1).

Another interesting point concerns the number of studies where the IQ
scores of children have been compared, not to the social class of the
parents, but to the IQ scores of one or both parents. According to a recent
review, the number of such studies is now greater than 40 (Bouchard and
McGue 1981). One may note here that, instead of obtaining an IQ score
for the parent(s), it would have been much easier to record their social
class.

Table 2.1 *Illustration of the avoidance of the term 'social class'. Terms used in the titles of 24 references on the influence of the social class of parents on intellectual development of children are classified below*

	No.
Underprivileged homes	1
Environment, Nurture	2
Cultural differences, Cultural background	3
Socially composite, Certain social factors, Social factors	3
Socio-economic differentials, Socio-economic correlates, Economic status, Socio-economic status, Social status, Socio-economic factors, Economic standing, Occupational rank	14
Social class	1
Total	24

2. The confusion between IQ scores and intelligence

Historical perspective: ethnocentric naïvety about intelligence

Everyone knows the phrase attributed to Binet, 'Intelligence is what my test measures'. Whether or not Binet made that statement is of little importance. What is important is that most psychologists using tests have talked as if they knew better but have acted as if IQ scores indeed measure intelligence. The issue raised here is not whether the differences revealed by the tests are acquired or inherited but whether they are the manifestation of a genuine inferiority or the manifestation of a social arte-fact.

Some psychologists claim that current IQ tests are essentially fair to the children of the various classes. In their opinion, the difference in mean IQ scores between the children of working-class parents and those of upper-middle-class parents reveals a real superiority of the latter group of children over the former. This opinion is based upon the conviction that the values embodied by the test are universal ones. According to this opinion, only by degrading the meaning of the word intelligence could one hope to bridge the gap between the two sets of IQ scores.

Other psychologists believe that at least part of the difference in mean IQ scores is an artefact because the tests currently used are biased towards the middle-class culture. According to these psychologists, however, all we need to do is to improve the content of the tests.

In current social practice, two elements of *the test situation* embody middle-class values, irrespective of the content of the test. The first element of the test situation is its lack of apparent connection with real life. From the tester's point of view, an absence of direct reference to the child's experience may appear as a guarantee of culture fairness. In reality, the gratuitous aspects of the test situation may appear normal to a middle-class child and bizarre to a working-class one. In the film 'E.T.' (*The extra terrestrial*), one child asks another, 'How do you explain school to an intelligent being?' The same could be asked about IQ tests. For a rational being like E.T., the test situation would appear absurd: an adult asks a child questions which are meaningless to the child and to which the adult already knows the answer. This sort of make-believe situation is typical of the middle-class culture and of the current school culture as a whole.

The second element of the test situation is its competitive nature. This competitive nature has been clearly stated by one of the founding fathers of American testing: 'In the actual race of life, which is not to get ahead, but to get ahead of somebody, the chief determining factor is heredity' (Thorndike 1916). 'Getting ahead of somebody' conveys the real meaning of the ordinal nature of IQ scales.

Binet was not the first scientist to try to construct an instrument to 'measure' human intelligence. Before him, authors devised various tests based on items like the reaction time to some stimulus or the ability to discriminate between neighbouring stimuli. According to Lawler (1978), Galton had built such a test, but when he found out that the man-in-the-street could do as well on his test as people that he considered *a priori* as more intelligent, he finally gave it up. This is not surprising considering Galton's ethnocentric view of human intelligence:

The natural ability of which this book mainly treats, is such as a modern European possesses in a much greater average share than men of the lower races. (Galton 1892).

In 1926 Florence Goodenough published a paper on racial differences in the intelligence of schoolchildren. Before reporting her own results, she reviewed some previous work, including data showing that the inferior scores are highly correlated to the persistent use of a foreign language by the parents of the children tested. Instead of interpreting this fact as evidence of a linguistic bias of the tests, she chose to conclude that 'a more probable explanation is that those nationality-groups whose average intellectual ability is inferior do not readily learn the new language'. Her own results, obtained with a non-verbal test (the Draw-a-Man Test) placed Indian and Negro children as well as children of immigrants from Southern Europe significantly below those of 'American' parents. Another author who was a pioneer in cross-cultural testing later wrote that 'doubts soon arose that "intelligence" tests could be "culture free" ' (Dennis 1966). Goodenough herself corrected her views on the culture fairness of her test, indeed of any test, by stating (Goodenough and Harris 1950):

The present writers would like to express the opinion that the search for a culture-free test, whether of intelligence, artistic ability, personal-social characteristics, or any other measurable trait is illusory, and that the naïve assumption that the mere freedom from verbal requirements renders a test equally suitable for all groups is no longer tenable. (The early study by Goodenough which reports the differences in standing on the Draw-a-Man Test by the children of immigrants to the United States from various European countries is certainly no exception to this rule. The writer hereby apologizes for it!)*

How did Goodenough come to change her opinion so drastically? The answer is provided by Dennis (1966) in the above-mentioned paper:

Doubts became stronger when some groups were found to test higher than American whites.

Indeed, Indian boys of some tribes had been found to score higher than upper-middle-class American children on the Draw-a-Man Test! (Dennis 1942; Havighurst *et al.* 1946).

A more recent example concerns the use of Piaget-type tests. The children of Africa usually scored below Geneva children and nobody questioned this result. When a research worker found, however, that some African children did 'surprisingly well' on some conservation test involving quantities irrespective of shape, she sought an explanation, and found one: these children were used to seeing their mothers distribute food (Bovet, private communication).

In short, White middle-class builders of IQ tests have always played the game according to the rule 'heads I win, tails you lose'. As a final example of self-serving ethnocentric naïvety, let us quote a passage from the concluding chapter of a genetics textbook (McKusick 1964):

No one would dispute the desirability and the scientific soundness of encouraging reproduction of intelligent persons who are an asset to society. For example, income tax relief for university faculties based on number of children would make good sense.

It seems that someone questioned the 'soundness' of the above proposal since it disappeared from the second edition of the textbook.

To conclude on the ethnocentric naïvety of testers, the validation of a test always rests on the judgement of the people who have the power to decide, i.e. the white middle class. As long as this is the case, the operational definition of human intelligence will have an intrinsic bias towards white middle-class values. We believe that, in a society built upon social inequality, no school system could ever use culture-fair tests. In that type

* We note that Negroes, Indians, and Spanish Mexicans are not mentioned in this apology.

of society, tests are used either to mask the reality of social heredity or to justify it. If a culture-fair test existed, it would serve neither of these two purposes.

Double-talk about IQ and intelligence

Let us now examine evidence of double-talk in the issue of the relationship between IQ and intelligence. Very few psychologists claim that scores obtained with IQ tests are a valid measure of intelligence. In fact, many authors writing on the subject explicitly warn their readers that IQ should not be confused with intelligence. Thus, one authoritative writer in the field of psychological testing states in the introductory chapter of her manual (Anastasi 1961):

Although intelligence tests were originally designed to sample a wide variety of functions in order to estimate the individual's 'general intellectual level', it soon became apparent that such tests were quite limited in their coverage. Not all important functions were represented. In fact, most intelligence tests were primarily measures of verbal ability and, to a lesser extent, of the ability to handle numerical and other abstract and symbolic relations. Gradually, psychologists came to recognize that the term 'intelligence test' was a misnomer, since only certain aspects of intelligence were measured by such tests.

In spite of this early realization, millions of schoolchildren have been subjected to 'intelligence' tests, and the results of these tests have been used to influence their place in the school system and eventually in the society at large. Professional psychologists sometimes claim that only lay people confuse IQ scores with intelligence. This claim is contradicted by both the social and scientific practice of psychologists who use IQ tests.

The names of tests give a good indication of their social misuse. In the eighth edition of the most authoritative compilation on tests (Buros 1978), IQ tests are listed and analysed under the heading 'Intelligence'. The two types of individual tests most often used and quoted are called the Stanford–Binet *Intelligence* Scale and the Wechsler *Intelligence* Scale respectively. In fact, of 6000 references accumulated up to 1978, three-quarters concern these two types of 'intelligence' scales. Let us note finally that, whatever their names, tests are said to measure 'intelligence' quotients. That the term IQ continues to be used in scientific circles, even when scores are no longer defined by the ratio of mental age to chronological age, is an indication of the social significance of that term.

Confusion between test scores and intelligence is also revealed in the titles of studies quoted in reviews of the nature–nurture question. Two lists of references are analysed below. The first list comes from the review

Table 2.2   *Confusion between IQ and 'intelligence' in the titles of studies of the genetic variability of IQ scores*

	Erlenmeyer-Kimling and Jarvik (1963)	Jencks (1972)
Number of studies	52	22
Number of titles mentioning a psychological trait:	41	17
'Intelligence', or 'intellectual' (%)	68	59
'Mental growth', 'mental development', 'ability', 'talent' (%)	15	23
Neutral technical terms (e.g. 'Stanford Binet scale', 'achievement test scores', etc.) (%)	17	18
Total	100	100

published in *Science* by Erlenmeyer-Kimling and Jarvik in 1963.[1] The second list was obtained from the references given by Jencks in Tables A1 to A8 of his book, *Inequality* (1972).

The first list of references contains 52 titles. Of these, eleven titles refer only to the type of subjects, e.g. 'Twins', while 41 use various terms to describe the pyschological traits studied. The second list of references contains 22 titles, of which 17 refer to some psychological trait. As can be seen from Table 2.2, only in one-fifth of the cases do the authors refer to the trait in some neutral technical way. In more than half of the cases, the word 'intelligence' itself (or sometimes 'intellectual') appears directly in the title of the study.

Jencks's book contains some additional illustration of the contradiction between the explicit message conveyed by technical terms and the implicit message conveyed by everyday words. The author titled his technical appendix: 'Estimating the heritability of IQ scores'. Yet, in the text of his book, we find terms like 'élite', 'competent', 'virtue' 'academically talented', 'low aptitude students', etc. without quotation marks or any other qualification. The most sophisticated type of double-talk concerning the word 'intelligence' is that of Jensen (1980), whose technical analysis boils down to the definition attributed to Binet ('intelligence is what my test measures').

As a final example of a semantic confusion associated with the use of a test, let us mention that the students in the United States who obtain the best scores on a scholastic test of English and mathematics receive a

---

[1] This list was kindly supplied by one of the authors.

National Merit Scholarship. The use of the word 'merit' in this context illustrates the confusion introduced by Protestant and capitalistic ethics between merit and success in some competition.

3. Technical misconceptions about IQ scores

The reification of IQ scores

Originally, Binet defined mental age by the number of items correctly answered by a child. If the number of points obtained on the test corresponded to the mean score obtained by nine-year-old children, the mental age of the subject was said to be nine years. If the score of the subject corresponded to the average of scores obtained by 10-year-old children, the mental age was said to be 10 years. The items of Binet's test were chosen in such a manner that the scores obtained by a cohort of children of a given age were distributed according to a bell-shaped curve approximating a normal distribution.

In 1914, Stern introduced the idea of mental quotient as the ratio of mental to chronological age. The intelligence quotient is this ratio, after multiplication by 100 to avoid decimals. For an age cohort, IQ scores have the same distribution as the mental ages, i.e. their distribution is approximately normal.

The final statistical refinement was introduced by Wechsler in 1949. During the standardization of the test, the correspondence between test scores and IQ is made in such a way that IQ scores have a normal distribution with a mean value of 100 and a standard deviation of 15. Thus, the IQ of 100 is *defined* as corresponding to the median score on the test; the IQ of 115 is *defined* as corresponding to the score surpassed by 16 per cent of the subjects, and so on. In his manual, Wechsler (1974) reminds the reader of this fact in the following way:

It is no longer a matter of discovering how many children test above or below a given IQ in the population, since the deviation IQ is by definition dependent on the normal distribution of the test scores.

As early as 1903, Pearson had stressed the fact that some mathematical relationships have nothing to do with biology but are the results of the statistical properties of numbers. As a French geneticist has recently pointed out, one has a tendency to confuse the properties of numbers with the properties of objects (Jacquard 1984). IQ scores are numbers which by construction are distributed according to the normal curve. Whatever intelligence is, it is neither an object like the lung nor a one-dimensional function like height. It is a process of the organism based on a complex material structure. Yet some authors still argue as if the normal distribution of IQ scores was a proof or an indication of the genetic origin of that distribution. Thus, an expert wrote in an invited report to a conference on mental retardation (Albee 1971):

Basic human intelligence is inherited in a normal polygenic way . . . today, tomorrow, next year, and next century, some $2\frac{1}{4}\%$ of all children born will be mentally deficient because of these polygenic factors.

The confusion between a one dimensional biological variable and intelligence is sometimes less explicit. The following is an example of such an implicit confusion (Herrnstein 1973):

Overall, the spread of performance conformed to the bell-shaped curve that statisticians call 'normal,' with about as many superior children as inferior, but with most crowding around the average. Many biological traits display normal distributions, so that the construction of intelligence tests has been guided by the expectation of normality. However, if the expectation were far wrong, IQ's would not show the useful statistical properties of normal distributions to the considerable extent that they do.

It is worth noting that the author does not talk about superior and inferior scores nor even of superior and inferior intelligence, but of superior and inferior 'children'.

To explain to someone unfamiliar with statistics that the normal distribution is not a biological fact, one of us recently performed the following exercise. We took a telephone directory and considered the last digit of each number. We grouped these last digits by sets of 22, added the 22 digits and multiplied the sum by 1.01. We called the result 'telephone quotient' and plotted the distribution of these telephone quotients, TQ. The result of this exercise, which was performed with the beginning pages of the 1982 edition of the Paris telephone directory yielded the expected bell-shaped distribution, with a mean value of 99.4. Perhaps Herrnstein should try the same exercise with a Boston directory!

From the scientific point of view, the technical errors about normal distributions amount to a confusion between the properties of objects and the properties of numbers. From the social and political point of view, these technical errors lead to a confusion between natural laws and an artificially-built hierarchy. The quotation of Albee's statement given above is more than an illustration of just another technical error. It is a clear illustration of an ideology where intelligence appears as a commodity in fixed limited supply.

The statement that IQ scores above 130 will always be in short supply is true, but it is as tautological as saying that, out of the 26 letters of the alphabet, there will always be only one letter A. The origin of this logical confusion may lie in the current correlation between IQ scores and material wealth. Although this correlation is far from what it would be in a meritocratic society, it is large enough to encourage the confusion between the distribution of IQ scores and the distribution of money. In reality, intellectual wealth does not have the same intrinsic properties as material wealth. To the extent that the total supply of material wealth is limited at a given time, the increase in wealth of some is correlated with the decrease in wealth of others. The opposite is true of intellectual wealth. By sharing this wealth with others, we become richer, not poorer, in particular because we will then have more people with whom we can exchange ideas.

The confusion between group differences and individual differences

The data presented on p. 18 show that, when socially significant criteria are used, tests discriminate highly between the children of contrasted social groups. Figures 3.9 and 3.10 of the next chapter are also informative on this point. When differences between groups are considered, two errors are to be avoided. Although these errors are contradictory, they are often made by the same people.

The first error consists in confusing the individuals of a group with some mythical average type (this is the essence of racist thinking). Any inequality between the two groups is then 'explained' by reference to a difference between mean values. The second error consists in minimizing the effects of the social class of origin. An extreme case of such minimization is presented by Eysenck, in two books written for the general public (Eysenck 1971, 1973). At the end of the first book, entitled *Race, intelligence and education*, he presents the curves reproduced in Fig. 2.2. Eysenck then makes the following comment:

'It will be seen that eradicating all environmental influences would not greatly affect the distribution of IQs'.

The same curves are presented in *The inequality of man* (1973). In that book, Eysenck's conclusion is stated even more clearly:

This truth may be put into diagrammatic form. Jensen (1972) has calculated the shrinkage to be expected in human variability in IQ if all environmental sources of variance were removed; Figure 6 shows the result, assuming a heritability of .80. . . . Figure 6 deserves close study by all those who hope to change people by changing society; it shows clearly the narrow limits within which such an enterprise must be confined at present, even if we could control all environmental sources of variation.

Eysenck's message is crystal clear: don't bother changing society, it would hardly make any difference. Even if we were to stick to IQ

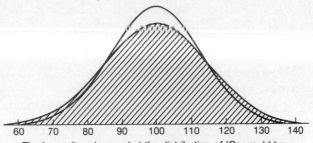

The heavy line shows what the distribution of IQs would be
theoretically if all variance due to environmental factors had been
eliminated and all differences in IQ were due entirely to
hereditarian influences. The shaded curve represents the normal
distribution of IQs in the present population.

Fig. 2.2 An example of confusion between within-group and between-group variance. This illustrates a mystification about the effect of social class of origin. (Figure and caption reproduced from Eysenck 1971).

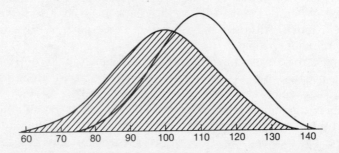

Fig. 2.3 The possible effect of a total control over social conditions. The shaded curve represents the distribution of IQ scores in the general population. The heavy line was drawn under the following assumptions: (*a*) broad heritability of 0.8, (*b*) variance *within* social groups of children entirely genetic, and (*c*) differences *between* groups entirely social.

distributions and to meritocratic values, this conclusion would be based on a technical mystification. This mystification lies in the lumping together of two types of variations: individual variations within a social group on the one hand, and mean differences between groups on the other. If we really had total control over social environment, the effect could be far from negligible, as indicated in Fig. 2.3.

The fact that the width σ_1 of the solid curve differs by only 10 per cent from the width σ_2 of the shaded curve is simply a mathematical consequence of:

1. The definition of the variance as the square of the width, σ^2.

2. The assumption made about the proportion of genetic variance: $\sigma_1{}^2/\sigma_2{}^2 = 0.8$ ($\sqrt{.8}$ is about 0.9)

On the other hand, the fact that the two curves have the same mean position does *not* result from Eysenck's assumption. To illustrate this point, let us make some simplifying assumptions. Let us assume that the genetic variance in IQ scores is indeed 80 per cent of the total variance and that, within a social class, the IQ score of a child is determined entirely by his genes. Under these conditions, the non-genetic part of the variance (the remaining 20 per cent) would be entirely due to the social class of the parents. Hence, by placing all children in social conditions currently reserved to a privileged group, one would bring the average IQ score to about 110. The solid curve would then be shifted to the right by a very substantial amount (see Fig. 2.3, p. 28).

Contrary to Eysenck's assertion, this assumed control over non-genetic conditions would have a considerable effect, even though the width of the IQ distribution would indeed be reduced by only 10 per cent. The change would come from the shift in the distribution rather than from the narrowing of that distribution. All the effects which are now attributed to the mean IQ gap between contrasted groups would vanish (assuming that their origin was indeed the IQ gap). Mild mental retardation would shrink to what is now observed in the privileged group. On the other hand, the possibility of access to advanced education would increase enormously, so that the current division between intellectual and manual work would disappear to a large extent, most children qualifying for intellectual work. Presumably, if these are the 'narrow limits' imposed by biology on the 'hopes' of social reformers, most of the reformers would settle for that. The technical aspects of the mystification embodied in the curves of Fig. 2.2 are analysed more fully in the appendix.

Confusing facts and values in the validation of IQ tests

In her manual on psychological testing, Anastasi (1982) writes:

The validity of a test concerns *what* the test measures and *how well* it does so. It tells us what can be inferred from test scores. In this connection, we should guard against accepting the test name as an index of what the test measures.

In order to be considered as valid a test must fulfil a certain number of criteria. The criteria usually discussed entail the following procedures:

—an examination of the content of the test (content validation);

—an examination of the way in which the test is constructed (construct validation), and

—an examination of the correlation between test results and some external criterion such as school success (criterion-related validation).

For a technical presentation of these procedures, we refer the reader to standard textbooks on tests. The following discussion is a non-technical critique of these procedures. We shall show that they leave the question of validity unanswered.

Content validation

By examining the content of a school achievement test, for instance an arithmetic test, one can determine what type of knowledge is being tested and at what level. This procedure, however, is not useful for so-called intelligence tests, since these tests assume no specific knowledge from the testee. On the issue of content validation, Anastasi (1982) writes:

Unlike achievement tests, aptitude and personality tests are not based on a specified course of instruction or uniform set of prior experiences from which test content can be drawn. Hence, in the latter tests, individuals are likely to vary more in the work methods or psychological processes employed in responding to the same test items. The identical test might thus measure different functions in different persons. *Under these conditions, it would be virtually impossible to determine the psychological functions measured by the test from an inspection of its content.* *

As pointed out in the above quotation an inspection of the content of the tests cannot be used to determine whether or not a test samples the psychological function named intelligence.

That the verbal content of tests increases the difference in test scores between children of lower- and upper-class parents has been known for a long time. And yet, the two individual tests most often used continue to have a strong verbal component. One would expect test makers to provide data concerning the *systematic* additional social bias thus introduced. On the contrary, in the case of the last edition of the WISC (Wechsler 1974, p. 35), the test makers have taken steps to discourage psychologists from taking this systematic bias into account.

Here again there is a confusion between systematic differences due to social class and random variations. By construction of the test, the verbal score has a mean of 100 and a standard deviation of 15 within the whole population; the same is true of the performance score and of the global

* Emphasis added.

score which is obtained by combining the two partial scores. The verbal scores, however, are more socially biased than the performance scores. Hence, there exists a systematic difference between verbal and performance scores for working-class children.

Clinical psychologists know that when there is a large discrepancy between different parts of a test, it may be more meaningful to consider each partial score separately rather than to combine them. Since working-class children tend to score systematically lower on the verbal part than on the performance part, some psychologists might be tempted to discard the verbal score for such children. And yet, the tables published by the test constructor seem to be designed to discourage psychologists from doing so. The table gives the gap between the verbal and performance scores below which the difference between the scores is not statistically significant *in the general population*. Since random individual fluctuations are large, they mask the systematic differences due to social class.

Construct validation

In choosing test items, Binet made sure that they had a good power of discrimination as a function of age. An item designed for eight-year-old children would have to be very easy for 10-year-olds and very hard for six-year-olds. Such age differentiation tells us nothing about intelligence. Height and the ability to lift weights also increase with age and yet give us no direct information about mental age.

This question of age differentiation is far from a trivial technical point. To illustrate the fundamental nature of this question, we shall first refer to a situation described by a French psychologist (Chiland 1971). During a clinical interview with a six-year-old child, the psychologist noted that the child showed no sign of inhibition or fear of the adult, which she interpreted as a sign of immaturity. Indeed, inhibition generally increases with age. But whether this is a sign of developmental maturity or the loss of a valuable human quality is not clear.

In the specific case of intelligence, if one chose to define it as the ability to ask 'why', one would have to conclude that intelligence generally declines after the age of four, so that IQ would be correlated to a *lack* of intelligence.

Other forms of construct validation include correlation with other tests and correlation between test items. Such procedures are obviously circular. As stated by Anastasi, 'In the absence of data external to the test itself, little can be learned about what a test measures'.

Criterion-related validation

An example of validation by an external criterion provides an illustration of the fact that this type of validation usually begs the question of which aptitude a test really samples. This example concerns a hypothetical 'medical aptitude test', whose scores would be correlated to future grades in medical school.

It is interesting to note that the case of a 'medical aptitude test' is the first example of validation presented by Anastasi (1982). Although she does state that the procedure would be used to select 'promising applicants for medical school', she fails to point out the crucial difference between 'successful' students and 'good' doctors.

The procedure of validation by correlation with university grades or with the judgement of teachers begs the fundamental question of which qualities are deemed desirable of a medical doctor. By answering a question of fact about medical studies as presently organized, one takes for granted the value of these studies. More generally, one begs the question of values concerning medicine and its place within society. Current medical studies do have a certain degree of efficiency when it comes to selecting hard-working people adapted to a competitive and technological society. Whether or not one considers these individuals as 'good' doctors, however, depends on one's view of medicine and of its place in society. One could choose to define a 'good' doctor as primarily one who is capable and willing to teach people to take care of their health.

In an analogous way, criterion validation of 'intelligence' tests concerns the correlation between IQ scores and success in school or in the so-called rat race. It tells us nothing about human intelligence. The criteria used to define intelligence and to validate intelligence tests depend largely on questions of values, not on questions of facts. Once you start doubting the intelligence of current school practice, the correlation between IQ scores and school success is more invalidating than validating of IQ tests. Another external criterion that can and has been used to invalidate tests is the systematic effect of the social class of the parents on the IQ scores of their children.

In conclusion, procedures used to validate 'intelligence' tests are as socially determined as the tests themselves. The high degree of sophistication of some of these procedures only serves to mask an unwillingness to face the social, psychological, and ethical questions posed by the construction and use of IQ tests.

4. Summary

The distribution of IQ scores of children of primary school age is characterized by the following facts. The variance of IQ scores within one social group accounts for roughly 80 per cent of the variance within the general population. When failure is defined as performing below the national norm, the probability of failure as a function of social class is the same whether the performance considered is related to IQ tests or to primary school.

We noted the rarity of good statistical data on the influence of the social class of parents on test and school results of their children. This rarity is in itself a fact worthy of careful consideration. Another socially significant fact is the historical persistence of the use of the word 'intelligence' in tests, in spite of the realization of the technical inadequacy of this term.

The biological view of the social heredity of IQ scores is essentially based on a confusion between independent sources of variations: variation *within* a social group of children and variation *between* social groups. The environmental view of the social heredity of IQ scores may be partly valid, but it is plagued by two conceptual confusions: the confusion between IQ scores and intelligence, on the one hand, and the confusion between social class and environment on the other.

Discussions about IQ usually fail to distinguish clearly between questions of facts and questions of values. In addition, they are often obscured by technical confusions. The principal technical confusions are:

—the reification of IQ scores;
—the above-mentioned confusion between social and individual differences, leading to a confusion between differences and inequality; and
—attempts to validate 'intelligence' tests while ignoring the choices of values implicit in these attempts.

The above confusions are not simply technical errors. Each has a social significance as well. The reification of IQ scores corresponds to a view of intelligence as a merchandise in rare supply. The confusion between the social and individual components of IQ scores is not simply a statistical confusion between random and systematic variations. It is a manifestation of a refusal to consider social class as a basic component of present reality. Finally, the circular nature of attempts to validate IQ scores stems from this same inability to question current social values.

Appendix: A note on the use of variance analysis to mask social differences (see Fig. 2.2)

Figure 2.2 illustrates a mystification about the effect of the social class of origin on IQ scores. From a technical point of view, this mystification derives from the confusion between group differences and individual differences. In order to clarify this technical issue, three points need to be made. The first point concerns the statistical independence of the two types of differences. The second concerns the fact that these two types of differences can arise from qualitatively different causes. The last point concerns the mathematical apparatus of variance analysis. Let us consider each of these points.

The first concerns the fact that the two types of differences are statistically independent. To illustrate this point, let us imagine two fictitious experiments on pairs of identical twins. In the first out of observations, we obtain test scores of twins, within a single social class. For the sake of this illustration, let us assume that, within a social class, IQ scores are determined solely by the genotype of the individual. In the case of identical twins, the scores would be identical within each pair so that the correlation observed within pairs would be 100 per cent. Let us now imagine another fictitious experiment with another group of identical twins. We now suppose that the twins have been separated at birth, and reared in contrasted social groups. Again for the sake of illustration, let us assume that the effect of a change in social class is to add 10 points to the IQ score. Under that hypothesis, the observed correlation within pairs would still be 100 per cent, as in the previous case. Although the *variance* of the distribution of IQ scores has been unaffected by the change in social class, the *mean* has changed.

The second point concerns the origin of the two types of differences. In the fictitious example given above, the differences within one social class are correlated entirely with the genetic differences within that class. Yet the mean difference of 10 points between the children of the two classes is caused entirely by the social differences between the groups.

The last point concerns the mathematical apparatus. Two mathematical artefacts combine to minimize the apparent effect of social class on IQ scores. The first artefact is the use of a variation score that combines within a single number a systematic variation due to group differences (10 IQ points in the above example) with random variation associated with individual differences. The second artefact is the use of an analysis of variance. In this type of analysis, only the squares of differences are being considered, so that the algebraic distinction between the two types of differences disappears. The metric of IQ scores has been built in such a way that 80 per cent of the variance in IQ scores is within a social class, the differences between classes only accounting for 20 per cent of the variance. Yet it is this 20 per cent which corresponds to the large social differences displayed in Fig. 2.1 and in Fig 3.9 and 3.10 of the next chapter.

The popularity of IQ scales among the powers that be probably stems from the fact that these scales incorporate group differences within the individual differences. The individual differences, which are intuitively attributed to inborn differences, tend to mask the systematic social differences. The trees of individual differences hide the forest of class differences.

Part II
How much *could* we boost . . . ?

In Part II the authors report original work performed in France within the National Institute for Health and Medical Research (INSERM). As the titles of both chapters indicate, the issue is that of biological or psychological limits to a democratic access to education. Specifically, the authors examine to what extent the massive exclusion of working-class children from academic tracks and from academic education can be correlated to their alleged genetic inferiority in 'intelligence'. As was pointed out in Chapter 2, IQ scores do not measure intelligence. Yet all genetic studies of 'intelligence' and most arguments about the social heredity of scholastic status are based on IQ scores. Hence the work presented in Chapters 3 and 4 also refers to IQ scores. Far from contradicting the critique of IQ presented in other chapters, the results presented here strengthen the view of IQ scores as socially conditioned indicators of status.

The study described in Chapter 3 arose in the context of the nature--nurture controversy over IQ and over scholastic differences between groups of contrasted origin. The authors report on the 'Intellectual status of working-class children adopted early into upper-middle class families'.

From a theoretical point of view, this study is unique in providing a direct quantitative answer to a question posed in 1913 by Richardson and reformulated by Jensen in 1969: 'How much can we boost IQ and scholastic achievement?' While the American psychologist was pointing the attention towards Black children, the authors, from a European perspective emphasize social class rather than race. How much could we boost achievement in primary school and IQ scores? Apparently a lot.

The title of Chapter 3 emphasizes the distinction between academic questions about genetic differences and socially meaningful questions. This distinction is even more relevant to the question examined in Chapter 4. The authors show that the questions that are socially most relevant are also the ones that are scientifically least ambiguous.

The work presented in Chapter 4 deals with the probability of access of children of manual workers to advanced education. This work is like a three stage rocket. In a first stage, the authors wondered about the social implications of the results of the adoption study presented in Chapter 3. Specifically, they wanted to investigate the possible consequences of certain ambiguities in the interpretation of these results as they bear on the issue of social heredity. In a second stage, they wanted to submit Herrnstein's theory of 'IQ in the meritocracy' to a quantitative test based on an analysis of educational data in 12 OECD countries. In the last stage, they discovered that the most significant issue is not the initiation of a new number game about some parameter measuring social effects or about the relative weight of fiction and reality in Herrnstein's model, but the quantitative analysis of educational waste.

Throughout their analysis, the authors use as an indicator of social discrimination the percentage of waste of academic potential among the children of the 'lower' half of the population, i.e. essentially the children of manual workers. If one chose to ignore the observations presented in Chapter 3, one could enquire whether social effects account for 100 per cent, for 50 per cent or even for 0 per cent of the usual IQ gap between the children of contrasted social groups. It will turn out that this enquiry is largely irrelevant to the question posed in the title of Chapter 4, when this question is formulated in terms of educational waste.

Once again, the real question is not the nature–nurture question but the ideas one has concerning democracy in education. According to the prevailing ideology, social equality within universities could only be achieved at the cost of a levelling down of intellectual standards. The analysis of educational data from 12 countries will show that precisely the reverse is true. Present inequalities can only be maintained at the cost of a large waste of educational potential.

The analysis presented in Chapter 4 brings a new perspective both on the nature–nurture controversy and on the IQ controversy. In the light of the present waste of educational potential, both controversies appear as Byzantine quarrels over the sex of angels.

3. How much *could* we boost scholastic achievement and IQ scores?

A direct answer from a French adoption study by
Michel Schiff, Michel Duyme, Annick Dumaret
and Stanislaw Tomkiewicz

We report here on an adoption study performed in France between 1972 and 1977. The research described here was first presented in a short article entitled 'Intellectual status of working-class children adopted early into upper-middle-class families' (Schiff *et al.* 1978). The final report on our study appeared in French in 1981 and a detailed summary of that report appeared in English in 1982. The present chapter is an English version of our final report* and has been divided into seven sections as follows:

1. Presentation of the study.
2. Subject group A (adopted children).
3. Subject group B (biological half-sibs of group A).
4. Presentation and analysis of the results.
5. Examination of biases.
6. Synthesis and interpretation of the results.
7. Conclusion.

This chapter can be read on three different levels. The reader anxious to have an overview of the study could start by reading Sections 1 and 6. The methodology of the study is described in Sections 2 through 5, as well as the detailed results of our observations. Finally, the methodological and computational details will be found in the appendices.

1. Presentation of the study

General context

In 1913, a British author named Richardson asked what would happen to the 'offspring of poor parents' if they were to live from birth in 'well-to-do and well-educated families'. The study presented here was designed to answer that question.

* We are indebted to Larry Litzky for translating our 1981 report.

The nature–nurture debate over IQ is almost as old as IQ tests, and the number of empirical studies of the variability of IQ scores is large. Correlations between IQ scores of related individuals have been computed and analysed in various situations: ordinary families, twins, twins reared 'apart', and adoption studies. These studies will be discussed in Chapter 6. None of these correlational studies provide any direct answer to the question posed by Richardson.

In 1969, Jensen formulated the question in a slightly different manner: 'How much can we boost IQ and scholastic achievement?'. From an analysis of existing data on various IQ correlations, Jensen estimated that genetic variability accounts for 80 per cent of the variance of individual IQ scores within the White population. From this estimate, he concluded that the failure of most Black children to do well in school was likely to be inherent in their genes.

The fallacy of this conclusion has been pointed out several times before. Jensen's genetic analysis has been criticized, both on theoretical grounds (Lewontin 1970; Feldman and Lewontin 1975; Layzer 1974) and on methodological ones (Kamin 1974). In fact, the alleged value of 0.8 for the heritability of IQ scores offers no answer to the question asked by Jensen in the title of his article. In Part III, the reader will find a discussion of the distinction between heritability within groups and heritability between groups. The distinction between heritability in the broad sense (genetic variability) and heritability in the narrow sense (genetic transmission) will also be discussed, as well as the distinction between heritability and lack of educability. Here let us only point out that, to our knowledge, no author has ever used heritability coefficients (broad or narrow) to make quantitative predictions about the effects of a change of social class. In this respect, it should be stressed that the only other observations providing a direct answer to Jensen's rhetorical question concern Black children (Scarr and Weinberg 1976), not White lower-class ones. In other words, our observations of the effects of a change of social class shortly after birth can be compared to no other estimate, either empirical or theoretical.

In most studies of adopted children, their mean IQ scores have been observed to be above average (e.g. Burks 1928; Horn *et al*. 1979; Skodak and Skeels 1949). This could be explained by the above average status either of the biological parents or of the adoptive parents. Methodological biases in the selection of the children have also been suggested (Munsinger 1975a). To our knowledge, in no study have authors tried to isolate the effects of the social class of adoption by controlling and contrasting the social status of the two sets of parents. We also note the scarcity of data on the scholastic achievements of adopted children, most authors choosing to focus on IQ scores rather than on socially more relevant indicators. In this latter respect, the work of Skeels (1966) is an outstanding exception.

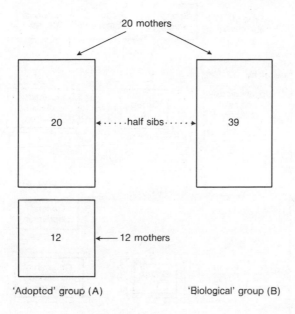

Fig. 3.1   The structure of samples A and B.

The experimental plan

The adopted children (group A) were selected in the following manner: abandoned at birth, they had been placed in adoptive homes before the age of six months. The biological parents were both unskilled, whereas the adoptive father occupied an 'upper-middle-class' position. Thirty-two subjects meeting these criteria were studied.

A second group was constituted by children of 20 of the 32 mothers. These children had grown up in their 'natural' milieu. This group has been designated as group B (biological).

The structure of samples A and B is shown in Fig. 3.1. The children concerned have the same mother and are, in general, half-brothers and half-sisters, i.e. they do not have the same father.

An auxiliary sample was constituted by schoolchildren taking the group tests at the same time as the study subjects. The totality of pupils taking the group tests at the same time as group A has been designated as a_t, and those taking the group test at the same time as group B as b_t. We shall see in what follows that samples a_t and b_t are too biased to provide unambiguous results.

The various comparisons which were made are presented in Fig. 3.2. This diagram brings out both the multiplicity of variables used to

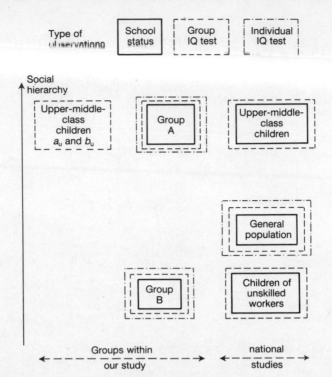

Fig. 3.2 Schematic diagram of the experimental plan.
The two left-hand columns concern the study groups; the right-hand column, groups studied in national surveys. The horizontal rows correspond to position in the social hierarchy. For each group the number and nature of observations made is indicated by the number and nature of rectangles according to the code indicated above the diagram.

determine the status of adopted children and the multiplicity of samples to which the group of adopted children was compared. The variables used are school status (solid line rectangles), IQ scores on a group test (broken line rectangles), and IQ scores on an individual test (dotted line rectangles). Groups A (adopted) and B (biological) are located at the centre of the diagram. Groups of schoolchildren studied in national surveys (school records and group tests) or in the standardization of a test (individual tests) appear on the right. On the left are shown the children of 'upper-middle-class' families who took the group test at the same time as subjects A (group a_u) or at the same time as subjects B (group b_u). The vertical position of the groups on the diagram corresponds to their position in the social hierarchy.

The study was conceived in 1971 and carried out between 1972 and 1977. Most of the analysis was done between 1977 and 1979. Initially, a strict separation had been planned between the three major phases of the study:

1. a pilot study and the working out of methods;
2. the definition of the sample of adopted children;
3. the application of methods worked out during the first phase to the subjects defined in the second.

In practice, however, there was a certain overlapping of these phases. The original experimental plan concerned the study of siblings raised in contrasting environments. We had hoped to compare children whose two biological parents were the same, one of these children having been adopted (subject A) and the other having been raised in his original milieu (subject B).

Two reasons led us to modify this plan. On the one hand, in the majority of cases it became clear that the biological father of subject A was not the same as that of subject B. On the other hand, the tracing of biological families turned out to be even more complicated than initially foreseen, and the completion of the project was thus made somewhat problematical. Consequently, the experimental plan had to be modified.

The criterion of a common father for children A and B was replaced by one entailing that the adopted child's biological father be at the bottom of the occupational ladder. Thus, without giving up the idea of a biological control group internal to the study, we shifted the focus of our experimental plan from the question of nature–nurture (siblings raised in contrasting environments) to a plan focusing on the question of social heredity (adopted children having moved up the social ladder). To a certain degree, we were able to achieve both objectives at the same time since, of the 32 mothers of the adopted subjects studied, 20 had one or more school-age children living in the original milieu.

Another modification involved the development of our reseach methodology. Because of difficulties encountered, we decided to give up the idea of using the same research methods for all subjects in favour of a more flexible methodology which could be adapted to each individual case. In spite of these modifications, we have maintained the spirit if not the letter of the above-mentioned separation: in each case the choice of subjects was made blindly, i.e. without our having any information whatsoever on the subject's school or psychometric performance.

2. Subject group A (adopted children)

Preliminary analysis of the files

For our study we required the collaboration of adoption agencies taking in a large number of infants abandoned at birth by parents of the lowest social strata. The study required agencies which practised a 'liberal' adoption policy, i.e. they often placed children in families early in life and/or across social class barriers.

In order to obtain a high proportion of parents from the lowest social strata we contacted public welfare services (DDASS[1]). After a pilot study, a questionnaire was sent out to 80 such services outside the Paris area. After analysing the 79 responses obtained, we undertook on-site analysis of abandonment files in nine agencies. Of the nine agencies consulted, six happened to have files which met the rather stringent criteria demanded by our study.

The choice of subjects was made in a 'funnel' selection process. Increasingly strict criteria were applied, starting first from lists of state wards and then, among these, from files of children who had been abandoned at birth.

During a first phase, we transcribed information concerning identity and administrative situation from registration lists. From this list of some 5000 state wards, we drew up a second list of state wards who had been abandoned during the first month of their lives. The corresponding 1136 files were then scanned, and we obtained a list of files worthy of being examined in detail.

Appendices 1–3 contain a statistical description of the files from among which the study candidates were selected. Appendix 1 describes the content of documents transcribed from welfare services starting from the 1136 cases of abandonment at birth as well as other documents on file concerning the subjects studied. Appendix 2 deals with the numerical code used at the end of the study to classify the occupations of the biological parents (and, when appropriate, those of the adoptive parents) of the 476 children abandoned at birth and for which the putative father's profession was known. The statistical profile of these 476 files is described in Appendix 3. The selection process is summed up in Table 3.1.

We looked for children for whom there was a maximum contrast between the socio-professional status of the biological parents and that of the adoptive parents. To this end, the occupations of both biological and adoptive parents were classified into four categories (see Table 3.2).

The first category, divided into classes 1 and 1a, corresponds to the high social status desired for the adoptive parents; the last category corresponds to those occupations desired for the biological parents, and the intermediate category permitted the elimination of a file. This classification resulted from a compromise between the quality of the sample (i.e. the

[1] DDASS: *Direction Départementale d'Action Sanitaire et Sociale* (Departmental Social and Health Bureau). From an administrative point of view, France is sub-divided into 95 *départements*, with one DDASS in each. An adoption agency is included in each DDASS.

Table 3.1   *Summary of the selection process*

	No.
Children abandoned at birth in 6 adoption agencies	1136
The occupation of the putative father is known	476 out of 1136
The biological parents were both unskilled workers	168 out of 476
Placement for adoption occurred before the age of 6 months	102 out of 168
High socio-professional status of the head of the adoptive family	43 out of 102
Subjects retained for the study of their school and psychometric status	32 out of 43[a]

[a] The analysis of the 11 candidates not retained is presented on pp. 75–76.

Table 3.2   *Classification of occupations into main classes. These categories were used to classify the files of the adopted children and to select those for whom there was the greatest contrast between biological and adoptive parents*

Class 1 – Upper-middle-class: Includes senior executives,[a] professionals (doctors, lawyers, accountants, etc.), businessmen (excluding shopkeepers and artisans), and certain middle-level managers.

Class 1a – Middle-class: Includes middle-level managers, junior executives, small businessmen, artisans, and certain highly skilled personnel and students.

Class 2 – Lower-middle-class: Lacking homogeneity, it includes shopkeepers, military and police personnel, sales representatives, office workers, skilled workers, farmers (male), and various semi-skilled personnel.

Class 3 – Lower-class: Includes unskilled workers, labourers, drivers, domestic personnel, farm hands, and various unskilled workers. For women, four supplementary groups were included in this category: salesgirls, farmers, illiterate or mentally deficient women, and women on welfare.

[a] See footnote 1 of Appendix 2, p. 95.

contrast between the two types of occupations) and its size.

A more precise classification of occupations was undertaken at the conclusion of the study to allow for comparisons with national surveys on school-age children (INED–INOP, 1973; Ministère de l'Education 1976). The occupations were then classified according to the INSEE* coding system with the aid of the INSEE manual published after the 1968 census (INSEE 1968). Details of this final classification are provided in Appendix 2.

* *Institut National de la Statistique et des Etudes Economiques* (National Institute for Statistics and Economic Studies).

Table 3.3 Socio-professional profile of the adoptive families of the 32 A subjects

No.	Socio-professional level (mother)			Socio-professional level (father)		
	Code[a]	Occupational level	Nature of activity	Code[a]	Occupational level	Nature of activity
1	n	None	At home	12	Junior executive	Technical
2	12	(ex) Junior executive	Medical/social services	10	Senior executive	Higher education
3[b]	12	(ex) Junior executive	Medical/social services	10	Senior executive	Higher education
4[b]	12	Junior executive	Secondary education	12	Junior executive	Intellectual
5	12	(ex) Junior executive	Secondary education	10	Senior executive	Technical
6	23	(ex) Employee	Office work	10	Senior executive	Technical
7	n	None	At home	10	Senior executive	Technical
8	n	None	At home	10	Senior executive	Commercial
9	10	Senior executive	Secondary education	10	Senior executive	Technico-commercial
10	10	Senior executive	Secondary education	10	Senior executive	Commercial
11	10	Senior executive	Higher education	10	Senior executive	Higher education
12	n	None	At home	13	Entrepreneur	Service
13	17	Junior executive	Primary education	10	Senior executive	Scientific
14	23	(ex) Employee	Office work	11	Professional	Professional
15	n	None	At home	10	Senior executive	Secondary education
16	n	None	At home	10	Senior executive	Technical
17	n	None	At home	10	Senior executive	Technical
18	n	None	At home	18	Contractor/artisan	Construction
19	n	None	At home	13	Businessman	Service
20	18	(ex) Artisan	Service	10	Senior executive	Administrative
21	n	None	At home	12	Junior executive	Administrative
22[b]	n	None	At home	13	Contractor	Construction
23	10	Senior executive	Medical/social services			***
24	n	None	At home	10	Senior executive	Technical
25	12	(ex) Junior executive	Medical/social services	10	Senior executive	Higher education
26	10	Senior executive	Secondary education	10	Senior executive	Higher education
27	12	Junior executive	Medical/social services	10	Senior executive	Technical
28	17	Junior executive	Primary education	11	Professional	Professional
29	12	(ex) Junior executive	Medical/social services	10	Senior executive	Technical
30	12	Junior executive	Primary education	10	Senior executive	Intellectual
31	12	(ex) Junior executive	Medical/social services	10	Senior executive	Commercial
32	n	None	At home	12	Junior executive	Commercial

n = none
[a] For a precise definition of socio-professional categories, see Appendix 2.
[b] Twins.
*** Adoptive mother was single.

In a few cases, our classification does not correspond exactly to that of INSEE. These disparities, which are analysed in the section dealing with biases, are due to the fact that the first classification was made during our initial study of welfare agency files whereas the final coding was made after the study of the subjects.

Definition of the sample

'Candidates for the study' were included in the sample if:

1. they were born between 1 January 1962 and 31 December 1969;
2. they were abandoned at birth (prior to the age of one month);
3. their biological mother's occupation was in class 3;*
4. their putative father's occupation was in class 3;
5. placement for adoption occurred before the age of 6 months; and
6. the head of their adoptive family was in class 1.

Of the 1136 abandoned-at-birth cases, 43 met the above criteria. Eleven files, which shall be dealt with in depth in the section devoted to biases, were not included in the study. The reasons leading to the exclusion of these 11 files from the study have no relation to the probability of school failure. The number of subjects studied was 32.

Profile of A subjects

Table 3.3 provides a coded description of the SES characteristics of each of the A children. The subjects were numbered from 1 to 32, 1 through 20 being attributed to A subjects for whom there was at least one corresponding B child of school age. A children for whom there was no corresponding B child were designated by numbers 21 to 32.

Age at the time of abandonment was determined by the official declaration of abandonment, usually signed by the mother when she left the place where she gave birth. Abandonment generally took place at the end of the first week of the child's life (age varied from one to 13 days, with a median age of seven days).

Of the 32 births, three concerned pairs of twins so that, in fact, there were 35 children in the group of adopted children. Throughout the study, each pair of twins was regarded as a single subject. These 'double' subjects are constituted by pairs of twins of the same sex adopted by the same family.

The birth weight is known for three-quarters of the subjects, and the

* Three mothers who had no occupation were included in the sample: two women on welfare and one mother of five children who was married to a labourer.

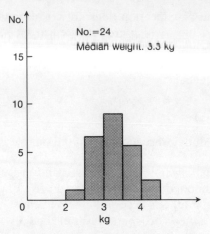

Fig. 3.3   Birth weight of 24 A subjects.

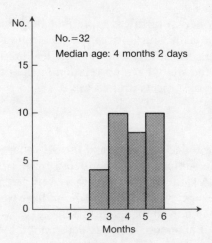

Fig. 3.4   Age of the 32 A subjects at the time of adoptive placement.

weight distribution, illustrated in Fig. 3.3, is normal. It should be noted that one pair of twins was born prematurely. In addition, one of the twin births was accompanied by circumstances indicating a considerable biological trauma.

The age at placement in the adoptive family is illustrated in Fig. 3.4. This age varies from two months, one day to five months, 25 days with a median value of four months, two days. The sex distribution is balanced; of the 32 subjects, 15 are male and 17 are female. Before the adoptive placement, most subjects were kept in state nursing homes; in other cases, they were taken care of by nursing families paid by the state.

The socio-professional levels of the adoptive parents are presented in Table 3.3. With respect to socio-professional category, the following correspondence exists between the classes defined at the beginning of the chapter and the two-figure codes presented in Appendix 2.

Class 1	Codes 11–13
Class 1a	Codes 15–19
Class 2	Codes 20–27
Class 3	Codes 30–36

The occupations of the adoptive mothers are as follows:

Without profession	13
Employees	2
Shopkeepers	1
Junior executives	11
Senior executives	5
	—
	32

Those of the adoptive fathers are as follows:

Employer (artisan)	1
Employer (medium-sized business)	3
Professionals	2
Junior executives	4
Senior executives	21
Father lacking	1
	—
	32

It will be noted that for one of the subjects, case number 18, the occupation of the adoptive father is in class 1a. On the basis of the adoption file, the adoptive father had been classified in class 1 (contractor). After the child had been tested and his school file known, it became apparent that the adoptive father's occupation had been overestimated (he was, in fact, an artisan having three employees). In conformity with our general policy with respect to biases, we did not exclude this subject as his history was already known.

The socio-professional categories of the biological parents are presented in Table 3.4. The mother's age and occupation are often known at two different times: at the time of birth of the A child and when one of her children begins primary school. The age indicated is the first one. The age of

Table 3.4   *Socio-professional profile of the biological parents of the 32 A subjects*

No.	Biological mother	Age[a]	Biological father (putative)	Age[a]
1	Worker	19	Car body shop worker	25
2	Factory worker	22	Worker	25
3	Factory worker	28	Mason	?
4	Housewife (5 children)	37	Labourer in masonry	38
5	Worker	27	Worker	27
6	Maid	19	Bulldozer operator	25
7	Farm worker	27	Worker in masonry	40
8	Maid	21	Turner	23
9	Maid	22	Worker	?
10	Maid	30	Worker	22
11	Worker, kitchen helper	30	Worker	32
12	Worker	24	Worker	25–30
13	Worker	19	Worker	20
14	Night attendant	28	Night work in postal service	44
15	Maid	23	Unskilled worker	31
16	Farm worker	34	Truck driver	30
17	Maid	23	Driver	30
18	Maid	23	Worker in carpentry	31
19	Salesgirl	22	Mechanic	23
20	Maid	29	Worker	37
21	Waitress	30	Mechanic	25
22	Welfare case	39	Assembler	54
23	Maid	27	Assembler in electricity	25
24	Welfare case	33	Labourer	26
25	Factory worker	17	Mechanic	19
26	Worker	20	Mechanic	30
27	Maid	22	Driver	?
28	Factory worker	24	Labourer	?
29	Salesgirl	19	Factory worker	25
30	Waitress	23	Waiter	30
31	Maid	24	Worker	28
32	Cleaning woman	33	Worker	32

[a] At birth of the A subject.

the biological fathers is such that their belonging to the working class may be considered as permanent. This is often also true for the biological mothers. At the time of birth of the A subjects, the average age of biological mothers is 26 years and that of the putative fathers is 29 years.

The terms used for the parental occupations are those used in the documents consulted. For the putative fathers and for the 12 mothers having no other children in the study other than child A, information concerning occupations is taken from the official declaration of abandonment. For the mothers of a B subject, the information is also drawn from school files.

The occupations of the biological mothers can be summarized as follows:

Workers	12
Domestic personnel	12
Waitresses, salesgirls, night attendant	5
Without occupation	3 (including 2 welfare cases)

As for the putative fathers, the summary of their occupations is the following:

Unskilled workers	26
Truck drivers and heavy equipment operators	4
Other unskilled occupations	2

There is nothing exceptional in the composition of the adoptive families. Two of these families took in two subjects each so that, in fact, there were only 30 adoptive families. It should be noted that in one case (adoption by a single woman) there was no father and that, according to school teachers, there were two instances of families breaking up (separation or divorce). For each of the 32 subjects, the number of children in the adoptive sibship varied from one to four with an average of 2.2 children. In only five cases were the subjects the only child. The position of the subject in the adoptive sibship varied randomly. At the birth of the A child, the adoptive mother and father were, on the average, 36 and 37 years old respectively.

To summarize: the group of adopted children is made up of 35 children living in 30 different families. Each of the three pairs of twins was considered as a single subject so that there are statistically 32 subjects. The ratio of boys to girls is normal. The birth weight distribution is also normal. Abandoned at about the age of seven days, the subjects were taken in by their adoptive families at about four months. All of the putative fathers are unskilled workers; the mothers are also at the bottom of the occupational ladder. On the other hand, half of the adoptive mothers and the majority of the adoptive fathers occupy relatively high positions (senior or junior executives, professionals). Two-thirds of the adoptive fathers are senior executives; Table 3.5. provides a list of these characteristics.

Ethical considerations and policy

Not to cause harm to the study subjects was and remains one of our major concerns. The ethical aspects of the research were analysed at the beginning of the study even before we had solved the methodological problems. The results of this analysis led us to propose a set of precautions which

Table 3.5 *Summary of the characteristics of the 32 A subjects*

Number	Age at abandonment (days)	Twins	Birth weight (kg)	Age at placement (months/days)	Sex	Socio professional category code[a] A mother	A father	B mother	B father	Sibship Rank	Size
1A	8		2.90	5/18	F	n	12	32	32	2	2
2A	6		3.30	3	F	12	10	32	32	3	3
A1 3	6	×	2.35	3/3	M	12	10	32	32	1	3
A2	6	×	2.10	3/3	M	12	10	32	32	2	3
A1 4	7	×		5/26	F	12	12	n	32	3	4
A2	7	×		5/26	F	12	12	n	32	4	4
5A	6		3.50	3/26	F	12	10	32	32	2	4
6A	8			2/1	F	23	10	33	33	2	2
7A	1			5/25	M	n	10	34	32	1	1
8A	6		2.90	4/14	F	n	10	33	32	1	1
9A	4			5/16	M	10	10	33	32	2	2
10A	6		3.80	3/27	F	10	10	33	32	2	2
11A	4		3.10	3/3	F	10	10	32	32	1	2
12A	6		3.50	5/3	F	n	13	32	32	2	2
13A	6		3.40	4/3	M	17	10	32	32	1	2
14A	8		4.20	5/6	M	23	11	33	35	2	3
15A	8			4/22	M	n	10	33	32	1	1
16A	9		2.60	4/4	F	n	10	34	33	2	2
17A	8		3.08	3/17	F	n	10	33	33	1	2
18A	13			4/1	F	n	18	33	32	2	2
19A	9		2.88	2/21	F	n	13	30	32	2	3
20A	10			3/11	M	18	10	33	32	1	2
21A	10			3/1	M	n	12	33	32	1	1
A1 22	10	×	2.80	5/14	F	n	13	36	32	1	2
A2	10	×	3.50	5/14	F	n	13	36	32	2	2
23A	10		3.34[b]	5/25	M	10	–	33	32	2	2
24A	5		3.30	5/22	F	n	10	36	32	3	3
25A	10		2.95	2/13	F	12	10	32	32	3	4
26A	9		3.45	4/21	M	10	10	32	32	1	1
27A	10		3.30	2/11	M	12	10	33	33	1	2
28A	6		3.30	3/29	M	17	11	32	32	1	3
29A	7		3.68	3/16	F	12	10	30	32	2	2
30A	1		4.00	4/25	M	12	10	33	33	1	2
31A	6		3.80	4/2	M	12	10	33	32	1	2
32A	2		2.50	5/17	M	n	12	33	32	1	2

n = none
[a] For an explanation of occupational codes, see Table 3.2 and Appendix 2.
[b] At 10 days.

received the approval of the National Association of Adoptive House-holds, of the personnel concerned at the Ministry of Health, and of people funding the research programme. This approval was instrumental in enlist-ing the co-operation of the adoption agencies.

Our guiding principle was that of minimal interaction with the children and their families. We never met the children's parents, either biological or adoptive, and did not reveal the special status of the children to teaching and administrative personnel. With the exception of a few persons working at the Ministry of Health and the Ministry of Education, the only people informed of the study subjects' special status were school doctors and per-sonnel of adoption agencies.

It seemed to us that if we told the adoptive parents, and *a fortiori* the biological parents, of the special status of their children as the subjects of an adoption study, this might disturb both parents and children. Conse-quently, we decided to study the scholastic and psychometric status of the children without informing the parents in advance.

The group tests were always given to an entire class at a time. With respect to more individualized information (individual test and school record) we used the following procedure to avoid singling out a child: three children were selected apparently at random or according to socio-professional criteria.

Collecting the data

Precise information was available for all the adoptive families of the study (identity, address, telephone number, etc.). However, as this information dated from the time of adoption, it was occasionally over 10 years old. We were, nevertheless, able to trace each subject's adoptive family, in large part thanks to telephone directories. At the time of the study, all 30 fami-lies were listed in a telephone directory.

The school in which the child was enrolled was generally indicated to us by a social service external to the school. In six cases, this information was obtained through the answers to an impersonal and innocuous question-naire which, as a last resort, we had sent to several parents. The apparent subject of this questionnaire was school transportation.

Once the subject's school was known, we had to find out his grade and class. This information was usually obtained by correspondence. We asked the principal of the school to supply us with lists of students born the same year as the subject. Next, we requested the authorization to spend a few hours in a class to administer some tests. The 'choice' of the class was at times made *in extremis* in the principal's office after examining class rosters.

Access to the various schools was facilitated by the fact that we patiently followed hierarchial channels, requesting in each case the necessary authorization, first at the ministerial level, then at the level of the board of education, and finally at the school itself. On a few occasions we met with a certain reluctance, but this was overcome in each case, and we thus managed to be granted access to each school. Again, we emphasize that our requests to administer tests always concerned an entire class and never a particular child.

It should be remembered that the set of procedures employed (access to schools, 'choice' of the class, and of the children to be tested, test procedures and school information) had been worked out in a pilot study on subjects not meeting the study's criteria. The care with which these procedures had been worked out doubtlessly contributed to the fact that the subsequent study ran quite smoothly.

Our goal was to obtain two IQ scores, one from a group test, the other from an individual test. This goal was achieved in 95 per cent of the cases for the group test and 100 per cent for the individual test (see Table 3.10 p. 64).

The order of testing was always the same. A psychologist (A.D.) administered the group test to the entire class. Meanwhile, a colleague (M.D.) obtained from the teacher information on three children chosen from the class list apparently at random or on the basis of parental occupations. These three children were then tested individually. For the subject, the test was always administered in its entirety, and always by the same person (with the exception of a child who had been previously tested by a school psychologist, see below). For the two children who served as a 'mask' for the subject, the tests were administered by one or the other of the two psychologists and were not administered in full.

The group test selected was the one most frequently used in the current school system and for which the influence of social class had been studied. This test, the *Echelle Collective de Niveau Intellectuel* (ECNI, Group Scale of Intellectual Level) had been standardized during a large national survey undertaken by the National Institute for Professional Orientation and Guidance in collaboration with the National Institute for Demographic Studies (INED–INOP 1973). The version of the test used depended upon the child's grade: Booklet I for first grade, Booklet II for second and third grades, Booklet III for fourth and fifth grades, and Booklet IV for sixth and seventh grades.

The administration of the group test was complete with, however, two exceptions. In the first case, the test had to be limited to the non-verbal items because of a shortage of time. In the second case, Booklet II had been brought along instead of Booklet I. This test was consequently also limited to the non-verbal items. We were, nevertheless, able to mark them, since the standardization of the different booklets had been made with a partial overlapping of age groups.

The age bracket of the subjects (born between 1962 and 1969) was selected to correspond with that covered by the school grades 1 to 7. However, as a result of testing programme delays, one subject was already in the eighth grade at the time the test was administered. In this case, we resorted to another group test, the 2A Scale, Cattell (1974). In addition, as the ENCI test had not been planned for children in special classes, one child who was in a remedial class was given an individual test only. One child absent the morning the group test was administered also took the individual test only.

The group tests were marked twice, each time independently. To minimize biases, we had decided to avoid any retrospective definition of samples. For this reason, the marking of the group test was delayed until the end of the study, when all decisions concerning the samples had been made.

For individual testing, the French version of the WISC (Wechsler 1965) was used. The test was always administered in its entirety under standard conditions by a qualified psychologist (A.D.). The final marking of items for which a personal judgement might have intervened was put off until the end of the study. As in the case of the group test, the final marking of items and the calculation of IQ scores were postponed until June, 1976, the date corresponding to the final verification of a subject's meeting study criteria.

The marking of items and the calculation of scores were done independently by two different psychologists, one external to the research team. The scores used were the average of the two scores. The disparity between the two series of scores is negligible (see Table 3.10).

With respect to the problem of social inequality, 'school status' is a more directly relevant variable than IQ score. Methodologically, this variable also presents certain advantages. On the one hand, it constitutes a datum that cannot be influenced by the personal biases of the researcher and, on the other, the probability of error is negligible given the quality of the information sources consulted. Information on school history is provided in Table 3.8.

The information sources used were the following:

—knowledge of a child's grade at the time of testing;
—school transcripts;
—school responses to a questionnaire updating school history that was sent out at the end of the study.

At the time of our visits to the various schools, three subjects were at least one year behind in school. The answers to the questionnaires sent out

at the end of the study brought to light another case of a child's being left
back. The number of children completely successful was thus brought
down to 28.

In 25 of these 28 cases the absence of 'school failure' is attested to not
only by our own observations and transcriptions made during our visits to
the schools, but also by a written document sent to us by the school administration. In the three cases where the school did not answer the questionnaire, success is attested to by our observations and transcriptions and by
the response we received to a second inquiry made by telephone (cases 29,
30, and 32).

In each case, the school history was updated either to the 1977–78 school
year or to the child's entry into sixth grade. (One history could only be
updated to the 1976–77 school year as the child had moved without leaving
an address.)

3. Subject group B (biological half-sibs of group A)

The definition of the B sample is, to a great degree, a result of the definition of the A sample, since the A subject was the point of departure for
the definition of the B subject by the fact of having the same biological
mother. Moreover, there are no differences between the two samples with
respect to ethical considerations, access to schools, and the study of school
histories. As far as the tests are concerned, the major difference results
from the decision to obtain IQ scores for only one B child per sibship (see
Table 3.6.).

Definition and description of the sample

In a report on the methodology of their adoption study, Skeels and Skodak
(1965) had stated that three qualities were needed for such investigations:
'Flexibility, Ingenuity, and Tenacity'. The success of the Skeels follow-up
had been an inspiration to us, and we named our research team the FIT
group. The tracing of the B subjects represented a *tour de force* which
nearly mobilized all the resources available for the study and by this fact,
threatened its very completion. The various difficulties were, however,
overcome, and we were able to constitute a valid sample of B subjects.

The tracing of the biological families took over three years and covered a
large part of France. It was undertaken by persons accustomed to dealing
with information requiring professional secrecy. We would like to pay tri-
bute to the ingenuity and tenacity of these persons and in particular to two
social workers, D. Southway and N. Forma. Although both the telephone
and letters were used in doing this research, it was often necessary to give
of one's self and cover hundreds of kilometres just to obtain a small item of

information from a social service, an administrative agency, or an individual. These craftsmen's piecemeal procedures were, in the end, quite effective since with only one exception, we were able to trace all the subject A biological mothers for whom the identity was known. In four cases, the identity of the A subject's biological mother was not known and these mothers could not be traced.

With respect to children born before the A subject, their existence, and sometimes their identity was indicated in the A subject's abandonment file. In addition, we consulted a number of other independent sources to learn of the possible existence of other children and, in particular, of children born after subject A. The principal sources consulted were the following:

—DDASS* files on abandonment and other records, such as those concerning monthly family allowances;
—the records of various national social services to learn if the persons for whom we were able to provide the complete identity (name, date and place of birth) did or did not have dependent children;
—birth registrars at the mother's birthplace on occasion provided useful information regarding changes in the mother's marital status.

Table 3.6 describes the final results of this search. The first column indicates the mother's number in the same order as that for the A subjects. The table is then divided into three parts. In the central part, Subject A's birth date is indicated. Children born before Subject A appear on the left, those born after, on the right. Children abandoned or born outside of the 1958–70 period are represented by a number. The potential B subjects, i.e. those born in the 1958–70 period and not abandoned, are each represented by the year of their birth.

Thus, for example, mother 17 did not abandon any child other than Subject A. She had a child in 1961, abandoned Subject A at birth in 1964, and had two other children, one in 1965 and the other in 1967. She had no children before 1958 or after 1970.

Information concerning the 39 B subjects is presented in Table 3.7. There were no twins in this group. The sex distribution is balanced (20 girls and 19 boys). With respect to family milieu and social environment, the major sources of information consulted were files of adoption agencies and items on family information appearing in school records and on a family questionnaire which was included in the record.

The first column of Table 3.7 indicates the number of the sibship (corresponding to the numbers of the first 20 A subjects). The next column gives the B child's sex and year of birth. For one-quarter of the children, the

* See footnote, p. 42.

Table 3.6 *Synoptic table of the children of the 32 biological mothers of the A subjects*

	Children born before subject A			Subject A (1962–69)	Children born after subject A		
	Abandoned	Not abandoned			Not abandoned		Abandoned
No.	Abandoned	Born before 1958	1958–70ᵃ	Subject A (1962–69)	1958–1970ᵃ	Born after 1970	Abandoned
1			*1961*	1962	1964, *1965*, 1967	1	2
2		1	*1962*	1965			
3			*1963*	1963ᵇ, 1965ᵇ			
4			1959, 1960, 1961, *1965*	1968			
5		1	1962, 1963, *1963*	1964	1970	1	
6				1965		2	
7			*1967*	1968	1969	1	
8			*1964*	1965	1966	1	
9			*1963*	1968			
10			1960, *1968*	1969			
11		1	1960, 1962	1968	*1969*	2	
12			*1967*	1968		1	
13			*1966*	1968			
14			1962, *1966*	1968			
15			1958, *1965*	1965			
16		3		1963	*1964*, 1965, 1967	1	
17			*1961*	1964	1970, 1967	2	
18	1			1967	1965		2
19	2		*1959*	1964	1970		1
20	2			1968			2ᵇ
21	5			1966			
22	1	1		1962ᵇ			
23	7			1968			
24				1963			
25				1969			
26				1963			
27				1963			
28	2		*1961*	1962			
29				1966			
30			1966, *1967*	1969			
31			1967, 1962	1969			
32			3 children				

ᵃ In each sibship, the B subject tested is that for which the birth date appears in italics.
ᵇ Two twins.

family head's job qualification is superior to that of Subject A's biological father. However, the family situation is often unstable, as the fourth column indicates. The legal status of each B child appears in the last column of Table 3.7. A breakdown of the legal categories is presented below:

Legitimate child born during a marriage	22
Born before marriage, later legitimized by father	1
Natural child, later legitimized by husband	7
Natural child of a single mother	7
Adulterine child	2
	—
Total	39

A summary of the social and familial characteristics of the 39 B children, appears in Table 3.16.

Collecting the data

When a sibship contained more than one B child, we tested only one, selecting preferably the one closest in age to the corresponding A subject. The children thus selected are represented in Table 3.6 by an italic birth date. In two cases the child selected was not the closest in age (families 1 and 10): this modification corresponds to the choice of a child with a more 'normal' family life than the B subject closest in age (see Table 3.7). This choice was made *a priori* before test results and school history were known.

As far as the individual test is concerned, in 90 per cent of the cases the score comes from a WISC administered by us. The two scores coming from another individual test administered before the study correspond to the two oldest children who were no longer enrolled in school.

In the case of the group test, we proceeded as with the A children:

—For children in the normal track from first to seventh grade, we used the ENCI with the booklet corresponding to the subject's grade.
—For one child who was in the eighth grade, the ENCI was replaced by the Cattell 2A Scale.
—For children in 'slow learner' classes and for one of the two children in remedial classes, we used test scores supplied by the school.

In the latter cases, the absence of an ENCI test score is directly linked to the child's failing situation and consequently the elimination of these subjects from the comparisons would have biased the results rather heavily.

Table 3.7 *Familial and social milieu of the 39 B children*

No.	Sex and year[c]	Socio-professional milieu	Living with[d] . . .	Legal status[a]
1B1	F 61	Worker	Paternal grandparents	N
1B2	F 64	Worker	2 parents	R
1B3	M 65	Worker	,, ,,	L
1B4	M 67	Worker	,, ,,	L
2B	F 63	Worker	(Nurses[b]) (mother + aunt + uncle)	N
3B	M 62	Worker	(Grandmother) (mother + second husband)	N-L
4B1	M 59	Worker	(2 parents) (father + uncle + grandmother)	L
4B2	F 60	Worker	,, ,,	L
4B3	F 61	Worker	,, ,,	L
4B4	F 63	Worker	,, ,,	L
5B1	M 62	Worker	(2 parents) (mother + second husband)	L
5B2	M 63	Worker	,, ,,	L
5B3	F 65	Worker	,, ,,	L
5B4	M 70	Worker	2 parents	L
6B	M 63	Mother, worker; stepfather, military personnel	Mainly maternal grandparents	N-L
7B	M 69	Farm labourer	Nurse[b] paid by mother	N
8B	M 67	Worker	Alternately: mother + stepfather, grandparents	N-L
9B1	F 64	Skilled worker	(Nurse[b]) (mother + stepfather)	N-L
9B2	F 66	Skilled worker	2 Parents	L
10B1	F 60	Mother, domestic personnel; grandparents, shopkeepers	(Grandparents) (mother)	N
10B2	M 63	Mother, domestic personnel	(Nurses[b]) (mother) (institutional home)	N

No.	Sex and year[c]	Socio-professional milieu	Living with[d] . . .	Legal status[a]
11B1	M 60 ⎫	Worker	(2 Parents) (father + companion)	N–L
11B2	M 62 ⎬	Worker	,,	L
11B3	M 68 ⎭	Worker	(Nurses[b]) (mother) (institutional home)	A
12B	F 67	Worker	(2 Parents) (mother + grandmother) (mother + second husband)	L
13B	F 66	Worker	(Widowed mother) (grandparents) (mother + second husband)	L
14B1	F 62	Mother, domestic personnel	Maternal grandmother	A
14B2	F 66	Mother, domestic personnel	Stable nurse[b]	N
15B1	M 58	Mother, domestic personnel	(Mother) (mother + husband)	N–L
15B2	F 65	Father, military personnel	(2 Parents) (father)	L
16B	M 64	Farm labourers	(Widowed mother) (mother + companion)	L
17B1	M 61 ⎫	Artisan	(Nurse[b]) (mother + husband)	N–L
17B2	M 65 ⎬	Artisan	2 Parents	L
17B3	F 67 ⎭	Artisan	,,	L
18B	F 70	Domestic personnel	2 Parents	L
19B1	F 65 ⎫	Employee	2 Parents	L
19B2	F 67 ⎬	Employee	,,	L
19B3	M 70 ⎭	Employee	,,	L
20B	F 59	Mother domestic personnel	Grandparents	N

[a] Legal status: R, born before marriage; officially recognized at the time of marriage; L, legitimate child born during a marriage; N, natural child of a single mother; N–L, natural child subsequently legitimated by a marriage; A, adulterine child.
[b] 'Nurse' is a translation of the French term *nourrice*; see footnote, page 87.
[c] Brackets indicate children raised together.
[d] Parentheses indicate chronological succession of family situations.

The school history is known for the 39 B children. The information provided in Table 3.9 for each child comes from several sources:

1. For the 20 B children tested, the sources are the same as for the A children:
   —The child's grade at the time of our visiting the school;
   —school transcripts;
   —updating by correspondence at the end of the study.
2. For the 19 B children not tested, the school history was obtained by correspondence, as was the updating.

The updating allowed us to know the school history up to either the beginning of sixth grade or of the 1977–78 school year. It should be noted that in three cases (1 B^1, 15 B^1, and 20 B) school failure is not known from the school history but only by the child's situation at the beginning of the sixth grade (one year behind in each case with, in two cases, the child entering a remedial class). Finally let us point out that in 23 out of the 24 cases of failure, the reality of failure is confirmed by a written document which was not transcribed by us (i.e. by responses to an updating questionnaire filled out and returned by the school).

4. Presentation and analysis of the results

The results have first been presented for each of the 74 study children, thus providing the reader with the means to verify our statistical analysis. In the interest of clarity, the details of this analysis have been relegated to the appendices. Next, we have presented 12 comparisons of three different types (see Fig. 3.2). The A subject group is compared to the B subject group. It is also compared to samples studied in national surveys, both of the general population and of social groups comparable to those of our study subjects. Finally, in the special case of the group test, we tried to use two samples internal to the study. The totality of these comparisons is summed up in Table 3.13.

For the A children, each pair of twins is treated as a single subject. This choice, which had been made at the beginning of the study, is not only in conformity with the logic of statistics; it also avoids giving excessive weight to the three sets of twins whose geminate situation *a priori* leads to lower IQ scores (see p. 46 and Zazzo 1960).

Raw data for each child

School history details for children A and B are presented in Tables 3.8 and 3.9. The child's scholastic situation is specified for each grade up until the

school year indicated in the last column: skipping grades, normal pro-
motions, being left back once or twice, placement in special classes
(remedial or 'slow learner' classes).

At the time this study was undertaken, a number of different terms were
used in the French education system for special classes for pupils not
advancing at the 'normal' rate. The French terms may be understood with
the aid of the following table:

	Permanent exclusion from the 'normal' tracks	*Temporary exclusion from the 'normal' tracks*
	'slow learner' classes	'Remedial' classes
Primary level	*Classes de perfectionnement*	*Classes d'adaptation*
Secondary level	*Section d'éducation specialisée* (SES)	*Classes de Transition, Classe Allégée –6ème III*

(As indicated, classes entailing permanent exclusion have been designated
as 'slow learner' classes in English; those entailing only temporary exclusion have been designated as 'remedial' classes.)

Turning once more to Tables 3.8 and 3.9, one notices that the number of
x's indicates the number of years spent in the corresponding grade. The
first instance of repeating a grade is indicated by italics as is placement in a
special class. Lastly, the figure in the penultimate column gives the number
of years that the child is behind at entry into sixth grade. Thus, subject 1 A
enters 'on time' into a normal sixth grade class at the beginning of the
1973–74 school year whereas subject 1 B, at the same date, enters one year
late into a remedial sixth grade class.

It will be observed that, with the exception of subjects 16 A and 7 B, the
last grade for which we have information corresponds to the entry into
sixth grade or to the last year of the study (1977–78 school year).

Tables 3.10 and 3.11 present the test scores for the A and B children
respectively. It should be remembered that for the B children, testing was
limited to one child per sibship.

The left side of the table concerns the individual test, in all cases, the
WISC, with the exception of two B children who were no longer enrolled
in school. The right side concerns the group test. The test used was the
ENCI, except for two children in eighth grade at the time of testing (who
took the Cattell test) and except for children in special classes (who had
already been tested by the schools). The last column gives the average of
the scores obtained on the two tests.

Table 3.8 *School history of the 35 A children*

| No. | Grades | | | | | | Last school year |
	1	2	3	4	5	6^a	
1 A	x	x	x	x	x	0	73–74
2 A	x	x	x	x	x	0	76–77
3 A_1	x	x	x	x	x	0	74–75
A_2	x	x	x	r	xx		74–75
4 A_1	xx	x	•	r	x	+1r	77–78
A_2	x	xx	x	x	x		77–78
5 A	x	x	x	x	x	0	77–78
6 A	x	x	x	x	x	0	75–76
7 A	x	x	x	x	x		76–77
8 A	x	x	x	x	x	−1	77–78
9 A	x	x	x	x	x		75–76
10 A	x	x	x	x			77–78
11 A	x	x	x	x			77–78
12 A	x	x	x				77–78
13 A	x	x	x	x			77–78
14 A	x	x	x	x			77–78
15 A	xx	x	x	xx	x	+2	76–77
16 A	x	x	x	x			76–77

| No. | Grades | | | | | | Last school year |
	1	2	3	4	5	6^a	
17 A	x	x	x	x	x	−1	74–75
18 A	x	x	x	x	x	0	77–78
19 A	•	•	•	•	x	0	75–76
20 A	x	x	x	x	x	0	74–75
21 A	x	x	x	x			77–78
22 A_1	x	x	x	x		0	77–78
A_2			x				77–78
23 A	x	x	x	x	x	0	75–76
24 A	x	x	xx	xx	x	+2	76–77
25 A	x	xx	x		x		77–78
26 A	x	x	x	x	x	0	75–76
27 A	x	x	x	x	x	0	77–78
28 A	x	x	x	x	x	0	77–78
29 A	x	x	x	x	x		77–78
30 A	x	x	x		x		77–78
31 A	x	x	x	x			77–78
32 A	x	x	x				76–77

^{a} Number of years behind (+1, +2) or ahead (−1, −2) in grade 6.
Symbols: •, one year in grade according to age in some later grade; x, one year in grade according to age according to school file; xx, grade repeated once; xxx, grade repeated twice.
Special classes: r, remedial; s, 'slow learners'.
xx, first instance of repeating; r and s, first instance of placement in a special class.

Table 3.9 *School history of the 39 B children**

No.	1	2	3	4	5	6ᵃ	Last school year
1 B1		•		x	x	+1r	1973–74
B2	•			x	x	0	1975–76
B3	x	x	x	x	x	0	1976–77
B4	x	x	xx	x	xx		1977–78
2 B	x	x	x	x	•	+1	1975–76
3 B	•	•	•	•	xx	0	1973–74
4 B1	•	•	•	•	xx	+1	1971–72
B2	x	xx	x	x	x	+1	1972–73
B3	xx	x	x	x	x	+1r	1973–74
B4	x	x	x	x	x	0	1974–75
5 B1	xx	x	x	x	x	+1r	1974–75
B2	xx	x	x	x	x	+1r	1975–76
B3	xx	x	x	x	x	+1	1977–78
B4	x	x					1977–78
6 B	x	xxx	s	s	s	+2s	1976–77
7 B	x	x		s			1976–77
8 B	xx	xx	x				1977–78
9 B1	x	x	x	x	xx	+1	1976–77
B2	x	x	x	x	x	0	1977–78
10 B1	xx	xx	s	s	s	+2s	1973–74
B2	xx	s	s	s	s	+1s	1975–76
11 B1	xx	s	s	s	s	s	1973–74
B2	x	x	x	x	x	0r	1973–74
B3	xxx	s	x	s	x		1977–78
12 B	xx	s	s	s			1977–78
13 B	xx	x	x	x	x		1977–78
14 B1	x	x	x	x	x		1973–74
B2	x	xx	x	x	x	0	1977–78
15 B1				x	x	+1	1970–71
B2	•	•	•			0	1976–77
16 B	x	x	xx	•	•	+1r	1976–77
17 B1	•	•	•	x	x	0	1972–73
B2	x	x	x	x	x	0	1976–77
B3							1976–77
18 B	x		x	x	x	−2	1976–77
19 B1	x	x	x	x	xx	+1	1977–78
B2	x	x	x	x	x		1977–78
B3	x	x					1977–78
20 B						+1r	1971–72

* For explanation of symbols see Table 3.8.

Table 3.10   *IQ scores of the 35 A children*

	Test number I				Test number II				
No.	Test	Source	Age (yrs/ mths)	Score	Test	Source	Age (yrs/ mths)	Score	Mean score
1A	WISC	A.D.	12/5	119	ECNI IV	A.D.	12/5	110	114.5
2A	WISC	A.D.	10/5	103	ECNI III	A.D.	10/2	110	106.5
3A$_1$	WISC	A.D.	12/1	106	ECNI IV	A.D.	12/1	104	105
3A$_2$	WISC	A.D.	12/1	112	ECNI IV	A.D.	12/1	98	
4A$_1$	WISC	School	7/7	93	–	–		–	92.7
4A$_2$	WISC	A.D.	10/7	97	ECNI III	A.D.	10/7	88	
5A	WISC	A.D.	7/10	116	ECNI III	A.D.	7/10	109	112.5
6A	WISC	A.D.	11/3	105	ECNI IV	A.D.	11/3	92	98.5
7A	WISC	A.D.	10/6	112[a]	ECNI III	A.D.	10/6	108	110.2
8A	WISC	A.D.	6/7	124	ECNI I	A.D.	6/7	126	125
9A	WISC	A.D.	10/0	110	ECNI III	A.D.	10/0	111	110.5
10A	WISC	A.D.	7/2	107[b]	ECNI I	A.D.	7/2	99	102.7
11A	WISC	A.D.	7/0	117	ECNI I	A.D.	7/0	129	123
12A	WISC	A.D.	6/3	119	ECNI II NV	A.D.	6/3	123[b]	120.7
13A	WISC	A.D.	6/8	134[a]	ECNI I	A.D.	6/8	111	122.7
14A	WISC	A.D.	8/4	95	ECNI II	A.D.	8/4	102	98.5
15A	WISC	A.D.	12/5	116	ECNI III	A.D.	12/5	95	105.5
16A	WISC	A.D.	8/9	101	ECNI II	A.D.	8/9	94	97.5
17A	WISC	A.D.	11/11	121	ECNI IV	A.D.	11/11	113	117
18A	WISC	A.D.	9/3	104	ECNI III	A.D.	9/3	95	99.5
19A	WISC	A.D.	12/9	101	ECNI IV	A.D.	12/9	104	102.5
20A	WISC	A.D.	8/4	114	ECNI II	A.D.	8/4	113	113.5
21A	WISC	A.D.	9/10	114[a]	ECNI III	A.D.	9/10	101	107.7
22A$_1$	WISC	A.D.	7/0	116	ECNI I	A.D.	7/0	122	109.1
22A$_2$	WISC	A.D.	7/0	99[b]	ECNI I	A.D.	7/0	100	
23A	WISC	A.D.	12/9	120[b]	ECNI IV	A.D.	12/9	119	119.2
24A	WISC	A.D.	7/4	81	ECNI I	A.D.	7/4	94	87.5
25A	WISC	A.D.	12/8	91[a]	ECNI III NV	A.D.	12/8	83	87.2
26A	WISC	A.D.	6/6	121	ECNI I	A.D.	6/6	131	126
27A	WISC	A.D.	11/6	107	ECNI IV	A.D.	11/6	104	105.5
28A	WISC	A.D.	13/2	111	CATTELL IIA	A.D.	13/2	100	105.5
29A	WISC	A.D.	8/7	111	ECNI II	A.D.	8/7	94	102.5
30A	WISC	A.D.	6/8	114	ECNI I	A.D.	6/8	116	115
31A	WISC	A.D.	9/9	133	ECNI III	A.D.	9/9	125	129
32A	WISC	A.D.	6/6	106[b]	–	–		–	105.5

[a] One more point on the second scoring.
[b] One less point on the second scoring.

Table 3.11 *IQ scores of 20 B children (1 from each of 20 sibships)*

No.	Test number I				Test number II				Mean score
	Test	Source	Age (yrs/mths)	Score	Test	Source	Age	Score	
1B2	WISC	A.D.	11/9	109[a]	ECNI IV	A.D.	11/9	100	104.7
2B	WISC	A.D.	13/4	93	ECNI IV	A.D.	13/4	90	91.5
3B	WISC	A.D.	14/5	106	CATTELL 2A	A.D.	14/5	129	117.5
4B4	WISC	A.D.	13/1	87	ECNI IV	A.D.	13/1	100	93.5
5B3	WISC	A.D.	11/3	92	ECNI III	A.D.	11/3	96	94
6B	WISC	A.D.	13/1	78[b]	WISC	School	10/3	70	73.7
7B	WISC	A.D.	6/8	103	ECNI I	A.D.	6/8	94	98.5
8B	WISC	A.D.	9/1	93	ECNI II	A.D.	9/1	94	93.5
9B1	WISC	A.D.	12/4	86[a]	ECNI III	A.D.	12/4	92	89.2
10B1	NEMI[c]	School	10/2	71[c]	NEMI; PM47	School	7/1	77 } 90	77.2
11B3	WISC	A.D.	8/0	105[a]	ECNI I	A.D.	8/1	93	99.2
12B	WISC	A.D.	8/9	69	WISC	School	7/6	70	69.5
13B	WISC	A.D.	9/9	111	ECNI II	A.D.	9/9	107	109
14B2	WISC	A.D.	9/11	96	ECNI III	A.D.	9/11	101	98.5
15B2	WISC	A.D.	11/6	101	ECNI IV	A.D.	11/6	96	98.5
16B	WISC	A.D.	12/0	91	ECNI IV	A.D.	12/0	86	88.5
17B2	WISC	A.D.	11/7	98	ECNI IV	A.D.	11/7	107	102.5
18B	WISC	A.D.	7/1	96	ECNI I	A.D.	7/1	93	94.5
19B1	WISC	A.D.	11/2	106	ECNI III	A.D.	11/2	109	107.5
20B	TERMAN	School	13/2	91	ECNI IV	School	13/10	91	91

[a] One more point on the second scoring.
[b] One less point on the second scoring.
[c] Latest score (provided by the school in November 1977).

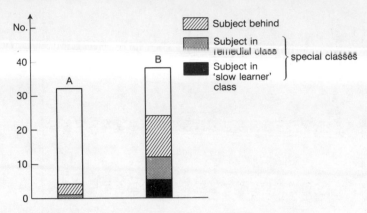

Fig. 3.5   Number of school failures observed, groups A and B.

Comparison of the A and B subjects

School failure, is defined as repeating a grade or being placed in a special class ('remedial' class or class for 'slow learners'; for an explanation of terms, see p. 61).

The gross failure rate is four out of 32 (13 per cent) for the A subjects and 24 out of 39 (62 per cent) for the B subjects. With specific respect to placement in special classes, the rates are one out of 32 (3 per cent) and 12 out of 39 (31 per cent) respectively. These results are presented diagrammatically in Fig. 3.5. The contrast between the two groups is considerable. In addition, this contrast increases as the severity of failure increases.

For a more precise comparison between the two groups, it is necessary to take account of the fact that the age distribution in the two groups is not the same. In relation to group A, group B contains more subjects just beginning school (13 per cent of the B subjects have completed only first grade as against 0 per cent of the A subjects) and more subjects who have completed fifth grade (72 per cent of the B subjects as against 50 per cent of the A subjects). We have compared, therefore, the rate of failure observed in the two groups for equivalent scholastic levels. Figure 3.6 represents the failures that have been accumulated up until a given scholastic level.

If the age distribution of the group B children is brought down to that of group A, the gross failure rate is reduced to 50 per cent (as opposed to 62 per cent before correcting for age), i.e. to 4 times the rate observable in group A. (See Appendix 5).

The distribution of scores obtained by the study subjects on each of the two tests is presented graphically in Fig. 3.7. The average scores are presented in Table 3.12.

The difference between groups A and B is highly significant as far as IQ scores are concerned. The two general averages differ by more than four

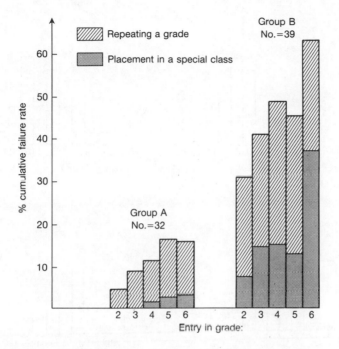

Fig. 3.6 Failure rates as a function of school level, groups A and B.

times the standard error of the mean difference (probability 3×10^{-5}). School failures provide a somewhat less precise statistic; the difference is nevertheless significant at the threshold of 0.1 per cent $\chi^2 = 11.4$ for one degree of freedom, see Appendix 5).

Comparison of the A subjects with schoolchildren of the general population

The results obtained for the A children may be compared to national norms, i.e. to the results obtained by children of the same age from the general population. This comparison may be made for each of the three indicators used (school failure, group test scores, individual test scores). Furthermore, in the first two cases, the results of large-scale national surveys may also be used to compare the A subjects' performance with those of the general population, both in their original social class and in their social class by adoption.

For group test scores, the survey used as a reference was undertaken on a representative sample of 120 000 schoolchildren from six to 14 years of age (INED–INOP 1973). For school histories, we used as a reference a survey undertaken by the Ministry of Education on a representative sample

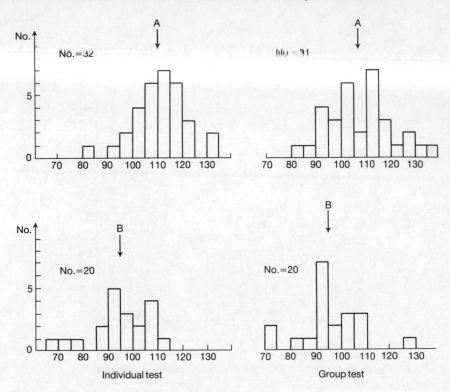

Fig. 3.7   Test score distribution, groups A and B.

Table 3.12   *Comparison of average IQ scores of group A and group B*

	Group A	Group B
Group test	106.8 ± 2.2	95.1 ± 2.9
Individual test	110.6 ± 2.0	94.2 ± 2.5
Average of the 2 tests	108.7 ± 2.0	94.6 ± 2.5

totalling 1/60th of French schoolchildren entering sixth grade in the 1974–75 school year (Ministère de l'Education 1976).

Comparisons with schoolchildren of the general population are presented first followed by comparisons with the children of unskilled workers and with 'upper-middle-class' children. The details of the calculations are presented in Appendix 4.

By the very construction of psychometric scales, half of the children of the reference population have a score below 100 and 16 per cent have a score below 85; in analogy with school failure, these two situations will be designated as 'mild failure' and 'serious failure'. At the end of primary school, the proportion of school failures is of the same order: the percentage of children behind in school at the entry into sixth grade varies from 42 per cent to 52 per cent according to year of birth. Prior to the elimination of certain remedial classes, 18 per cent of the children of a given age group entered sixth grade in this type of class. For children too young to allow for the observation of a complete primary school history (half of the A subjects), the risk of failure in the general population goes from 22 per cent for the youngest, i.e. those who have completed only two years of primary school, to 33 per cent of those who have completed four years of school.

To calculate the number of expected failures among 32 schoolchildren of the general population having the same age distribution as the A subjects, it suffices to add up the risk of school failure for each of the subjects as a function of his birth date and age at the time of the study. The number of school failures thus calculated is well above the number observed. (11.2 as opposed to 4; $\chi^2 = 7.1$, p = 0.005). As far as the distribution of test scores is concerned, the probability that it results from a statistical fluctuation is entirely negligible: the average of the two scores obtained by the A subjects (108.7 ± 2.0) is more than four standard errors above the average for the general population.

The results of the two national surveys mentioned above allow for the estimation of the performances of the two groups of schoolchildren of the general population whose parents have the same job qualification respectively as subject A's adoptive parents ('upper-middle-class' occupations)* and his biological parents (unskilled jobs). Socially these 'upper-middle-class' occupations correspond to the top 13 percentiles. (See Appendix 4).

We have seen that the performances of the A subjects are significantly above the national norms; they are *a fortiori* significantly higher than the scores observed in the general population for their original social class (16.5 failures for 32 subjects; average group test score 95 ± 1). They are, on the contrary, consistent with the performances observed in the general population for their social class by adoption (four school failures for 32 subjects; average group test score 110 ± 1).

According to national statistics, the proportion of school failures for children having the same distribution as the A subjects would be 52 per cent for the children of unskilled workers and 45 per cent for the children of workers in general (including foremen). With a rate of 50 per cent, the probability of observing four failures or less would be about 10^{-5}.

---

* With respect to 'upper-middle-class' occupations – the quotation marks have been used throughout the chapter as a reminder that this is a somewhat heterogeneous social group – their occupational levels have been matched with those of the adoptive parents (one artisan, three employers – medium-sized businesses, four junior executives and 22 senior executives, see p. 47).

**The special case of the group test: the comparison with
two intra-study samples**

Certain data of the study were collected solely with the aim of 'hiding' the
study subjects, i.e. to avoid singling out a child in his class. We thus collected class rosters including the parents' occupations in the majority of
classes that we visited and we had the entire class take the group test. *A
priori*, the children thus tested have no reason to be representative of the
general population nor even of children of their own social class. We were
therefore not planning to compare them with the study subjects.

An analysis undertaken shortly after the publication of our first article
confirmed that our *a priori* decision had been correct. As a superficial
interpretation of the figures might seem to reveal some internal contradiction with the other results of our study, we have reversed this decision and
we have presented the results of this analysis with all the reservations that
this retrospective decision entails (see pp. 80–84 and Appendix 6).

The internal sample available is made up of the children in the classes
of 31 A subjects (sample a_t)* and of those in the classes of 15 B subjects
(sample b_t). The occupations of the heads of the families (with the exception of the classmates of children 10 B and 20 B) appeared in the class roster
provided by the teacher. Apart from the two exceptions, the number of
occupations not declared is minimal (five per cent of the pupils).

The average ENCI test score estimated for the 'upper-middle-class' children is 116.2 in group a_u ('upper-middle-class' children tested at the same
time as the A subjects) and 107 in group b_u ('upper-middle-class' children
tested at the same time as the B subjects). Note that the a_u group average is
nine points higher than the average obtained by A subjects, while the b_u
group average is consistent with it. Also note that in both cases the averages concern 'upper-middle-class' children. The interpretation of these
results depends on which sample is more representative of 'upper-middle-
class' children. This point will be examined in the next section where biases
are discussed in detail.

Synthesis of the results

As was illustrated in Fig. 3.2, the performances of the A subjects were
used in 12 comparisons. These comparisons were of three types:

—comparison of the A subject with children of the same mother;
—comparisons with schoolchildren studied in national surveys;

---

* Although the sample is not quite complete (see Appendix 6), the index *t* represents the
totality of schoolmates; the index *u* represents 'upper-middle-class'.

—comparisons with 'upper-middle-class' children from two intra-study samples.

Except for the last type of comparison, intellectual performance was estimated in more than one way. The totality of these results is presented in Table 3.13. Other overall presentations of the results will appear in Section 6.

5. Examination of biases

We shall now examine the biases which might modify the interpretation of the results. We hope that the unusual length of the report of this examination will be seen as a reflection of the care we have brought to it and not as a reflection of an unusual accumulation of sources of bias.

We would like to insist upon the quantitative and reasoned character of the evaluations presented. During these evaluations we tried to make the best possible use of the information available by avoiding two pitfalls. The first would have consisted in making choices always biased in the direction of our results; the second would have consisted in always making choices biased in the opposite direction.

Group A

Group A is the most important group for the study as it appears in all the comparisons. We shall examine, in order, the criteria for selecting the subjects, the sampling of the subjects, and the methods of observation.

Criteria for selecting the subjects

Each of the six selection criteria, listed on p. 45 will now be examined in turn. The first criterion concerns years of birth, which raises the question of secular trends. The comparison of a sample with national samples that had been studied at different dates poses the question of drift in the performances of the population as a whole, a drift which would falsify the comparison. In the case of school failure, we were able to take account of variations in national norms (see Appendix 4). For test scores, however, no such updating was possible. We might have considered a restandardization in the case of the group test with the aid of samples a_t and b_t. Given the biases in the composition of these two samples (see pp. 80–84), the remedy would have been worse than the evil. It should be pointed out that for the A subjects and for the B subjects, the psychometric results were consistent with the rates of school failure (see Figs 3.9 and 3.10). This consistency makes it rather improbable that there be a significant drift specific to the tests. Moreover, a possible drift would have no effect on the comparison between groups A and B.

Table 3.13 *Recapitulation of the gross results of the study*

| | Group A (No. = 32) | Group B (No. = 39 or 20) | National surveys | | | |
			General Population	Unskilled workers	'Upper-middle-class'	Intra-study samples
School failures	4 out of 32	24 out of 39[a]	11.2/32	16.5/32	4/32	
Group test (score average)	106.8 ± 2.2	95.1 ± 2.9 (N = 20)	99.2	95 ± 1	110 ± 1	107 (b_u) 116.2 (a_u)
Individual test (score average)	110.6 ± 2.0	94.2 ± 2.5 (N = 20)	100			
Average of the two tests	108.7 ± 2.0	94.6 ± 2.5 (N = 20)	99.6			

[a] Equals 16.1 out of 32 after correction for age and date.

The second criterion concerns abandonment at birth. *A priori*, the risk of handicaps linked to pregnancy or to the perinatal period is greater for the A subjects than for children of the general population. This increase in risk is due, in particular, to the presence of three geminate pregnancies, one of which was particularly traumatic.

The third criterion concerns the occupational levels of the biological mothers. The main comparison of the study is that of the A children with children of unskilled workers of the general population. In that comparison, the way in which the biological mothers were selected introduces a slight bias *against* the A children. This is because the wives of unskilled workers are not all unskilled, as were the biological mothers listed in Table 3.4.

Criterion (*d*) concerns the occupational levels of the biological fathers. In principle, the putative fathers are all unskilled workers. In Appendix 7, which is devoted to the examination of uncertainties and biases in the socio-professional category definitions, we will show that the occupational levels of the putative fathers have been slightly under-estimated by the classification described in Appendix 2. This slight bias compensates for the bias in the opposite direction specific to the biological mothers.

We examined the bias that might have been associated with the fact that subjects A and B generally had different fathers. It was precisely because of this difference that we took care to include the lack of occupational qualifications for the father as one of the subject A definition criteria whereas, on occasion, a subject B father did have a certain level of qualification. In these circumstances, if the father's occupational level did introduce a *systematic* genetic bias, it would be in favour of group B and not of group A. As to the effect of the *random* genetic variations, it is included in the IQ dispersion, i.e. in the statistical error. Finally, we considered the possibility of a genetic contamination of group A which might have been hidden by errors in the father's occupational level: a mother declaring, for example, that the father was a worker when, in reality, he was an engineer. Given all available information, what might have been the genetic contamination of sample A by biological fathers more qualified than the consulted files indicated?

Let us consider first a hypothetical study in which we would have looked for A subjects whose biological mothers had been unskilled and whose fathers had held 'upper-middle-class' occupations. In the general population, the gap separating the children of unskilled workers and 'upper-middle-class' children is 15 IQ points. For the purposes of this discussion, let us assume that half of this gap can be attributed to genetic differences. Moreover, each of the two parents contributes in the same way to the additive value of genotypes, i.e. each contributes a half. If the biological fathers of the A children had all held 'upper-middle-class' occupations, this would have constituted a genetic advantage for the A group of 15/4 = 3.7 IQ points at most. In our records this situation is rare.

In reality, in order for a significant contamination to have occurred, *two conditions would have had to be met simultaneously*.

First, there would have had to be more couples crossing class barriers among the biological parents than in the general population. (This is in contradiction with the analysis of the files of children abandoned at birth presented at the end of Appendix 7.) Secondly, the biological mothers would have had to frequently conceal the occupational qualifications of the fathers and to have done so in such a way as to have avoided the exclusion of a file. (The absence of information or a slight qualification would have led to the exclusion from the sample.) Even if a highly improbable estimation is made of the number of engineers concealed under the designation 'bulldozer operator' or 'worker', the analysis of the sociological profiles presented in Appendix 7 shows that the risk of contamination does not go beyond five per cent. The corresponding effect would be 1/20th of the maximum contamination: that being 3.7/20 = 0.2 IQ points.

Criterion (e) concerns placement for adoption before the age of six months. Among the 168 abandoned-at-birth cases meeting criteria (a) through (d) listed on p. 45, 60 per cent fulfilled criterion (e). This criterion has two consequences.

First, the choice of adopted children as subjects eliminates children who are organically deficient at birth. The proportion of organically deficient children may be higher among abandoned children than in the general population where it is about one per cent. We would like to point out, however, that severely deficient children do not appear in the school statistics which served as a reference for the study and that the B child afflicted with an organic deficiency (deafness) was eliminated from the study. The elimination of organically deficient children, therefore, biases neither the comparison with samples studied in national surveys nor the comparison with sample B.

The second consequence of criterion (e) might be the selection of the most 'alert' children. This effect is examined in detail in Appendix 8 simultaneously with that associated with the criterion (f). Criteria (e) and (f) taken together (early placement in an 'upper-middle-class' family) reduced the number of 'candidates' for the study from 168 to 43. The final effect of this reduction in the number of candidates is dependent on three factors. The first factor is the extent to which rigorous selection of babies through the use of baby tests would affect the mean development quotient. The second factor is the extent to which such a development quotient is a predictor of later IQ scores. The last factor concerns the extent to which children to be adopted were indeed selected by baby tests. The effect of each

Table 3.14 *Reasons for the exclusion of 11 files from the study*

Reasons for abandoning search	Subjects	Addresses
Abroad	Traced	2 out of 2 found
Identity of mother lacking	Traced	5 out of 6 found
Occupation inconsistent with study criteria	Not traced	3
	Total	11 files excluded from the study

of the three factors is examined in Appendix 8. Using conservative values for each factor, their combined effect is estimated to be 0.8 IQ points.

From this bias, it is necessary to subtract the biases in the opposite direction linked to pregnancy conditions, the absence of maternal care during the first months of life and, finally, the handicap linked to the three geminate births, one of which occurred in dramatic conditions. It is difficult to estimate the total effect of these handicaps, but it is permissible to think that they more than compensate for the slight bias calculated above.

The sampling of the subject

Once the criteria defining the theoretical sample were selected, two sources of bias had to be avoided. The first could stem from a link between the loss of subjects (because of refusal to co-operate, for example) and the variable under study (here, school failure). The second could stem from a redefinition of the sample that would be made *a posteriori*, i.e. after the variable under study was known (here, school and psychometric status). We will now consider each of these possible sources of bias.

Analysis of the 11 files excluded from the study

(*i*) Tracing the addresses. None of the 43 'candidates' was abandoned because of failure to trace the address. With respect to the 11 'candidates' whose files were not retained, the situation regarding the tracing of addresses is summed up in Table 3.14. (For a summary of the selection of files, see Table 3.1.) Not only was the tracing of addresses highly successful (39 found out of 40 traced), but the only case where the search was abandoned was unrelated to the status of the A child (B mother not identified).

(*ii*) Refusals to co-operate. Once we had located the subjects (A or B), we always succeeded in gaining access to the schools concerned. This achievement is due both to the efforts made to obtain the necessary authorizations and to the choice of procedures which avoided singling out particular children.

(*iii*) The 11 'candidates' not studied. The analysis of these cases shows that *a priori* their absence is unrelated to their school and psychometric status.

In two cases, the adoptive families moved abroad, one family, in fact, returning to their native country. *A priori*, these two cases present no greater risk of school failure than children enrolled in school abroad and who, by that very fact, are excluded from the national statistics serving as reference for the study.

Three files were added to the list of 'candidates' after the study had been completed. This addition occurred during the final analysis of the study, when efforts were made to code all occupations according to the INSEE instruction manual. In this systematic re-classification of professions, three borderline cases were found actually to meet the criteria for the study. These cases concern an adoptive father who was a junior officer, an adoptive father for whom the transcribed information was contradictory (sales representative and executive) and a biological father who was a cook. None of these files had been taken into consideration.

Finally, in six cases, the fact of having no information on the identity of the biological mothers led us to abandon 'candidates' for whom there was no hope of finding a possible biological correspondent.

In summary, none of the 11 cases not studied contained *a priori* a particular risk of biasing the status of the A child.

Blind definition of the sample

Each decision regarding a subject's inclusion in the study was made before knowing the child's school status. In the case of the 11 files described above, not only did we have no information on the intellectual status of the children when the decision was made to exclude the files from the study, but this status has remained unknown to this day. Apart from the case described on p. 80, we never went back on a decision to include or exclude a subject from the study.

The methods of observation

Except for the fact already mentioned that studies of school status rarely accompany psychometric studies, our methodology contains nothing of particular note. We have previously brought up the question of the efforts made to reduce the risk of errors and bias in the scoring of test results.
With respect to the administering of the individual test, our study is subject to the same hazards as all studies of this type. To the degree that the person administering the test was not external to our study, the absence of bias due to the expectations of the psychologist cannot be guaranteed since blind procedures were not use (attempts to use blind procedures turned out to be impractical). One point, however, is worthy of noting: comparisons made between various groups of children involve greater variations than those which distinguish pairs of fraternal twins from pairs of

identical twins (see Chapter 6). Consequently, our comparisons are *a priori* less sensitive to subjective biases than other generally accepted comparisons.

The use of a group test decreases the probability of subjective biases; this probability is small in the case of intra-study comparisons. However, one cannot exclude the possibility of bias which would lead to the over-estimation of study subject IQ scores in relation in national norms. As to the possibility of secular drifts mentioned on p. 71, the consistency of the three types of evaluations within both the A and B groups makes that possibility rather unlikely.

The information which is most directly relevant to the problem of social inequality (the presence or absence of school failure) is also methodologically the most reliable. Given the quality and the multiplicity of the information sources used, we think that the risks of bias and of errors in school history are even smaller than in the national survey which here serves as reference.

Group B

As in the case of group A, we shall examine, in order, the definition of the B sample and the possibilities of bias linked to the composition of the sample and those linked to observation methodology. Since Group B has been compared to Group A, it is with respect to Group A that possibilities of bias must be considered.

Definition of the B sample

The definition of the B sample has as its point of departure the A sample. It is composed of children (1) having the same biological mother as an A child; (2) under the legal custody of their mothers; and (3) within an age bracket allowing for the reconstruction of their school history. The following points will be examined below:

(a) Review of the situation of 12 B mothers.
(b) Tracing the B children of the other 20 mothers.
(c) Decision to test only one B child per sibship.
(d) Questions of paternity.
(e) Family milieu.
(f) Question of the comparison with group A. Should the 20 B sibships be compared to the 20 corresponding A subjects or to all of group A?

Review of the situation of 12 B mothers

The seven cases where the mother was traced and where there was no B child were as follows:

Cases 21 to 24 (numerous other abandonments). These are welfare cases totalling 22 abandonments. The mothers had no other dependent school-age children.

Cases 25 and 26 (no other child born of the same mother). In 1976, mother 25 was married; according to the social security centre where she was registered, she had no dependent children. Mother 26 was primiparous at the abandonment of child A in 1969. According to municipal records at her place of birth, she was not married as of 1976.

Case 27. The mother could not be traced even though her identity was known. In 1963 she was single and primiparous.

The remaining five mothers could not be traced:

Case 28 According to a welfare file, the mother went abroad, taking with her a child born in 1961. Her marriage abroad was confirmed by municipal records at her birthplace.

Cases 29 to 32. The identity of these four mothers was completely unknown; they gave birth 'in secret', i.e. without revealing their identities. Certain items of information (for example, the name of the hospital where they gave birth), suggested that it would be possible nevertheless to trace the mothers. These hopes, however, did not materialize.

In summary, in six cases there were no school-age children in the mother's custody. In five cases, no trace of the mother could be found. Finally, in one case, the mother took her child abroad with her.

Tracing the B children of the other 20 mothers

To know of the possible existence of B children, we used several sources of information. Three sources were systematically used: the adoption file in which the mother's situation is described, the school file of the B child tested (in which brothers and sisters are listed), and an informal interview with the child tested. In addition, welfare files were also consulted as well as other administrative documents concerning the mother. It seems unlikely that school-age children in the mothers' legal custody escaped our search.

Decision to test only one B child per sibship

This decision was made at the time when the tracing of the B subjects seemed very difficult, and we feared we would not be able to complete the study with the means available. As mentioned above, the tracing of the biological mothers was very laborious; in June 1976, at the time that the final report was to be sent to the Foundation that had subsidized a part of the study, we had only traced 10 biological sibships. As stated in Section 3, the choice of the B subject within the sibship was made *a priori* in the absence of information on the children's school status. The absence of bias was also verified *a posteriori* by comparing the school status of the 20 children tested with that of the 19 children not tested (see Table 3.9). The rate of failure is, in fact, slightly higher among the children *not* tested so that, in the comparison of test scores with group A, it is group B which is slightly favoured by the decision to test only one B child per sibship.

Questions of paternity

We have already noted that the difference in paternity between groups A and B can only tend to diminish the gap between the two groups (see p. 73).

Family milieu

The family life, particularly of the B subjects born before the A subjects, is often disrupted: 15 out of the 39 children never lived with two parents. This proportion is rather high, but it approaches that observed in a social category very close to the one studied: that is, domestic personnel, where the proportion of children having two married parents does not reach 60 per cent and where 38 per cent of the children live in a household where the family head is a woman (INSEE, 1954 census). Finally, with respect to socio-professional environment, there is a slight bias in favour of the B children in relation to the children of unskilled workers: two live with a skilled worker; two with a military man; three with a white-collar worker; and three with an artisan.

Question of the comparison with group A: 20 or 32?

Of the 32 mothers, only 20 had a child in the two samples. Should then the 20 B shipships be compared to the 20 corresponding A subjects or to all of group A? To answer this question, we compared the profiles of the 12 mothers without B children to the profiles of the 20 other mothers. The professional choice criteria are the same in the two groups. The presence of four welfare cases totalling 22 abandonments in the first group tends to favour the second group, so that, *a priori*, the comparison of the 20 sibships with the A children of *all* 32 mothers tends to favour group B. Following the logic of a comparison centred on groups rather than on individuals, this is the solution that we have chosen. In fact, the numerical results are almost identical when the comparison is restricted to the first 20 A subjects.

The methods of observation

Observation methodology is the same for the B subjects as for the A subjects. We would like to point out, nonetheless, that a linguistic handicap was observed among six of the 20 children tested; they spoke a German dialect at home. *A priori*, it is difficult to say to what degree this constitutes a bias in the comparison with the A subjects and to what degree it reflects the underprivileged status of the B subjects.

The linguistic handicap of the chilren of unskilled workers is a well-known phenomenon, although neither scholastic selection nor published statistics take account of it. In our study, the linguistic handicap observed among the six B children was not observed among any of the A children living in the same region near the German border.

We could have decided to eliminate the verbal scores from our analysis. Three reasons led us to reject this solution:

—This decision would have been made retrospectively;
—It would make it impossible to compare the gap between the A and B groups with the corresponding gap in the general population;
—Last but not least, we would like to point out that to eliminate the effects of a linguistic handicap from the observations would amount to eliminating a part of precisely that social effect which we were seeking to measure.

Samples a_t, b_t and groups a_u, b_u

Certain study data were collected solely to avoid singling out a child in his class. Sample a_t is made up of schoolchildren taking the group test at the same time as 31 of the A subjects; group a_u is made up of the sub-set of 'upper-middle-class' children in the a_t sample. Similarly, sample b_t is made up of schoolchildren taking the group test at the same time as 15 of the B subjects and the group b_u is made up of the sub-set of 'upper-middle-class' children of the b_t sample.

A priori one could expect that neither sample a_t nor sample b_t would be representative of the general population of French schoolchildren and that, consequently, neither group a_u nor group b_u would be representative of 'upper-middle-class' children. For this reason we had planned not to use these groups for the study and, thus, had decided not to mark the group tests of the a_t and b_t sample children. After our initial article had been sent to *Science*, one of the co-authors who was preparing a thesis based on data collected during the study (Dumaret 1979, 1985) analysed data relating to samples a_t and b_t, thus confronting everyone with a difficult choice. The decision regarding the study's 'decoy' children could no longer be questioned in a blind fashion. Once the results of group a_u and b_u were known, the decision was made unanimously to go back on our general policy and to add the data regarding the 'decoys' to the study, even though this had not been initially planned.

A much more difficult series of choices concerned the presentation and interpretation of the new data thus introduced into the study. In making these choices we were guided by historical precedents described in Chapter 6. On the one hand, we had to avoid presenting the new data in such a way that it would go unnoticed. On the other hand, we had to avoid giving it excessive importance which would obscure the value and meaning of the other results. Intuitively, it might seem that, the a_u sample 'upper-middle-class' children were better matched to the group A children than were the 'upper-middle-class' children of the other sample. The analysis of samples a_t and b_t is presented in Appendix 6. The results of this analysis show that the intuitive point of view is not necessarily the best.

The new results concern the comparison of the A group with two groups of 'upper-middle-class' children (a_u and b_u). If one wanted to interpret these comparisons to make statements about the presence or the absence of genetic differences, one would need to know: (*a*) how well the groups being compared were matched in terms of environment, and (*b*) how well these groups were matched in terms of ascertainment. We examine each point in turn.

Let us first consider the question of environment. From the point of view of family environment, the A subjects could only be matched by other adopted children (for a discussion of this point, we refer the reader to Chapter 6). From the point of view of school environment (as distinct from family environment), the a_u sample is matched to the A group, while the b_u sample is not.

Let us now consider the bias in ascertainment. As we have seen, the A group is representative of the population of 'upper-middle-class' adopted children. What about the a_u and b_u samples? Since these two samples differ by nine IQ points, they cannot both be representative of 'upper-middle-class' children. The proportion of upper-middle-class children is abnormally high in the a_t sample, as indicated below. That proportion is 39 per cent in sample a_t while it is 15 per cent in the general population and 10 per cent in sample b_t (for more details, see Fig. 3.11 in Appendix 6).

In the a_t sample there is considerable variation in social composition and this variation is associated with a considerable variation in the mean score observed for upper-middle-class children. Within the a_t sample, the mean score expected from the social composition alone varies from a low 97 (classmates of subject 22 A, see Table 3.27 in Appendix 6) to a high 108 (classmates of subject 9 A). Three sub-samples of the a_t sample were formed by ordering the 31 classes according to increasing values of the expected IQ score. Each sub-sample contained about 100 upper-middle-class children. After a slight correction to go from upper-middle-class

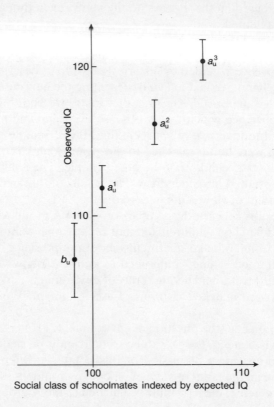

Fig. 3.8   Mean IQ scores of 4 samples of 'upper-middle-class' children.
The abcissa indicates the mean social class of schoolmates as indexed by the mean expected IQ of these schoolmates. The ordinate shows the mean score observed for the b_u sample and for three sub-samples of the a_u sample. By construction, the four samples are socially equivalent. The mean IQ scores of children appears to be as highly correlated to the social class of their schoolmates as to their own social class.

children to 'upper-middle-class'* ones, these groups of children constituted the sub-samples a_u^1, a_u^2 and a_u^3. The difference in mean IQ scores for these sub-samples is presented in Fig. 3.8, together with the value for sample b_u. The results shown in Fig. 3.8 are as follows. First of all, the striking fact is that the mean IQ scores of schoolchildren seems as highly correlated to the social class of their schoolmates as to their own social class.† The results also show that, once we take into account the social class of the school-mates, the mean IQ scores for 'upper-middle-class' children within the *a*

---

* For the significance of the quotation marks, see footnote on p. 69.
† An analogous result was reported by Guterman (1980)

and *b* samples become consistent. When these values are extrapolated to a standard distribution of schoolmates, they also become consistent with the value observed for the A sample.

In other words, the mean IQ score observed for the A subjects is consistent with the mean score which would be observed for 'upper-middle-class' children whose schoolmates had the same social distribution as the general population.

This is as far as comparisons with samples a_u and b_u can bring us. To go further, one would need to know the answer to the following questions:

(*a*) To what degree is there a greater tendency among 'upper-middle-class' adoptive parents than among other 'upper-middle-class' parents to choose highly selective schools?

(*b*) In 1977, what was the social distribution of schoolmates of French grade schoolchildren of 'upper-middle-class' parents?

The problem in the comparison between adoptive and non-adoptive families is the same as in other adoption studies: the inter-correlation between the various variables may be significantly different in adoptive and ordinary families. Before concluding this discussion, we would like to make two comments.

Comment one

This concerns the differences observed between 'upper-middle-class' children who happened to be in the same classes as the A subjects (group a_u) and the 'upper-middle-class' children who happened to be in the same classes as the B subjects (group b_u). Although these children are from the same social class, the difference between the group test scores is above nine points; this difference varies in the same direction as the degree of social segregation observed in the samples. In contrast to the other comparisons of Table 3.13, the comparison with groups a_u and b_u is ambiguous. With respect to normal primary school enrollment, this ambiguity may be expressed as a continuum between two extreme hypotheses:

Hypothesis *A*: The 'upper-middle-class' children of group a_u are representative of 'upper-middle-class' children of the general population.
Corollary (1): The A children present, in relation to 'upper-middle-class' children, a significant inferiority on the IQ score scale.
Hypothesis *B*: Group b_u 'upper-middle-class' children are representative of 'upper-middle-class' children of the general population.
Corollary (2): The A children present, in relation to 'upper-middle-class' children, no significant difference on the IQ score scale.

Let us note that, even if a choice could be made between hypothesis A and hypothesis B, i.e, between corollary (1) and corollary (2), this would not be sufficient to eliminate the ambiguity of the interpretation. In the case of corollary (1), we would not know if the degree of difference observed were due to the effect of abandonment and adoption or to the genetic effects; similarly, in the case of corollary (2), the possibility of genetic effects could not be ruled out.

In summary, the comparison of the adopted children with samples a_u and b_u is subject to a double ambiguity.

Comment two

Our observations show that if the children of workers were placed in the same family and social environment as the adopted children in our study, their psychometric and school failures and, in particular, serious failures, would diminish greatly. Without contesting this fact, one might seek to limit its import by issuing the following hypothesis: the effect of the adoptive family milieu would be so favourable that it, and not the adoptive family's social class, would account for the observed decrease in failure risk.

A priori, it may be thought that, in contemporary France where adoption is a marginal phenomenon, the specific situation of the child abandoned and then adopted would constitute a psychological handicap rather than an advantage. We have nonetheless seen in this section that, from a scholastic point of view, the adoptive situation may present a certain advantage. Recent observations by one of us on 100 children who had been abandoned at birth and whose school situation was examined at around the age of 15, indicate that the adoptive situation as such does not constitute a substitute for social privilege: the variability of the school status of adopted children with their social class by adoption persists throughout the entire social spectrum (Duyme 1981).

In conclusion, we do not claim that group b_u is better matched than group a_u to our experimental group. What we do state is that the data drawn from samples a_t and b_t can only be ambiguous and that consequently they should only be used to illustrate how difficult it is to demonstrate the presence or absence of genetic effects. The results presented in Fig. 3.10 show that this methodological ambiguity is of little consequence to the analysis of the heredity of school failure.

The statistical weight of our observations

To conclude this discussion of our results, we would like briefly to bring up the statistical questions. Certain readers may be surprised that valid conclusions can be drawn from observations concerning 32 subjects. In fact,

the statistical weight of a result depends both on the number of observations and on the result itself. If the effect observed had been small, it
would not have been significant. A massive effect may, on the contrary, be
brought to light by a small number of observations.

In our study, the comparisons which are the most pertinent for social
heredity and the most significant from a statistical point of view are those
where the results obtained by group A are compared to the expected
results given their socio-biological origin. The results reported in Fig. 3.9
and above all, those reported in Fig. 3.10 place in perspective the real
importance of statistical uncertainties in the interpretation of our observations (error bars in the figures correspond to one standard error, see
Appendix 4).

To appreciate the statistical significance of the effect observed, one may
likewise consider the result most vulnerable to statistical uncertainties in
the comparison of the A children and the children of unskilled workers: the
number of school failures observed among the A subjects is four out of 32
instead of the 16 expected, given the biological parents' occupations. The
probability of obtaining such a discrepancy by chance alone is 10^{-5}.

6. Synthesis and interpretation of the results

Summary of study methodology

The experimental plan was described in Section 1. The principal sample is
made up of children whose parents were both unskilled workers. Abandoned at birth, these children moved up the social ladder owing to an early
adoption into an 'upper-middle-class'* family. The effect of the social
change has been estimated by comparing the adopted subjects to schoolchildren of the general population and to children of their original social
class. This effect has also been estimated by comparing the adopted subjects to children of the same mother who were living in their 'natural'
milieu.

The sample of adopted children (group A) was described in Section 2.
Sample A was selected from among the files of six public adoption agencies
comprising 168 children who had been abandoned at birth between 1962
and 1969 and whose parents were unskilled workers. One-quarter of these
children were placed before the age of six months into 'upper-middle-class'
families. The occupational levels of both biological and adoptive parents
are summed up in Table 3.15. Thirty-five adopted children, including three

* For the significance of the quotation marks, see footnote, p. 69.

Table 3.15   *Summary of the occupational levels of the biological and adoptive parents of the 32 A children*

Biological parents		Adoptive parents	
Fathers			
Unskilled workers	26	Artisan	1
Drivers	4	Businessmen	3
Others, unskilled	2	Professionals	2
	32	Junior executives	4
		Senior executives	21
		No father	1
			32
Mothers			
Workers	12	Employees	2
Domestic personnel	12	Shopkeepers	1
Waitresses, salesgirls	5	Junior executives	11
		Senior executives	5
Without occupation	3*	No occupation	13
	32		32

* Including two welfare cases.

pairs of twins, constituted the 32 A subjects of the study. The intellectual status of each subject was estimated in three different ways. School success was defined by the fact of never repeating a grade in primary school and not being placed in any special class. IQ scores were obtained with an individual test (WISC) and with a group test (ECNI).

Section 3 described the biological control group (group B). The B subjects are the school-age children of 20 of the 32 biological mothers of the A subjects. The school history of the 39 school-age children of these 20 biological mothers was studied in the same way as that of the A subjects. In each of these 20 sibships, one B child was designated according to age to undergo the same testing programme as the A children.

The social environment and family situation of the 39 B children is summed up in Table 3.16. Though the socio-professional category of the B children is slightly above the level of unskilled workers, their family situation resembles that of domestic personnel in the general population.

The results presented in Section 4 were discussed at length in Section 5. The discussion of biases focused on group A which enters into all the comparisons.

Being an unwanted child and being abandoned introduced a slight biological handicap among the A subjects which compensates for the slight

Table 3.16   *Summary of the characteristics of the familial and social milieu of the 39 B children*

Socio-professional status of the head of the family	
Domestic personnel	7
Unskilled workers	22
Skilled workers	2
Military personnel	2
White-collar workers	3
Artisan (self-employed)	3
	39

Family situation	
Children living or having lived with:	
2 parents (including 11 having always lived with 2 parents)	24
The mother	4
Grandparents	7
A nurse[a] or in an institutional home	4
	39

" In French, *nourrice*. This term is used throughout this chapter in its non-medical meaning, i.e. a woman who has the general care of a child or children. It should be pointed out that the *nourrice* is a veritable institution in France, especially among the working class.

advantage that might be introduced by the criterion regarding placement in an adoptive family. A detailed evaluation of this last possibility of bias showed that its effect on the average of IQ scores was under one point.

In the comparison with 'upper-middle-class' children or with the children of manual workers, certain uncertainties in the socio-professional categories introduced a lack of precision in the definition of the reference samples within the general population. This uncertainty concerned a fraction of the interval separating two adjacent categories: senior and junior executives in one case, skilled and unskilled workers in the other.

Going from the 43 files meeting our criteria to the sample in fact studied (32 subjects) introduced virtually no bias. The only case where the tracing of a subject A's address was abandoned is without relation to the child's status. With respect to access to schools, permission was never denied us. Finally, the reasons for the exclusion of 11 files from the study were unrelated to the children.

In the sample definition procedures, we paid particular attention to avoiding the bias that might have resulted from a retrospective definition. All subject-related decisions were made before subject status was known:

no subject was excluded after having been studied, and the status of the 11 cases excluded remains totally unknown to us.

In the estimation of test scores, the biases are, *a priori*, the same as in any psychometric study. The possibility of a bias due to observer prejudice is greatest in the case of the individual test; it is minimal for the group test and virtually non-existent for the status indicator having the greatest social significance (school history).

The examination of an intra-study sample (the children in the same classes as study subjects A and B who also took the ECNI group test) brings out the possibility of an over-estimation of the A subjects' psychometric performance in relation to the general population. Given the biased character of this internal sample, it was not possible to undertake a re-standardization of the ECNI test.

A possible shift of the psychometric scales used would not change the gap observed between groups A and B. Moreover, it would be without effect on the comparisons relating to school history.

Summary of the results

In the analysis of national surveys presented in Chapter 2, a distinction was made between mild and serious failures. We have designated as 'school failure' the fact of obtaining results inferior to those obtained by the average school child. For an 11-year-old child, school failure consists of still being in primary school (below grade six) or of being in a special sixth grade class. With respect to the tests, failure consists in obtaining a score below the national average.

Among all failures, those which are socially most significant have been designated as 'serious failures'. For children in sixth grade, 'serious failure' is defined as being placed in a special class. This type of failure concerns 18 per cent of all schoolchildren. For test results, 'serious failure' was defined by the fact of obtaining a score at least one standard deviation below the national average. By definition, this type of failure concerns 16 per cent of all schoolchildren.

The gross results of our study have been summed up in Table 3.13. In the present overall presentation of the results, we use the same type of metric as was used in Chapter 2 to compare the results of national surveys. This type of presentation has three advantages: (1) the three sorts of observations (school history, group test scores, and individual test scores) may be compared with each other. This provides a useful check on the internal consistency of our observations; (2) with respect to school failure, we obtain, moreover, a direct comparison with national surveys at the entry into sixth grade, i.e. with a relatively homogeneous age group. This allows for a better appreciation of the social significance of our results;

(3) finally, this mode of analysis allows for an estimation, with the greatest statistical precision, of school failures which are socially most significant and which we have designated as 'serious failures'.

The totality of our results is presented in Table 3.17; the statistical uncertainties which would have encumbered the table have been presented in Figs 3.9 and 3.10.

Table 3.17 is organized in the following fashion. In the columns, the results concern consecutively school histories, the average score for the two tests, group test results (generally ECNI) and individual test results (generally the WISC). For each of these variables we have presented, in order, the gross results and the corresponding failure rates. On the different lines, we have considered successively children raised by unskilled workers, children raised in 'upper-middle-class' families, and children of the general population.

Figures 3.9 and 3.10 are organized in the same fashion. From left to right we have considered consecutively school history, the average of the two test results, group test results and individual test results. Figure 3.9 concerns the totality of failures; Fig. 3.10 gives the corresponding rates of serious failure. The groups of children considered are the children of unskilled workers (highest failure rate), children of the general population (intermediate rate) and 'upper-middle-class' children (lowest rate).

For the A subjects of the study, statistical uncertainties are represented by an error bar corresponding to one standard error. For subjects of national surveys, rectangle height corresponds to an uncertainty of ± 1 point on a scale with a 15 point standard deviation (white rectangles represent 'upper-middle-class' children and black rectangles the children of unskilled workers). As for the 'upper-middle-class' children who took the group test at the same time as the study subjects, the uncertainty in the comparison with the A subjects is represented by the gap between the two groups (a_u and b_u).

The totality of our observations can be summarized as follows (see Fig. 3.9). The intellectual status of the A subjects was estimated in three different ways. The comparisons with other groups gave the following results:

1. In five cases, the A subjects can be compared to children of unskilled workers reared in their own social class. Their status is largely superior in all five comparisons.
2. In three cases, the A subjects can be compared to the national norm for the general population. With the three indicators used, the status of the A subject was clearly above the national norm.
3. In four cases, the A subjects can be compared to children of 'upper-middle-class' parents reared in their own social class. In three of

Table 3.17 *Synthetic presentation of the totality of the comparisons*

Children's social class	Sample	School history			Results on the 2 tests			Group test (ECNI)			Individual test (WISC)		
		No. failures[a]	Failure rate (%)	Rate of serious failures (%)	Average of 2 scores	Failure rate (%)	Rate of serious failures (%)	Score	Failure rate (%)	Rate of serious failures (%)	Score	Failure rate (%)	Rate of serious failures (%)
Unskilled workers	B subjects of the study	16.1	66	33	94.6	64	23	95.1	62	21	94.2	67	25
	National surveys	16.5	67	34	–	–	–	95.0	62	21	–	–	–
'Upper-middle-class'	A subjects of the study	4	17	3	108.7	25	4	106.8	29	5	110.6	22	3
	National surveys	4	17	3	–	–	–	110.0	21	3	–	–	–
	Group a_u	–	–	–	–	–	–	116.2	10	1	–	–	–
	Group b_u	–	–	–	–	–	–	107.0	28	5	–	–	–
National norms		11.2	46	18	99.6	50	16	99.2	50	16	100	50	16

[a] Reported for 32 children of the same age as the A subjects.

The columns show the different types of variables. For each variable we have given consecutively the gross results, the failure rate, and the rate of serious failures (for the definition of failure rate, see p. 69). The statistical uncertainties are given in Table 3.13 (for the gross results), in Fig. 3.9 (for failure rate), and in Fig. 3.10 (for the rate of serious failures).

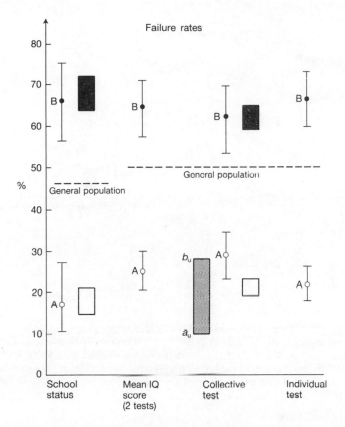

Fig. 3.9 Totality of study results expressed in terms of failure rates (mild and serious).
From left to right: failure rate at the entry into sixth grade (entering late, or in special remedial or slow learner classes); psychometric failure rate (score below the national average) for the average of scores on the two tests and for each of the tests. The results obtained by the A subjects (*white circles with error bars corresponding to one standard error*) may be compared with those obtained by children of the same mother (*black circles with error bars*) and with those obtained by children of the general population in national surveys (*dashed line*). For school history and the group test, we may also compare the results with those observed in national surveys in the social class of origin (*black rectangles*) and in the social class by adoption (*white rectangles*). Finally, in the case of the group test, we have the results for two groups of 'upper-middle-class' children who took the test at the same time as the study subjects (*grey rectangle*). See also Fig. 3.10.

these cases, the A children have an equivalent status. In the fourth comparison, the status of the A children is significantly lower.

Comparisons between groups A and B are the most direct comparisons

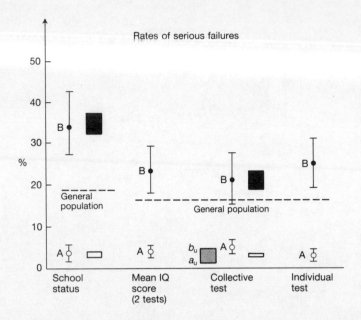

Fig. 3.10   Totality of study results expressed in terms of serious failure rates.
For school history, serious failure is defined by entering sixth grade in a remedial or
slow-learner class; for the tests, serious failure is defined as a score more than 15
points below the national average. To estimate these rates from the total failures
observed, we used the proportion of serious failures in the total of failures (see
Appendix 4).

both from a methodological point of view (intra-study comparisons) and
from a genetic point of view (equivalent gene pools for the fathers, identical gene pools for the mothers). The comparison between groups A and B
brings out more clearly than ever before the combined effect of social class
and family milieu for an equivalent 'socio-biological' origin.

Comparisons of group A with national norms more than those of the
preceding type, permit us to situate observations concerning the A subjects
in the context of the problem of social heredity. They are, however, more
vulnerable to methodological uncertainties as far as test scores are concerned. Fortunately, the risks of methodological biases are fairly small in
comparisons made with the indicator most closely related to social heredity, i.e. school failure, and also in the case of psychometric failures we
have designated as serious.

Contrary to what we suggested in our preliminary article (Schiff *et al.*
1978), the lack of significant difference between the A group and 'upper-
middle-class' children in three comparisons should *not* be interpreted as indicating a lack of genetic difference between the groups compared. *Mutatis*

mutandis, the significant difference observed in the fourth comparison should *not* be interpreted in the opposite way. The bias in ascertainment intrinsic to the fourth comparison has been analysed in Section 5.

7. Conclusion

The contribution of our study consists in trying to answer, in as direct and quantitative a way as possible, the more than half-century-old question about the limitations on children's development imposed by the alleged biological handicap associated with their social origin.

We have studied the school status and IQ scores of 32 subjects: children who were abandoned at birth and placed at an early age in an adoptive family. By birth, these children were at the lowest rung of the social ladder. Yet, their position in the school system and their IQ scores are close to those which were recorded by national surveys for their social class by adoption.

Our methodology does not allow one to exclude the possibility of a genetic difference between social classes[6], but our results demonstrate the importance of the social contribution to the school and psychometric failures of children of working-class families. To the rhetorical question 'How much *could* we boost scholastic achievement and IQ scores?', we can confidently answer, 'Enough to eliminate the bulk of the failures currently observed'.

The interpretation of previous studies has often been plagued by a variety of confusions. In particular, the question of why two children in the same family differ has been confused with the question of why it is the children of unskilled workers who fail most frequently in school. We hope that our study will contribute to making it more obvious that one must not look to the genetics of IQ for explanations about the reproduction of social inequalities.

Let us note, finally, and this point is fundamental, that *if one impugns all studies of adopted children as a scientific means of evaluating the effect of social class, only one other means for studying this effect remains: eliminate social injustice*. The data and the analysis presented in the next chapter concern the effect of social injustice on academic achievement.

Appendix 1. Contents of documents in our archives

The documents collated and used in the study were filed in volumes. The content of these volumes is briefly described below in five sections.

---

[6] We shall see in Chapter 6 that all adoption studies designed to evaluate environmental effects are similarly inconclusive about genetic effects.

1. The selection process

Volume 1 (pages numbered from 1 to 1072),
Files examined and rejected. Transcription in standard form of social and familial information on the adoptive and biological families.

2. Characteristics of the A and B subjects of the study

Volume 2 (pages numbered from 1 to 873).
These documents consist of transcriptions and, on occasion, photocopies. There were two types of information (not always present in a given file), (*a*) legal information: birth certificate, official act of abandonment, placement contract, new birth certificate, etc., and (*b*) familial and social information on the biological and adoptive families.

3. Information on school enrolment, subjects A and B

Volume 3a: 32 A subjects (pages numbered from 1 to 400).
Volume 3b: 39 B children (pages numbered from 1 to 435).
The information on school enrolment is of three types: (*a*) information records on our visit to the school, (*b*) primary school file, and (*c*) updating questionnaire at the end of the study.

4. Group tests

Volume 4a: A subjects (pages numbered from 1 to 368).
Volume 4b: B subjects (pages numbered from 369 to 548).
Volumes 4c to 4t: children in the same class (about 10 000 pages, not numbered).

5. Individual tests

Volume 5a: A subjects (pages numbered from 549 to 826).
Volume 5b: B subjects (pages numbered from 827 to 976).

Appendix 2. Final coding of occupations

The classification described here is based essentially on that of INSEE (1968). The information provided below makes clear the content of the categories we used in the final classification of occupations of the parents, without violating the anonymity of the subjects. In Table 3.3, a compromise was reached between the necessity of protecting the subjects and that of informing the reader.

The following list is a complete transcription of all of the occupations (or, as in the case of code 36, the social level) recorded in the files of the 476 cases of abandonment at birth where the occupational level of the putative father was known.

The fact that this is a literal compilation explains the strange character of some of the terms. The code numbers used here are different from those of the INSEE classification.

Class 1

Code 10. Senior executives[1]

Advertising agent, commercial attaché, pilot, depot manager, company manager, works manager, personnel manager, chemist, divisional controller, manager (w.f.p.[2], assistant bank, administrative, commercial, business, advertising, regional, company, factory, technical), managing director, company manager, engineer, inspector (architecture, bank, postal service, police, social security), interpreter, assistant professor, university instructor, senior officer, secondary school teacher (with the exception of music and physical education), psychologist, assistant factory director.

Code 11. Professionals

Lawyer, surgeon, tax adviser, legal adviser, dentist, certified public accountant, doctor, notary, veterinarian.

Code 12. Junior executives of Class 1

Insurance agent, social worker, clerk (of notary, of lawyer), guidance counsellor, air traffic controller, headmaster (mistress) (nursery school, public school), building manager, nurse (head, registered), inspector (insurance, factory, technical, at company x), journalist, physical therapist, police officer, teacher (physical education or music), midwife.

Code 13. Industrialists, contractors

Real estate agent, sales agent, contractor (building, transportation, public works), industrialist, company president (12 workers).

Class 1a

Code 15. Students

High school diploma (secondary school certificate level), undergraduate, bachelor's degree.

---

[1] As the list of occupations in this code category indicates, the term 'senior executives' is used in its most general sense and should be understood as referring to a specific socio-professional level rather than to a precise set of posts within a business hierarchy. Similarly, the term 'junior executive' should be understood as referring to a socio-professional level. The French terms, *cadre supérieur* and *cadre moyen* have this general connotation.

[2] The initials w.f.p. shall be used throughout the remainder of this appendix to indicate 'without further precision' where no information other than the general term was provided regarding occupation.

Code 17. Junior executives of class 1a (primary school teachers, technicians, etc.)

Assistant manager accounting department, technical assistant, technical agent, trained personnel in company *x*, bank branch office head, head accountant, export department head, production department head, department head, stock portfolio manager, sales manager, accountant, agricultural adviser, postal service controller, draughtsman (draughtswoman), director of youth centre, steward, instructor (instructress), student instructor, student nurse, nurse, primary school teacher, kindergarten teacher, surveyor, instructor, administration officer, junior officer, professional orientation, trade union representative, pharmacist assistant, computer programmer, home economics teacher, prospector, geophysicist, technician.

Code 18. Small businessmen, artisans

Manager (driving school, cleaners), contractor (wood and coal, painting, plumbing, roofing), artisan (roofer, carpenter, painter, plumber), jewelry maker, taxi driver, hairdresser owner, cabinet maker, garage owner, printer.

Code 19. Diverse

Assistant manager, production agent, actor, works foreman, dressmaker, dancer, drug company representative, postal service employee (secondary school certificate level), musician, insurance writer, townhall secretary, medical secretary, overseer of children's home, pharmaceutical company representative.

Class 2

Code 20. Merchants

Antique dealer, butcher, café proprietor, pork-butcher, merchant (w.f.p.), café keeper, grocer, manager (co-operative, store, automobile branch office), watchmaker, hotel proprietor, animal dealer, pedlar, haberdasher, stationer, nightclub operator, proprietor of automobile business, restaurant proprietor, automobile representative, tailor (merchant), barkeeper.

Code 21. Army, police

Officers are coded 12 and 10.
Adjutant, sergeant, CRS*, policeman, 'gendarme'†, soldier (w.f.p., A father only), retired veteran, Women's Army Corps (WAC), sergeant, sergeant-in-chief, non-commissioned officer.

Code 22. Commercial representatives and employees (men)

Commercial agent, head salesman, shoe company employee, representative, salesman.

---

* CRS, *Compagnie Républicaine de Sécurité*, élite police unit whose duties are analogous to American National Guard.
† Soldier employed in police duties, particularly in rural areas.

Code 23. Employees (men and women)

Agent (Air France, tax office, customs, postal service, National Electricity Board, hospital, mortgage, laboratory, municipal, railroad), assistant accountant, administration clerk, typist, employee (w.f.p., administration, bank, office, tax office, National Lands Service, National Electricity Board, Public Housing Service, mortgages, laboratory, municipal, town hall, postal service, railroad, treasury), accountancy student, invoice clerk, civil servant (w.f.p.), printing employee, receptionist, retired railroad employee, secretary, switchboard operator, stenographer–typist, works (on railroad, in company *x*).

Code 24. Foremen

Foremen (w.f.p., workshop, construction, head foreman, warehouse, mine), overseer.

Code 25. Skilled workers

Railroad switchman, CAP* (hairdresser, dressmaker), tile-layer, work team head, pebble-dasher, hairdresser, assistant supervisor (construction), outfitter, dressmaker, roofer (w.f.p., zinc-worker), print shop employee, fitter (w.f.p., tin shop, bathroom appliances), mechanic–electrician, carpenter, carpenter–cabinet maker, model maker, assembler (dairy appliances, heating), skilled worker (male and female), plasterer, plasterer–painter, plumber, tailor.

Code 26. Farmers (men)

Farmer, farm owner, works on father's farm.

Code 27. Diverse, semi skilled

Chemist's assistant, dental assistant, assistant infant welfare specialist, baker, cashier, bookkeeper (woman), chef, train conductor, convoy supervisor, checker (w.f.p., electrical appliances), cinema ticket taker, demonstrator (woman), hotel operator trainee, employee (male or female; arsenal, firm *x*, truck manufacturer, hospital, factory), beautician (female), canteen manager, horticulturist, master gardener, warehouse keeper, operator (w.f.p., film, cinema, telephone), military radio technician, garage receptionist, TV announcer (woman), assistant station master, stewardess, heating technician, works in (laboratory, advertising), salesgirl–finisher.

Class 3

Code 30. Salesgirls

Grocery store employee, florist, pastry shop waitress, works in parents' shop, salesgirl.

Code 31. Farmers (women)

Farmer, farm operator, daughter of farmers, works on her mother's farm.

---

* CAP, a French diploma *Certificat d'Aptitude Professionnelle* certifying completion of a two-year programme in a vocational high school.

Code 32. Unskilled workers (men and women)

Assistant assembler, fitter (w.f.p.), fitter–mechanic, road mender, automobile bodyshop worker, roofer, factory forwarder, electrician, blacksmith, miller, mason, labourer, machinist, stock-room keeper, mechanic, miner, flour–miller, assembler (w.f.p., electrician, in tyres, in transistors), unskilled worker (w.f.p.), worker (w.f.p., automobile, butcher, shoes, knife-works, printing (woman), leather goods, carpentry, mason, mines, metallurgy, caster, painter, driller, plastic, on a press, factory), painter (w.f.p., building, plaster, cars), photo-engraver, shoe stitcher, polisher, assistant in metallurgy, adjustor, mechanical adjustor, ironer (woman), without any skill, sawyer, locksmith, welder, upholsterer–decorator, weaver, turner, turner–miller, cooper.

Code 33. Drivers and service personnel

Assistant cook, nurse's helper, hospital worker, hospital assistant, hospital orderly, bartender, maid, driver (w.f.p., of bus, of truck, deliveryman), bulldozer operator, cook, household employee, restaurant employee, chambermaid, cleaning woman, maid, kitchen helper, orderly, waiter (café, hotel), servant, hospital helper, deliveryman, dishwasher, waitress, construction material transporter, works (in a tavern, in a restaurant).

Code 34. Farm workers (men or women)

Lumberjack, domestic, farm worker (man or woman).

Code 35. Diverse, unskilled

Rural family helper, laboratory aide, laboratory helper, postal service auxiliary, apprentice, rag-picker, janitor, iron-manager, child day-care worker, sick-nurse, caretaker, laboratory helper (woman), legionnaire, sailor, sailor–fisherman, itinerant merchant, cinema usher, newspaper delivery girl, seasonal, works in (slaughterhouse, bus company *x*, construction, at home, colourings, tulle, piping), night-work in postal service, basket maker, night attendant.

Code 36. Illiterate, mentally deficient, on welfare

Already abandoned another child (without indication of occupation), mental age 8–10 years, mentally deficient, slightly retarded.

Code n. Without occupation

Raises her children, without occupation, keeps father's house.

Code x. Occupation unknown

No occupational or intellectual information.

Code y. Asocial (B mother)

Prostitute.

Code e. Students (B mothers)

Schoolgirl, technical high school student, home economics student, high school student (female), preparing high school certificate.

Table 3.18   *'Funnel' selection process in each of the six adoption agencies*

Agency	Early abandon- ments 1962–69	+ occupation of B father known	+ low occupations of 2 B parents	+ early placement	+ adoptive family in class 1	No. of subjects
a	73	5	2	2	1	1
b	59	10	3	2	2	2
c	70	29	11	6	3	2
d	148	72	15	10	1	1
e	400	147	57	22	13	10
f	386	213	80	60	23	16
Total 6 agencies	1136	476	168	102	43	32

Table 3.19   *Breakdown of occupations into large classes. We have considered the 476 cases of abandonment at birth for which the occupation of the putative father is known. Italics indicate those which met study criteria for the corresponding column*

Class	B mothers	B fathers	A mother	A fathers
1	3 (1%)	40 (8%)	31 (6%)	*154 (32%)*
1a	33 (7%)	56 (12%)	51 (11%)	93 (20%)
2	97 (20%)	164 (35%)	67 (14%)	144 (30%)
3	*264 (55%)*	*216 (45%)*	32 (7%)	44 (9%)
Outside	*79 (17%)*	0	295 (62%)	41 (9%)
Total	476 (100%)	476 (100%)	476 (100%)	476 (100%)

Appendix 3. Statistical profile of the 476 cases of abandonment for which the occupation of the putative father is known

To specify the nature of the files from which the 'study candidate' files were selected and to prepare for the discussion about biases, we present a statistical profile of the 476 cases of abandonment for which the occupation of the putative father is known.

1. The 'funnel' selection process

Tables 3.18 specifies, for each of the six adoption agencies, the 'funnel' selection process which was summed up in Table 3.1.

Table 3.20 *Breakdown of occupations into detailed categories. We have considered the 476 cases where the occupation of the putative father is known*

Code	Occupations	B mothers	B fathers	A mothers	A fathers
10	Senior executives	1	26	13	110
11	Professionals	0	4	4	20
12	Junior executives of class 1	2	7	14	14
13	Industrialists, contractors	0	3	0	10
	Total: class 1	3	40	31	154
15	Students	15	32	0	0
17	Junior executives of class 1a	13	15	46	68
18	Small businessmen, artisans	0	6	5	14
19	Diverse, high-level	5	3	0	11
	Total: class 1a	33	56	51	93
20	Merchants	3	21	8	16
21	Army, police	0	16	1	20
22	Representatives, salesmen	–	24	–	20
23	Employees	66	42	49	31
24	Foremen	0	2	1	16
25	Skilled workers	12	27	5	17
26	Farmers (men)	–	13	–	12
27	Diverse, semi-skilled	16	19	3	12
	Total: class 2	97	164	67	144
30	Salesgirls	30	–	5	–
31	Farmers (women)	10	–	7	–
32	Unskilled workers	66	144	7	38
33	Drivers and service personnel	132	44	4	4
34	Farm workers	3	11	0	0
35	Diverse, unskilled	8	17	9	2
36	Illiterate, mentally deficient, or on welfare (B mother)	15	–	–	–
	Total: class 3	264	216	32	44
x	Occupation unknown	25	–	159	7
n	Without occupation	44	–	103	0
a	Absent or no adoption	–	–	33	34
e	Student (B mother)	9	–	–	–
y	Asocial (B mother)	1	–	–	–
	Total: alphabetical code	79	0	295	41
	General total	476	476	476	476

Table 3.21 *Placement of the child according to the occupation of the putative father. In the 476 cases where the occupation of the putative father is known, the latter has little influence on the fate of the children abandoned at birth. The italics correspond to study criteria.*

	Early placement in an adoptive family of category						Late placement in an adoptive family of category						Not Adopted	Total
	1	1a	2	3	x	Total	1	1a	2	3	x	Total		
B father: class 1	6	9	10	1	2	28	1	1	7	1	0	10	3	41
B father: class 1a	17	12	9	4	0	42	4	0	6	2	0	12	1	55
B father: class 2	39	29	30	8	4	110	14	6	21	6	1	48	7	165
B father: class 3	54	22	41	16	0	133	22	12	20	7	0	61	21	215
B father: all categories	116 (24%)	72 (15%)	90 (19%)	29 (6%)	6 (0%)	313 (66%)	41 (9%)	19 (4%)	54 (11%)	16 (3%)	1 (0%)	131 (27%)	32 (7%)	476 (100%)
Both B parents: low	43 (26%)	13 (8%)	32 (19%)	14 (8%)	0 (0%)	102 (61%)	16 (10%)	13 (8%)	16 (10%)	7 (4%)	0 (0%)	52 (31%)	14 (8%)	168 (100%)

2. The distribution of occupations

The distribution according to large classes is presented in Table 3.19. We observe that unskilled occupations predominate among the biological parents (55 per cent of the B mothers and 45 per cent of the B fathers are in class 3), whereas among the adoptive families, class 1 occupations predominate (32 per cent among the adoptive fathers as opposed to eight per cent among the biological fathers). It will also be noted that categories x (occupation unknown) and n (without occupation) have been excluded in the case of the biological fathers following the definition itself of the 476 cases reported here.

Table 3.20 presents a more detailed breakdown of occupations.

3. Other children of the same mother

Table 3.22 provides a breakdown of the number of children born before the subjects and who had been abandoned. We observe that half of the cases of abandonment at birth concern primiparous mothers. In the cases where a mother had had another child, only rarely had this child been abandoned.

4. The placement of children according to the occupation of the putative father

Table 3.21 presents another type of breakdown of the 476 cases. The future of children after abandonment depends little on the occupation of the biological father both with respect to the probability of early adoptive placement and with respect to being placed in an 'upper-middle-class' family. Among the 168 children whose two biological parents lack occupational qualifications, 43, i.e. one out of four, were placed early in a class 1 family. This factor of four is brought up in the discussion of selection biases and in Appendix 8.

Appendix 4. Comparison of group A results with national survey results

We present details on the following:

1. Comparison of the study subjects with various national samples for IQ scores;
2. National statistics concerning school history;
3. Calculation of the number of school failures as a function of social origin;
4. Statistical analysis of the results.

1. Comparison of the study subjects with various national samples for IQ scores (Section 4 and Table 3.13)

The comparison with different national samples was presented in the text in three different forms:

—In the synthetic Table 3.13, average IQ scores were compared.

Table 3.22 *Breakdown of the 476 cases of abandonment at birth according to the number of children of the same mother*

Primiparous and multiparous mothers	Cases
No indication	52
Primiparous mother	194
1 other child	123
2 other children	49
3 other children	25
4 other children	20
5 other children	3
6 other children	5
7 other children	2
8 other children	3
Total	476

Abandonments prior to that of the subject	Cases
No indication	52
First abandonment	402
1 other abandonment	8
2 other abandonments	5
3 other abandonments	1
4 other abandonments	4
6 other abandonments	2
8 other abandonments	2
Total	476

—In Fig. 3.9, failure rates were compared, where failure was defined as having obtained a score below the national average.

—In Fig. 3.10, the rates of serious failure were compared, where serious failure was defined as having obtained a score at least one standard deviation below the national average.

(a) Comparison of average IQ scores

From the individual scores presented in Tables 3.10 and 3.11, the following average and dispersion values are obtained:

	Group A	Group B
Group test	106.8 ($\sigma = 12.2$)	95.1 ($\sigma = 12.9$)
Individual test	110.6 ($\sigma = 11.3$)	94.2 ($\sigma = 11.3$)
Average of both tests	108.7 ($\sigma = 10.7$)	94.6 ($\sigma = 11.3$)

Table 3.23   *IQ scores as a function of socio-professional category of head of family*

Socio-professional category	Proportion of schoolchildren (%)	Average of scores	Standard deviation
General categories			
Farmers and farm workers	16.3	95.6	13.2
Workers and foremen	42.4	96.6	13.5
Employees, army, police	11.3	101.8	13.7
Merchants and artisans	8.7	103.0	13.9
Upper-middle-class	15.0	108.9	13.8
Not declared	6.3	93.1	14.8
Total	100	99.2	15
Specific categories used in the study			
Unskilled workers (biological fathers)	23.4	94.8	13.5
Junior executives ⎫	6.5	107.9	13.7
Senior executives ⎬ (adoptive fathers)	5.0	111.5	13.6
Professionals and ⎭	3.5	107.4	14.0
industrialists			

Source: INED–INOP (1973, p. 41).

In the standardization samples, the ECNI group test average was 99.2 and the WISC individual test average, 100.

In the INED survey which used the ENCI group test, the average scores obtained by six- to 14-year-old schoolchildren in the various social categories were as shown in Table 3.23. Given the uncertainties in the classification of occupations analysed in Appendix 7, we have chosen the reference value of 95 ± 1 for the mean IQ of children of unskilled workers.

With respect to social class by adoption, 1975 census data permit us to estimate that, at the time of the study, i.e. on the average in 1976, senior executives and professionals represented 10 per cent of the male working population 35–44 years of age (INSEE 1978); this group represented three-quarters of the adopted subjects. It may be estimated, therefore, that the totality of 'upper-middle-class' occupations (22 senior executives, two professionals, three industrialists, four junior executives, one artisan) represented the top 13 percentiles of the socio-professional hierarchy.

At the time of the standardization of the ECNI test, i.e. in 1965, 'upper-middle-class' occupations were held by 15.9 per cent of the active male population from 35 to 44 years old, and senior executives represented six per cent. We have seen that the children of these two groups obtained average scores of 108.9 and 111.5 respectively. By the process of linear interpolation between ranks in the professional hierarchy and the average of children's scores, we obtain a mean of 109.7 for children whose fathers are in the top 13 percentiles of the socio-professional hierarchy.

When the calculation is made directly, without taking into account the recent 'devaluation' of skilled occupations, the average obtained for 'upper-middle-class' children is 110.2 which is in agreement with the above estimation, given the biases in the second estimation. Hence the final estimation reported in Table 3.13: 110 ± 1.

(b) Comparison of failure rates (Figs. 3.9 and 3.10)

We have assimilated the score distribution to a continuous distribution which is assumed to be normal. Given the distribution of average m and a standard deviation, σ the probability of failure was obtained with the aid of a table of the normal distribution starting from the number of deviations $t = (m - m_0)/\sigma$ where m_0 is the national average. In the calculation of error bars, we did not take account of statistical errors in the dispersion.

In the general population the failure rate is, by definition, 50 per cent. For the social classes of origin and by adoption, we used the previously defined values of 95 ± 1 and 110 ± 1 with dispersions equal to 13.5 and with the value of 99.2 for m_0.

2. National statistics concerning school history

School results, like test results, have been presented in three different forms. In the synthetic Table 3.13, the number of failures observed was presented (being behind or being placed in a special education class) for 32 schoolchildren having the same age distribution as the 32 A subjects. In Fig. 3.9, these results were expressed in terms of failure rates at the entry into sixth grade. In Fig. 3.10, these same results were expressed in terms of exclusion rates (placement in special education classes).

The comparison of our observations concerning the A subject with those made in national surveys requires knowing the risk of failure both as a function of social class or origin and as a function of school level reached. In fact, only one-half of the A subjects had completed primary school at the time of the updating of school histories; the other half were still in third, fourth, or fifth grades.

(a) School statistics at the entry into sixth grade

The most recent statistics are those resulting from the third survey of the Ministère de l'Education (1976). This survey concerned 12 899 children born the first day of an even numbered month and entering sixth grade during the school year of the survey (1974–75). According to data published in the survey report (pp. 13 and 116) the school failure risks (being behind or being placed in special education classes) for children of this age group were as follows:

Social class	Risk of school failure (%)
Farm workers	66.8
Workers and foremen	59.0
of which – unskilled workers	67.2
Employees	42.5
Proprietors of businesses and industries	38.6
of which – industrialists and large businessmen	33.0
artisans and shopkeepers	39.7
Junior executives	24.5
Professionals and senior executives	12.8
of which – professionals	9.7
– senior executives	13.5
General population	46.2

Table 3.24   *National data relative to the first four primary grades (1973–74 school year)*
The figures in the upper part of the table show the probability of not repeating a given grade as a function of father's occupation. The figures in the lower part are cumulative probabilities indicating the chance of entering a given grade early or on time

	Probability of passing 'normally'			
	1st grade	2nd grade	3rd grade	4th grade
Farm workers	0.730	0.908	0.825	0.855
Workers and foremen	0.815	0.863	0.875	0.870
Employees	0.877	0.906	0.909	0.898
Businessmen	0.913	0.931	0.915	0.903
Junior executives	0.956	0.950	0.949	0.927
Senior executives and professionals	0.969	0.981	0.972	0.960
General population	0.861	0.900	0.899	0.890

	Cumulative probabilities			
	Entering 2nd grade	Entering 3rd grade	Entering 4th grade	Entering 5th grade
Farm workers	0.730	0.663	0.547	0.468
Workers and foremen	0.815	0.703	0.615	0.535
Employees	0.877	0.794	0.722	0.648
Businessmen	0.913	0.850	0.778	0.702
Junior executives	0.956	0.908	0.862	0.799
Senior executives and professionals	0.969	0.951	0.924	0.887
General population	0.861	0.775	0.697	0.620

Source: Ministère de l'Education (1975, pp. 27–32).

(b) School statistics on primary school

The latest data published come from the second survey of the Ministère de l'Education (1975). From this data we have obtained the success rates and the cumulative rates presented in Table 3.24.

The probability of going through grades one to four without academic mishap is given in the first part of the table, as a function of social origin. The second part presents the probability of arriving 'early' or 'on time' into grades two to five. They were obtained by multiplying the probabilities of success for each of the previous grades. We shall see in Section 2(*d*) below that, in the case of the sixth grade, this approximate calculation yields failure rates very close to those actually observed.

(c) Variation in rates of repeating over time

The evolution of rates of repeating is reproduced in Table 3.25 from data published by the Ministry of Education.

By cross-multiplying the rates of success of a single diagonal in each of the five primary grades, we obtained the following values for rates of success at the entry

Table 3.25   *Chronological evolution of success rates in each of the primary grades. Each line corresponds to two successive academic years. The column indicates the grade which is passed without repeating. The year of birth of children who pass without having ever repeated previously is indicated. The figure under that year gives the probability of not repeating the grade. The school history of a given age class is read diagonally from top to bottom and from left to right. We have indicated in italics children born in 1962. Thus, 82.1% of the children born in 1962 did not repeat 1st grade, 88.2% did not repeat 2nd grade and so on*

Source	School year	1st grade	2nd grade	3rd grade	4th grade	5th grade
a	1967–68 to 1968–69	1961 0.814	1960 0.873	1959 0.878	1958 0.859	1957 0.836
a	1968–69 to 1969–70	*1962* *0.821*	1961 0.877	1960 0.883	1959 0.870	1958 0.843
a	1969–70 to 1970–71	1963 0.814	*1962* *0.882*	1961 0.890	1960 0.890	1959 0.846
a	1970–71 to 1971–72	1964 0.827	1963 0.892	*1962* *0.900*	1961 0.893	1960 0.858
b	1971–72 to 1972–73	1965 0.813	1964 0.918	1963 0.939	*1962* *0.915*	1961 0.860
b	1972–73 to 1973–74	1966 0.820	1965 0.919	1964 0.937	1963 0.919	*1962* *0.883*
b	1973–74 to 1974–75	1967 0.833	1966 0.932	1965 0.945	1964 0.930	1963 0.887
b	1974–75 to 1975–76	1968 0.832	1967 0.929	1966 0.944	1965 0.937	1964 0.892
b	1975–76 to 1976–77	1969 0.832	1968 0.927	1967 0.947	1966 0.922	1965 0.892
b	1976–77 to 1977–78	1970 0.847	1969 0.933	1968 0.937	1967 0.917	1966 0.884

[a] Sénat. Commission des finances. *Execution du budget pour 1977 du Ministère de l'Education*, question no. 8.
[b] Ministère de l'Education (1978). Service des Etudes Informatiques et Statistiques. *Document de Travail* no. 155, January.

into sixth grade as a function of the year of birth. In conformity with the results presented in 2(d), we have subtracted 0.5 per cent from the product of the five rates of success.

Children born in	Success rate (%)
1961	48.3
1962	52.2
1963	55.1
1964	58.5
1965	58.5
1966	58.3

Let us note that the evolution over time of rates of repeating is known only for the general population and not for the children of the various social clases. We shall see that, given that the available statistics are recent, corrections are quite minimal for the totality of A subjects and nil for the B subjects.

(d) The relation between repetition in primary school and failure rates in the sixth grade

The comparison between the data on primary school history and data on the entry into sixth grade confirms that, to a very good approximation, success rates are cumulative.

With the aid of data from Table 3.25, we have compared the product of the rates of success in the five primary grades with the success rates observed in the last two surveys at the entry into sixth grade. As the figures below indicate, the result of this comparison is satisfactory.

	Survey no. 2	Survey no. 3
Average year of birth	1961.5	1962.5
Calculated success rate (%)	50.7	54.2
Observed success rate (%)	50.1	53.8
Difference (%)	− 0.6	− 0.4

3. Calculation of the number of school failures as a function of social origin

Let us consider groups of 32 children having the same age distribution as group A and the same balanced sex distribution as group A. What would the number of failing students be as a function of the social class of these groups? First, we have presented the results without taking account of the birth date (except for the group representing the general population).

Although laborious, these calculations are straightforward. Cases where the child has entered sixth grade (children born between 1962 and 1966) must be distinguished from those where the child is too young (children born after 1966). In the first case, the probability of success is that which has been tabulated in Section 2(a); in the second, the probabilities are those presented in the second part of Table

3.24. With respect to the latter, it should be noted that the socio-professional categories are less detailed than those for the entry into sixth grade.

The risks of failure at some point during the school career are simply one minus the probabilities of complete success. Thus, multiple failures for a child are included simply as 'failure'. To know the number of failing children as a function of attributed social class, it suffices to break down the probabilities corresponding to each child; this breakdown has been presented in Table 3.26.

The first column gives the year of birth, for example, 1962 for subject 1 and 1969 for subject 32. The second column gives the case numbers of the subjects. The third column gives the A subject's last grade. The fourth column gives the socio-professional category of the adoptive parents of the A subject of the same number, for example, junior executive for subjects 1 and 32. The following column gives the number of subjects having the same characteristics and who have been placed on the same line, e.g. 1 for the first line which corresponds to subject 1 and 4 for the fourth line which corresponds to subjects 3, 15, 25, and 27. The column 'upper-middle-class' corresponds to those children of the general population of the same social class as the corresponding A subject, e.g. junior executive for subject 1 and senior executive for the subject of the following line. The following columns correspond to the various hypotheses which have been employed for the social class of diverse groups of 32 subjects, ranging from the group of senior executives and professionals to the group of unskilled workers. The last two columns correspond to the general population.

For the general population, the calculation was made in two different ways. In the next to last column, we used data from surveys 2 and 3; for the subject of the first line, for example, the probability of failure reported in Section 2(a) is 0.462 at the entry into sixth grade; for subject 32, the probability is 0.225 (the complement to 1 of 0.775; see the last line of Table 3.24). In the last column, we took account of birth date: the two figures corresponding to the above examples become 0.478 (the complement of 0.522, see 2(c)) and 0.224 (the complement of 0.776, see Table 3.25).

In the case of incomplete school histories, unskilled workers have not been distinguished from the category 'workers and foremen.' However, the data reproduced in Section 2(a) show that at the entry into sixth grade, the failure rate for unskilled workers is very close to that of farm workers (67.2 per cent instead of 66.8 per cent). For incomplete school histories, therefore, we have used data relative to farm workers.

The next to last line of the table gives the average number of subjects failing in school as a function of attributed social class. This number varies from 3.2 for the category of senior executives and professionals to 17.6 for the category of unskilled workers.

In the case of the general population, the expected number of failures amounts to 12 if year of birth is not taken into account and to 11.2 if it is. To take account of year of birth in an approximate way, we have applied a rule of three to the figures of the next to last line: they were multiplied by 11.23/12 = 0.936. The results of this multiplication appear in the last line of the table.

A calculation analogous to the preceding one concerning 39 children having the

Table 3.26 *Breakdown of the risk of failure as a function of social class for 32 schoolchildren having the same age distribution as the A subjects of the study*

Year Subject	Last grade	Socio-profes. category	No.	Upper-middle-class	Sr. ex. prof.	Jr. exec.	Business-men	Employees	Workers	Unskilled workers	General pop. without corr.	with corr.
1962 1	6	Jr. ex.	1	0.245	0.128	0.245	0.386	0.425	0.590	0.672	0.462	0.478
1962 23	6	Sr. ex.	1	0.135	"	"	"		"	"	"	"
1962 28	6	Prof.	1	0.097	"	"	"		"	"	"	"
1963 3, 15, 25, 27	6	Sr. ex.	4	0.135	"	"	"		"	"	"	0.449
1964 6, 17	6	Sr. ex.	2	0.135	"	"	"		"	"	"	0.415
1964 19	6	Industr.	1	0.330	"	"	"		"	"	"	"
1965 4	6	Jr. ex.	1	0.245	"	"	"		"	"	"	"
1965 2, 7, 9	6	Sr. ex.	3	0.135	"	"	"		"	"	"	"
1966 21	6	Jr. ex.	1	0.245	"	"	"		"	"	"	0.417
1966 29	6	Sr. ex.	1	0.135	"	"	"		"	"	"	"
1967 16	4	Sr. ex.	1	0.076	0.076	0.138	0.222	0.278	0.385	0.453	0.303	0.267
1967 31	5	Sr. ex.	1	0.112	0.112	0.201	0.298	0.352	0.465	0.532	0.380	0.328
1967 18	5	Artisan	1	0.298	"	"	"		"	"	"	"
1968 14	4	Prof.	1	0.076	0.076	0.138	0.222	0.278	0.385	0.453	0.303	0.277
1968 22	4	Industr.	1	0.222	"	"	"		"	"	"	"
1968 5, 8, 10, 13, 20, 24	4	Sr. ex.	6	0.076	"	"	"		"	"	"	"
1969 12	3	Industr.	1	0.150	0.049	0.092	0.150	0.206	0.297	0.337	0.225	0.224
1969 32	3	Jr. ex.	1	0.092	"	"	"		"	"	"	"
1969 11, 26, 30	3	Sr. ex.	3	0.049	"	"	"		"	"	"	"
Total, without correction for date				4.28	3.20	6.02	9.52	11.04	15.32	17.58	12.00	11.23
Total, with correction for date				4.0	3.0	5.6	8.9	10.3	14.3	16.5	11.2	

same age distribution as the B children showed that the corrective factor corresponding to birth dates was nearly equal to 1 in the case of group B: the number of failures expected for 39 school-children of the general population is 15.5 according to surveys 2 and 3 and 15.4 if birth data is taken into account.

4. Statistical analysis of the results

The statistical uncertainties have been presented in Table 3.13 for IQ scores, in Fig. 3.9 for failure rates, and in Fig. 3.10 for the rates of serious failures. We shall specify here how these uncertainties were estimated.

For the IQ scores, the uncertainty was obtained by dividing by $\sqrt{N}$ the standard deviation observed. To estimate the failure rate, we did not use the observed standard deviation value but a slightly higher invariable value ($\sigma = 13.5$). The mean IQ score for the A group is above the cut-off point for failures while the mean IQ score for the B group is below this cut-off point. Hence, by using a broader distribution, one overestimates the proportion of failures for the A group and the proportion of success for the B group. This tends to reduce the gap between the two groups and thus produces a conservative estimate of the effect observed.

As can be seen from the last line of Table 3.26, the number of school failures observed in the A group coincides exactly with the number expected for children of 'upper-middle-class' parents. The rate of 4/32 = 12.5 per cent must be corrected for age to correspond to entry into the sixth grade. Using the national statistics presented in Section 2(*a*), the weighted average rate of failure for 32 'upper-middle-class' children is 17.3 per cent. To estimate the interval corresponding to a standard error, we drew, from the results of the last line of Table 3.26, the curve of the χ^2 as a function of the expected failure rate: the horizontal line, $\chi^2 = 1$, intersects this curve at the abscissa 27 per cent and at the abscissa 10.5 per cent.

We proceeded similarly for group B, starting from data on the last line of Table 3.26, for a group of 39 children. In this case, the χ^2 curve may be drawn only on one side; we obtain for the length of the lower error bar the value of 9.5 per cent; the same value was used for the upper error bar.

To calculate the height of the rectangles on the left of Fig. 3.9, we proceeded by a rule of three starting from ECNI test failure rate error bars for A and B children and from the corresponding rectangles for 'upper-middle-class' children and for the children of unskilled workers. Thus, for example, we have the following values for the upper error bars and for the half-heights of the rectangles:

School failure rates, A children (%)	$27 - 17.3 = 9.7$
ECNI failure rates, 'upper-middle-class' children (%)	$23.4 - 21.2 = 2.2$
ECNI failure rates, A children (%)	$34.5 - 28.7 = 5.8$

From whence the half-height of the rectangle for school failure for 'upper-middle-class' children: $9.7 \times (2.2/5.8) = 3.7\%$.

Finally for serious school failures, there is a one-to-one correspondence between the failure rate and the rate of serious failures for a given social class. The use of this correspondence permits us to estimate the rate of serious failures from the totality of failures observed. In relation to direct estimation, this procedure has the following three advantages:

(a) At the time of the study, the distinction between remedial sixth grade classes and ordinary sixth grade classes was in the process of changing, thus making comparison between groups A and B hazardous;

(b) The only serious failure observed in group A concerns the pair of twins, subject 4 whose birth was accompanied by considerable biological trauma;

(c) The greatest statistical precision is obtained by using the totality of information available.

The data reported in Fig. 2.1 of Chapter 2 permit one to draw the curve of serious school failure rates as a function of failure rates. Thus, to the failure rate of 67.2% (children of unskilled workers), there corresponds a rate of serious failure of 34.2%. As far as error bars are concerned, they have been obtained by a rule of three as for the totality of school failures.

Appendix 5. Comparison of the school failure rates of groups A and B

From the data in Tables 3.8 and 3.9, the following values for cumulative failure rates are obtained and are presented in Fig. 3.6:

Entry into	A subjects		B subjects
2nd grade	1.5/32	= 0.047*	12/39 = 0.308†
3rd grade	3/32	= 0.094	14/34 = 0.412
4th grade	3/26	= 0.115	16/33 = 0.485
5th grade	3/18	= 0.167	14/31 = 0.452
6th grade	2.5/15.5	= 0.161*	17/27 = 0.630

With respect to primary school history, the distribution of the 32 A subjects at the end of the study is as follows:

6 are in 3rd grade
8 are in 4th grade
2.5 are in 5th grade*
15.5 are in 6th grade

If the B group had the same number of subjects and the same age distribution as the A group, the number of failures in group B would be:

---

* The half subjects concern the pair of twins, subject 4.

† Three B children arrived 'late' into sixth grade without our knowing which grades they had repeated (1B1, 15B1, 20B). We have assumed that the repeated grades in these three cases were distributed uniformly, i.e. one repeating first grade, one repeating third grade, and one repeating fifth grade.

$$6 \times 0.412 + 8 \times 0.485 + 2.5 \times 0.452 + 15.5 \times 0.630 = 17.25 \text{ or } 53.9\%$$

This last result may be slightly corrected to account for the decrease in the risk of repeating with time. As we saw in Appendix 4, to move from the reference sample (surveys 2 and 3) to sample A, the failure rate must be multiplied by 0.936; this factor is practically equal to 1 for group B. After correction, the preceding rate becomes, therefore, $53.9 \times 0.936 = 50.4\%$ or 19.7 failures for 39 subjects. The χ^2 corresponding to the comparison of the two groups (four failures, 28 successes in group A; 19.7 failures, 19.3 successes in group B) amounts to 11.4 (p <0.001).

The corrected gross rate, 50.4 per cent, is very close to the gross rate expected for the children of unskilled workers ($16.5/32 = 51.5\%$, see Table 3.26 in Appendix 4). To calculate the failure rate extrapolated to the entry to 6th grade for group B, we started from the corresponding rate for the children of unskilled workers (67.2%, see Section 2(a) of Appendix 4) which we corrected by a rule of three: 67.2% $\times$ (50.45/51.5) = 65.8%. Such is the percentage reported in Fig. 3.9.

Appendix 6. Samples a_t, b_t, and groups a_u, b_u

The definition of the samples and the principal results were presented in the text. The details presented here concern:

1. The sociological structure of samples a_t and b_t
2. The relation observed between social segregation and IQ scores, when the social class of origin is controlled (upper-middle-class children)

1. The sociological structure of samples a_t and b_t

A detailed classification of occupation was first undertaken by using the occupational list described in Appendix 2. Occupations were then re-grouped according to categories used in the survey published by INED–INOP (1973). The socially privileged group was defined by categories 1, 2, and 3 of the following list of occupations:

1. Senior executives
2. Professionals and industrialists
3. Junior executives
4. Artisans and merchants
5. Employees, army, police
6. Workers and foremen
7. Farmers and farm workers
0. Occupation not listed.

The distribution of percentages of privileged children in samples a_t and b_t is presented in Fig. 3.11. It can be seen that, from a sociological point of view, the two samples differ considerably.

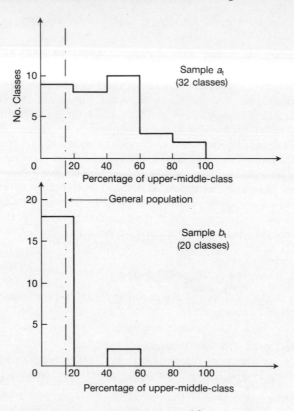

Fig. 3.11 Sociological structure of samples a_t and b_t.

2. The relation observed between social segregation and IQ scores, when the social class of origin is controlled (upper-middle-class children)

The distribution of social classes in samples a_t and b_t is presented in Table 3.27. The second column of the table gives the number of pupils in each class (excluding subjects A and B). Columns 3 to 10 give the occupations of family heads according to the categories defined above.

In the INED survey, the relation between average IQ score and the occupation of the head of the family was the following (INED–INOP 1973, pp. 40–1):

Occupation of the head of the family	Children's average score
Senior executives	111.5
Professionals and industrialists	107.4
Junior executives	107.9
Artisans and merchants	103.0
Employees, army, police	101.8
Workers and foremen	96.6
Farmers and farm workers	95.6
Occupation not listed	93.1

These data allow us to isolate the specific effect of the social class of schoolmates, as distinct from the social class of the pupils themselves. In the last column but one of Table 3.27, we characterized the social class of the schoolmates of the subjects by the average IQ score expected from the distribution given in the preceding columns. As was already apparent from the data presented in Fig. 3.11, the average

Table 3.27 *Social structure of the classes of the A subjects (Sample a_t) and of the B subjects (Sample b_t)*

Subject	No.	1	2	3	4	5	6	7	0	Mean occupational class indexed by expected IQ score	Average IQ score observed for categories 1, 2, 3
1 A	32	8	1	4	2	4	10	0	3	102.8	108.5
2 A	20	1	0	1	0	2	9	0	7	97.2	99.0
3 A	28	9	4	2	1	8	4	0	0	105.5	115.4
4 A	24	8	1	3	0	3	7	1	1	103.9	112.2
5 A	16	2	1	2	3	2	4	1	1	102.1	103.0
6 A	32	3	1	5	7	8	7	0	1	102.7	113.8
7 A	31	13	8	4	0	1	3	2	0	107.2	114.8
8 A	24	1	0	5	2	2	14	0	0	100.5	114.8
9 A	24	11	6	3	1	3	0	0	0	108.5	124.6
10 A	32	3	1	4	0	4	14	0	6	99.7	125.5
11 A	25	15	2	2	0	1	5	0	0	107.5	129.2
12 A	25	1	4	5	4	6	5	0	0	103.5	112.1
13 A	26	5	0	1	1	3	14	1	1	100.6	114.8
14 A	30	17	5	1	2	4	1	0	0	108.3	109.6
15 A	28	1	0	2	1	6	18	0	0	99.3	113.7
16 A	29	0	0	2	4	6	13	1	3	98.9	118.0
17 A	29	6	4	4	2	4	9	0	0	103.9	114.1
18 A	28	6	1	3	0	4	11	0	3	101.8	108.7
19 A	21	2	0	2	0	5	11	0	1	100.2	95.5
20 A	20	3	0	2	1	10	3	1	0	102.8	117.0
21 A	22	1	0	2	0	7	9	0	3	99.5	105.0
22 A	11	0	0	0	0	2	5	4	0	97.2	–
23 A	27	10	2	4	0	7	3	0	1	105.8	119.8
24 A	21	5	1	3	1	4	7	0	0	103.6	116.9
25 A	7	1	0	2	0	0	3	1	0	101.8	123.0
26 A	20	5	2	8	0	2	3	0	0	106.4	129.3
27 A	29	6	3	7	0	5	4	0	4	103.9	118.1
29 A	19	5	1	2	1	3	7	0	0	103.4	103.6
30 A	19	2	0	3	1	8	5	0	0	102.5	119.6
31 A	20	0	0	3	1	3	13	0	0	99.4	106.7
32 A	26	0	1	2	2	5	15	0	1	99.2	108.7
Sample a_t	745	150	49	93	37	132	236	12	36	102.8	115.9

Table 3.27—*contd.*

Subject	No.	\multicolumn{8}{c}{Distribution of occupations}	Mean occupational class indexed by expected IQ score	Average IQ score observed for categories 1, 2, 3
		1	2	3	4	5	6	7	0		
1 B_2	21	0	0	3	0	4	14	0	0	99.2	114.0
2 B	23	0	1	3	0	4	15	0	0	99.4	100.2
4 B_4	20	1	0	1	1	4	9	3	1	98.9	109.5
5 B_3	11	0	0	0	0	1	7	2	1	96.6	–
6 B	12	0	0	1	0	0	4	7	0	97.0	65
7 B	16	0	0	1	3	1	7	1	3	98.1	124
8 B	28	3	0	1	1	5	16	0	2	99.5	100.7
9 B_1	31	0	0	1	2	5	21	0	2	98.0	120
13 B	25	0	0	2	0	11	12	0	0	99.8	112.5
14 B_2	20	1	1	1	1	5	5	6	0	99.8	110.7
15 B_2	23	1	0	1	0	8	12	0	1	99.4	104.0
16 B	20	0	0	0	2	1	10	7	0	97.1	–
17 B_2	31	2	0	3	1	6	15	4	0	99.7	113.2
18 B	7	0	1	0	0	0	6	0	0	98.1	115
19 B_1	21	1	0	1	1	3	15	0	0	98.9	81.5
Sample b_t	309	9	3	19	12	58	168	30	10	98.8	105.9

social class of schoolmates is both higher and more variable in sample a_t than in sample b_t.

Since the social composition within sample a_t is so variable, this sample was divided into three sub-samples according to the average expected score. The average score of 'upper-middle-class'* children was derived from that observed for upper-middle-class-children (categories 1, 2, and 3 of Table 3.27) by using the following equations:

1. δ = observed average – expected average for upper-middle-class children
2. average for 'upper-middle-class' children = corresponding expected value + δ

Using this procedure, we obtained the results presented in Table 3.28 for 'upper-middle-class' children of samples a_t and b_t. The scores displayed in the text in Fig. 3.8 are those of sub-samples a_u^1, a_u^2, a_u^3 and of sample b_u.

Appendix 7. Uncertainties and biases in the classification of occupations

Three types of problems will be examined. The first is of a general nature and concerns the difficulty of making a precise comparison between classifications made

* For the significance of the quotation marks, see footnote, p. 69.

Table 3.28 *Variation of the mean score of upper-middle-class children with the social origin of their classmates*

| Name of group | No. | Upper-middle-class children | | | 'Upper-middle-class' children[a] (estimated average score = 110.0 + δ) | Social origin of classmates indexed by average expected IQ score |
		Average score expected (1)	Average score observed (2)	δ = (2) − (1)		
a_u^1	98	109.5	111.4	1.9	111.9	100.7
a_u^2	92	109.6	115.8	6.2	116.2	104.3
a_u^3	102	109.9	120.3	10.4	120.4	107.6
a_u	292	109.7	115.9	6.2	116.2	102.8
b_u	31	108.9	105.9	−3.0	107.0	98.8

[a] For the significance of the quotation marks, see note p. 69.

under different conditions: the same term does not necessarily cover the same reality. The second problem is the difficulty of making a precise separation between skilled and unskilled workers. The third concerns the possibility of errors in the mothers' declaration regarding the occupation of the A child's father.

1. Uncertainties in the classification of occupations

In Fig. 3.12 we have presented the proportion of schoolchildren of the principal urban groups in the two national surveys which served as reference for the study.

The Ministry of Education survey post-dates that of the INED by 10 years, so that the major differences (increase in the proportion of upper-middle-class children, decrease in the proportion of children of unskilled workers) is due in part to the increase in the number of qualified personnel which took place during the decade. However, even when one takes into account the evolution of occupations, around 10 per cent are missing from among the children of workers in the Ministry survey. It is not possible to know if this results from a subject classification error or from the loss of workers' children who, for one reason or another, were not enrolled in school.

The preceding considerations illustrate the difficulty in pin-pointing locations on the social spectrum and the somewhat illusory character of such pin-pointing. In situating the parents (both biological and adoptive) on the social spectrum, we have, therefore, allowed for a certain margin of uncertainty. This margin has been evaluated as one-quarter of the distance separating two adjacent groups (skilled and unskilled workers, or senior and junior executives). On the children's IQ score scale, this uncertainty corresponds to one point on either side of the value calculated according to the parents' social class.

2. The division between skilled and unskilled workers

This division is difficult to make and was not attempted in the Girard *et al.* survey (1963). In principle, the A subjects' putative fathers are all unskilled workers (see

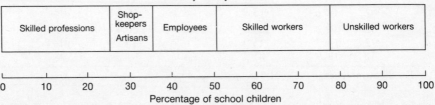

Fig. 3.12 Difficulty of making a precise comparison according to socio-professional category.

The comparison of percentages in the two national surveys serving as references for the study illustrates both the increase in the number of skilled personnel in 10 years and the difficulty of pin-pointing a group's location on the social spectrum. The total of 100 per cent corresponds to the five principal urban groups.

Table 3.4). An examination of the 476 cases where the occupation of the putative father is known, however, brings out an abnormally high proportion of unskilled occupations in relation to the totality of blue-collar workers (84 per cent, see Table 3.20).

This excess of unskilled occupations is doubtlessly due, in part, to the nature of the population. However, two artificial sources of this excess were also noted.

—In three cases (i.e. nine per cent of the subjects) use of the INSEE manual brought to light an under-estimation of occupational qualifications (an automobile body shop worker, a mason, a fitter–electrician).
—In conformity with the INSEE manual, persons qualified simply as workers without any other information were classed as unskilled workers. Ten subjects, i.e. 31 per cent of group A, are in this situation.

In conclusion, the classification adopted led to a slight underestimation of the putative fathers' occupational status; the corresponding bias is in the opposite direction to the bias concerning the biological mothers (who have even fewer qualifications than the wives of unskilled workers). Hence, the uncertainty of one point on the mean score expected given parental occupations includes this possibility of bias.

3. Erroneous indications by the mother

To conclude, we will examine a possible 'genetic' contamination of group A due to erroneous declarations by mothers who might, for example, have qualified as 'worker' a father who, in reality, was an engineer. For such a bias to appear in our study, two phenomena would have to occur simultaneously and often. First, the number of contrasting couples (mother lacking qualification, father highly qualified) would have to be significant in relation to couples forming within the same social class. Secondly, in these socially contrasting couples, a considerable proportion of mothers would have to hide the father's qualification, not by abstaining from supplying information, nor by calling a 'technician' a 'foreman' (which would have led to excluding the file from the study) but by qualifying as 'worker' a father who was an engineer.

Let us examine first the question of socially contrasting couples. According to data in the 476 cases analysed in Appendix 3, the distribution, in per cent, of the occupational qualifications of the partners of mothers without occupational skill is as follows:

—Rural and urban workers, farmers	71
—Employees	12
—Artisans, merchants, army	8
—'Upper-middle-class'	9

The partners of mothers without occupational skill belong mostly to the working classes. To obtain an upper limit to a possible contamination, let us suppose that when the partner holds an 'upper-middle-class' occupation and when the mother gives information on the father, she places the father in the working classes one time out of three; to the nine per cent of 'upper-middle-class' occupations named by the mothers would correspond then 4.5 per cent dissimulated among the 83 per cent of working class fathers; the contamination of the working classes by 'upper-middle-class' occupations would then be 4.5/83 = 5.4%.

To continue our estimation, let us suppose that this dissimulation takes place uniformly throughout the various strata of the working class and let us now examine the genetic bias that an 'upper-middle-class' father would bring.

The advantages (social and, possibly, genetic) of having both parents in the social category 'upper-middle-class' correspond to 15 IQ points; for the sake of this calculation, let us attribute half of this advantage to the socio-biological class of the two parents. Since each parent supplies half of the gene pool, the genetic advantage attributable to an 'upper-middle-class' father would be 3.7 points (one-quarter of 15). On the average, the bias introduced by a contamination of 5.4 per cent of 'upper-middle-class' fathers would be, therefore, 0.2 IQ points. Let us emphasize, in conclusion, that this is a conservative estimate since it is based on a series of conservative hypotheses.

Appendix 8. The selection of infants in the public adoption agencies

The possible bias introduced in the average test scores by the selection of 'well-developed' infants may be expressed as the product of three factors multiplying the standard deviation:

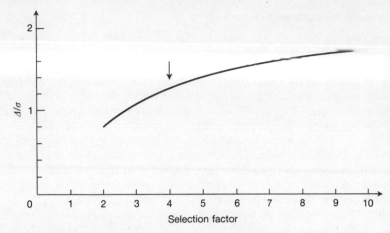

Fig. 3.13   Effect of truncation of a normal distribution.
The curve shows that, for a selection coefficient of four, the effect of selection is not
very sensitive to the value of the coefficient (see text).

$$\delta = \sigma \Delta e \varrho$$

where δ is the effect of the selection on the test score average;

σ is the standard deviation of the normal distribution of IQ scores;
Δ is the maximum effect of the psychometric selection of the most highly developed infants; Δ is a dimensionless number indicating the effect of truncation on
the mean of a normal distribution in units of σ;
e is the efficacy of the selection which was actually made by the adoption
agencies; e is a dimensionless number (see below)
ϱ is the correlation between development quotient at around 3 or 4 months and
test scores between 6 and 14 years.

1. The maximum effect of a selection by a factor of four

Given a normal distribution of scores of a standard deviation σ, what would be the
difference between mean values, with and without selection?

The effect of such a selection may be calculated with the aid of a table of truncated normal distribution (Falconer 1981). The result of this calculation is represented in Fig. 3.13 for the various values of the selection coefficient. The result is
relatively insensitive to the exact value of the coefficient; for a selection factor of
four, the maximum bias introduced in a distribution is 1.27σ.

2. The real effect of selection

Two facts contribute to reducing considerably the effect of the selection made. On
the one hand, only one of the six adoption agencies consistently used psychometric
estimations; this was agency f, which supplied half of the subjects. However, other

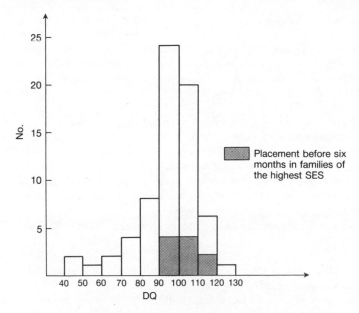

Fig. 3.14   Actual selection observed on a set of development quotients.
Data obtained in the Duyme (1981) survey. The subjects placed early in families of
the highest socio-professional category (dark rectangles) are far from being those
with the highest development quotients (DQ). In these data, selection efficacy is 40
per cent (see text).

factors intervened in the placement decisions: preferences expressed by the adoptive family regarding age, sex, physical appearance, etc.; priority granted to families who had been waiting a long time; the number of children already adopted;
judgements made about the infant's 'temperament' and that of the members of the
adoptive family.

We do not have available systematic estimates of development quotients for the
168 infants abandoned at birth whose parents were of a low socio-professional
category, nor for the 43 children placed before six months of age into families of a
high socio-professional category, nor even for the 16 subjects coming from agency
f. However, we do have at our disposal a detailed transcription of the files of that
agency at a period when numerical psychometric estimations were made fairly systematically.

This detailed transcription was made within the framework of another study carried out by one of us (Duyme 1981). This study deals with the scholastic future of
all children abandoned at birth in 1961 and 1962 in two agencies, including agency
f. In the latter, 72 children had been abandoned at birth in the 1961–62 period.
With the exception of one child who had undergone surgery, all children had been
the subject of early psychometric evaluations, 94 per cent of which are numerical.
These evaluations are represented in Fig. 3.14. The position on the histogram gives
the last numerical evaluation of the development quotient before six months.

Of these 72 cases, 11 were placed before six months in families of the highest socio-professional category. (There were five categories in the study.) Ten of these children were evaluated in a quantitative manner. In the histogram, we have represented these 10 children separately as shaded rectangles. We may observe that the selection with the aid of development quotients was incomplete since these 10 cases do not correspond to the 10 highest values of quotients measured.

The facts observed are as follows:

—Development quotients were, indeed, used to make a selection.
—This selection was incomplete.
—It had bearing on placement date more than on the adoptive family's social category; after analyzing the criteria of early placement, the choice of the highest socio-professional category increases average development quotients by only one point (i.e. average IQ scores are increased by 0.1 point; see below).

The numerical data which permit us to estimate the efficacy of the selection are as follows:

(a) The selection rate for subjects adopted before six months into families of the highest category is $72/11 = 6.5$.
(b) The average value of the development quotient in the interval above 50 is 93.8 (median value 96).
(c) For the 10 subjects placed before six months into a family of the highest socio-professional category and who were tested, the average development quotient was 102.2.
(d) For the 10 children having the highest development quotient, the average is 114.5. (In the case of a maximal selection of a coefficient of 6.5, the expected development quotient average would be 117.0.)

The comparison of the values calculated in (b) and (c) gives the effect of the selection that was actually made. The comparison between the values in (d) and (b) gives the effect of a perfect selection. The efficacy of the actual selection is, therefore:

$$\frac{(102.2 - 93.8)}{(114.5 - 93.8)} = 40\%$$

In the sample used in our study, there was no systematic evaluation of development quotients. A 40 per cent efficacy represents, therefore, an upper limit to the actual efficacy of an early psychometric selection in our study.

3. The correlation between development quotients and test scores

When the correlation is zero, the selection of development quotients has an effect of zero on the IQ scores. When the correlation is ϱ, an increase of x standard deviations in the development quotients corresponds to an increase of ϱx standard deviations in the IQ scores.

Excluding those studies dealing with the early detection of serious (but rare) biological anomalies, there is, to our knowledge, no study bringing out a value for ϱ significantly different from zero for very early evaluations of psychometric develop-

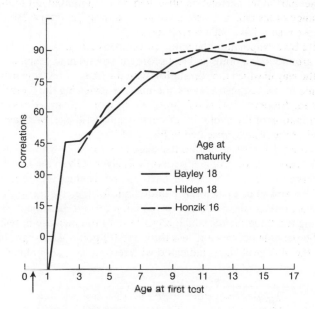

Fig. 3.15 Correlation between an early test score and a final score obtained at the age of 16 or 18.
Adapted from Bloom (1964). For our subjects, selection took place at around 0.3 years (indicated by an arrow in the lower left hand corner of the figure).

ment. In a recent review of these questions, McCall (1972) gives a median value of 0.01 for the correlation between test scores prior to six months and those between five and seven years. Another authoritative author on this subject (Bayley, 1970) writes:

The findings of these early studies of mental growth of infants have been repeated sufficiently often so that it is now well-established that test scores earned in the first year or two have relatively little predictive validity (in contrast to tests at school age or later), although they may have high validity as measures of the children's cognitive abilities at the time.

In the absence of a direct measure of ϱ, an indirect measure may be obtained by extrapolating from values measured at an age older than four months.

Before proceeding with this evaluation, we would like to point out that the ϱ values reported in the literature are all over-evaluated as far as our problem is concerned. In fact, to obtain a value corresponding to this problem, it would be necessary to proceed in the following manner. One would begin by testing children at a very young age. They would then be randomly distributed throughout the population.

Such an experiment is, obviously, impossible in practice. Either testing was done before adoption and the subsequent selective placement contributed to the observed correlation, or it concerns children remaining in their original milieu. In the latter case, part of the correlation observed is to be imputed not to the child but to the constancy of his milieu which is the same during the interval separating the two tests whose results have been correlated.

To evaluate by extrapolation the value of the correlation between development quotients at around four months and test scores at around nine years, it is necessary to examine the way in which the correlation with the final score value increases with age at the time of the first test. Among the authors reviewing the literature that we have consulted, Bloom (1964) is the only one to have attempted a synthetic and graphic presentation of the evolution of correlations with age. We have borrowed from this author the results presented in Fig. 3.15.

It will be noted that the correlation decreases very rapidly with the age at which the first of the two tests used for comparison was given. Given the fact that the correlation observed is due, wholly or in part, to the artefact indicated above, the value $\varrho = 0.1$ seems to us to be a reasonable limit for the actual correlation in the absence of this artefact (the mean age at selection for our 32 subjects is 0.3 year). By multiplying the three factors which contribute to the increase in test scores we obtain for the possible bias a value less than one IQ point. This slight bias is compensated by the biological biases indicated with respect to abandonment at birth.

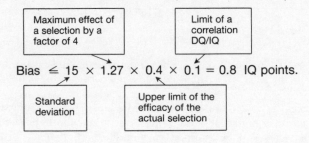

$$\text{Bias} \leq 15 \times 1.27 \times 0.4 \times 0.1 = 0.8 \text{ IQ points.}$$

4. How much *could* we boost access to universities?

Michel Schiff, Julia Schulz, and Josue Feingold

In 1980, one of us published an article entitled, 'School failure is not in the chromosomes' (Schiff 1980). In a letter to the editor, a reader of that article reacted in the following way (*Psychologie* 1981).

I wonder about all this noise about 'school failure among working-class children' . . . Why all the uproar today? Where does it lead? Should we destroy our culture and our civilization because they are not immediately accessible to people from the Third World and to people from the culture of poverty? Should we slow down our élite while, in the eastern countries brains are being selected as ferociously as athletes' muscles? Must France regress so that the Third World people can feel at home?

It is interesting to note that the article that produced such a strong reaction concerned the children of blue-collar workers and not ethnic minorities. Actually, the idea that hordes of 'have-nots' are threatening to destroy civilization has a long history and is still fairly widespread today. The belief that democracy will lead to the ruin of advanced education is part of that general idea. According to that idea, if the children of working-class parents were given wider access to university education, this would mean the end of higher learning. An analysis of educational statistics will lead us to the opposite conclusion. If access to advanced education were made socially less discriminatory, this could lead, instead, to a rising of the corresponding intellectual level.

According to the prevailing ideas, the massive increase in the number of students in secondary and tertiary education in the last 40 years has led to equal educational opportunity. Whatever social inequalities remain are then attributed to differences in innate ability between the children of the different social classes, as revealed by differences in the distributions of IQ scores.

As should be apparent to the reader of the previous chapters, we do not agree with this interpretation of inequality. In our opinion, as long as it is White middle-class people who decide who is intelligent and who is not, any outcome of that decision is *a priori* suspect. As long as teachers, filled both with goodwill and with ethnocentric naïvety, view human intelligence through their own school training, the academic failure of working-class children will be built into the school and social system. We are aware, however, of the fact that this is a minority opinion. Therefore, in order to communicate with readers unfamiliar with these ideas, we shall at first stay within the more conventional ideology.

The most explicit form of that ideology is Herrnstein's *IQ in the meritocracy* (1973). In a first step, we shall show that, even if one accepted the system of values implicit in the meritocratic model, this model would correspond to some mythical society rather than to the present one. In a second step, we shall change our perspective and use the meritocratic model as a mathematical tool for estimating the effects of social discrimination in education. Because of its underlying assumptions, this model under-estimates the effect of social discrimination, so that our estimates will be on the conservative side.

Although no author claims that IQ is the sole determinant of the heredity of social class, explanations proposed for that heredity have tended to focus on 'innate intelligence' (Gottesman 1968; Eysenck 1973; Herrnstein 1973). The assumption is made that the rank of an individual in society, and particularly within the educational system, is determined to a large extent by a capacity named IQ, and that this capacity has a sizeable heritable component. We present here a method of testing this meritocratic assumption. A one parameter version of the meritocratic model of social heredity will be confronted with data on unequal access to education in 12 OECD countries. Despite its conservative assumptions, this model will suffice to demonstrate the existence of a large waste of academic potential.

Concern over the waste of educational potential has been expressed before, in particular during the post-Sputnik era. Quantitative evaluations were also proposed (e.g. de Wolff and Härnqvist 1962; Sewell and Shah 1967; Halsey *et al.* 1980). The specific results of our analysis are the following:

(*a*) By using ordinal scales to measure educational achievement and social class, we were able to show that the amount of social discrimination and of social waste is essentially the same in the major Western countries.

(*b*) We evaluated in a quantitative manner the increase in the percentage of waste as the educational level increases.

(*c*) We showed that, at the highest levels of education, even the nature–nurture parameter concerning social class differences in IQ was essentially irrelevant.

Some of the results and conclusions presented here have been published elsewhere in French (Schiff 1980, 1982*b*; Schiff *et al.* 1981*a*). Short summaries also appeared in English (Schiff 1981, 1982*a*). The bulk of the data to be analysed here consists of statistics about the influence of parental social class on the probability of access to university. This type of influence will be compared to the influence of the social class of parents on IQ scores and with the alleged effect of the social class of parents on the 'innate intelligence' of their children.

This chapter is divided into five sections. In Section 1, we stress the basic limitation of a meritocratic model. Even if wealth were completely correlated with genes, economic inequality would still be a structural phenomenon. In Section 2, we show that even under the unrealistic assumption that IQ scores represent an innate ability, 'IQ in the meritocracy' does not account for social inequalities in access to the bachelor's degree observed in the United States. In Section 3, we analyse a series of French educational data. This analysis shows that (*a*) The percentage of waste due to social discrimination increases as one goes up the educational ladder, and (*b*) at the university level the question of genetic differences between groups becomes irrelevant to the issue of waste. In Section 4, we present a methodology for comparing educational waste in various countries. The percentages of waste turn out to be uniformly high in all countries. The numerical analysis presented in Appendix 1 shows that our estimate of that percentage is conservative. In the final section, we show that multiparametric models of social heredity either have no quantitative scientific basis (biological 'models'), or ignore the very existence of social class (psychological descriptions using individual variables).

1. Biological models can never 'explain' economic facts

In his book, *IQ in the meritocracy*, Herrnstein (1973) presented Jensen's evidence for a large value of the heritability of IQ. In a chapter entitled 'The specter of meritocracy', he then wrote:

Against this background, the main significance of intelligence testing lies in what it says about a society built around human inequalities. The message is so clear that it can be made in the form of a syllogism:
1. If differences in mental abilities are inherited, and
2. If success requires those abilities, and
3. If earning and prestige depends on success,
4. Then social standing (which reflects earnings and prestige) will be based to some extent on inherited differences among people.

Unless it is formulated in a quantitative manner, the syllogism reproduced above is at best a trivial tautological statement. The fact that a quantity A has *some* correlation with a quantity B and that quantity B has *some* correlation with a quantity C may mean that quantity A has *some* correlation with quantity C. But what is the value and the meaning of that correlation? Even if different from zero, it may well be insignificant, either numerically or in terms of causality.

Let us first examine the numerical aspects of the syllogism. To expose its inadequacy, one may formulate a similar one:

1. If Peter knows French, and
2. If John knows some of Peter's French vocabulary, and
3. If Mary knows some of the same words as John,
4. Then Mary knows some French. (Even if she only knows 'Parlez-vous français?')

Actually, Mackenzie has shown that even the weak statement that social standing is based to 'some extent on inherited differences among people' does not follow from the preceding statements of Herrnstein's 'syllogism'. Given three variables a, b, and c, and the correlation r_{ab} and r_{bc}, the correlation r_{ac} does not follow from the other two correlations; it only lies within the range:

$$r_{ab}\, r_{bc} \pm \sqrt{r_{ab}^2\, r_{bc}^2 - r_{ab}^2 - r_{bc}^2 + 1}$$

(Jensen, 1980, p. 302). Using conservative values for the correlations implicit in Herrnstein's statements, Mackenzie found that zero is included within the possible range of correlations between inheritance and social standing (-0.37 to $+0.93$, private communication).

The hierarchy of diplomas is also insufficient to 'explain' the unequal distribution of wealth and its reproduction from one generation to the next. In France, for instance, the proportion of university diplomas among junior executives is three times bigger than among industrialists (INSEE 1974); yet, their mean income is five times lower (CERC 1977).

Using a meritocratic model of economic success based on IQ, Bowles and Gintis (1973) have shown that available data are not consistent with this model. They state:

Our findings, based for the most part on widely available published data, document the fact that IQ is not an important cause of economic success; nor is the inheritance of IQ the reason why rich kids grow up to be rich and poor kids tend to stay poor. The intense debate on the heritability of IQ is thus largely irrelevant to an understanding of poverty, wealth and inequality of opportunity in the United States.

In our own analysis, we shall come to a similar conclusion in another area of social heredity, namely access to higher education.

We have just seen that available data contradict the meritocratic model of economic success. The main flaw of the meritocratic model when applied to economic data, however, concerns the fact that it takes for granted precisely what needs to be explained. In introducing his syllogism, Herrnstein talks about 'a society built around human inequalities'. But this is begging the question. Why should differences in mental and physical attributes be transformed into economic inequality? The very word Meritocracy, with its reference to the religious notion of merit, indicates a confusion between facts and values, between science and social choices. An illustration of that self-serving confusion is provided by a statement made by one of the early advocates of IQ tests (Goddard 1920, quoted by Kamin 1974):

These men in their ultra altruistic and humane attitude, their desire to be fair to the workman, maintain that the great inequalities in social life are wrong and unjust. For example, here is a man who says, 'I am wearing $12.00 shoes, there is a laborer who is wearing $3.00 shoes; why should I spend $12.00 while he can only afford $3.00? I live in a home that is artistically decorated, with carpets, high-priced furniture, expensive pictures and other luxuries; there is a laborer that lives in a hovel with no carpets, no pictures, and the coarsest kind of furniture. It is not right, it is unjust' . . .

Now the fact is, *that workman* may have a ten year intelligence while you have a twenty. To demand for him such a home as you enjoy is as absurd as it would be to insist that every laborer should receive a graduate fellowship. How can there be such a thing as social equality with this wide range of mental capacity? The different levels of intelligence have different interests and require different treatment to make them happy . . .

As for an equal distribution of the wealth of the world that is equally absurd. The man of intelligence has spent his money wisely, has saved until he has enough to provide for his needs in case of sickness, while the man of low intelligence, no matter how much money he would have earned, would have spent much of it foolishly and would never have anything ahead.

In that statement, Goddard is suggesting that if your mental age is 10 years, you are entitled only to $3 shoes; if it is 20 years, you may have $12 shoes. In other words, income should be proportional to the square of IQ! It actually turns out that, in the United States, IQ scores are only a minor determinant of income (Bowles and Nelson 1974). But even if the rank in the economic hierarchy happened to follow exactly the rank in the IQ hierarchy, this would still provide no answer to the main questions. Why is there an economic hierarchy in the first place? Why do people in the top decile of the distribution of income earn five times as much as people who are in the lower half of that distribution? Why are so many people living in poverty in the richest nations of the world?

Another confusion associated with the meritocratic model, and with individual models of social inequality in general, is the confusion between

Table 4.1 *Probability of access to higher education as a function of SES level and test level. Percentage of Wisconsin high school seniors who graduated from college (from Sewell and Shah, 1967)*

Socio-economic status levels	Males					Females				
	Test levels					Test levels				
	Low	Lower middle	Upper middle	High	Total	Low	Lower middle	Upper middle	High	Total
Low	0.3 (363)	7.9 (267)	10.9 (193)	20.1 (149)	7.5 (972)	0.2 (411)	1.3 (316)	2.5 (236)	13.8 (138)	2.7 (1101)
Lower middle	2.3 (300)	7.4 (324)	16.7 (275)	34.4 (253)	14.2 (1152)	0.9 (335)	5.3 (342)	8.9 (291)	20.8 (226)	7.9 (1194)
Upper middle	4.4 (273)	9.8 (277)	24.4 (316)	46.7 (289)	21.7 (1155)	2.4 (250)	9.3 (324)	12.1 (332)	24.9 (289)	12.4 (1195)
High	10.5 (134)	23.3 (232)	38.5 (299)	64.0 (442)	42.1 (1107)	7.9 (126)	15.3 (223)	36.4 (324)	51.1 (458)	35.0 (1131)
Total	3.2 (1070)	11.5 (1100)	23.9 (1083)	47.2 (1133)	21.8 (4386)	1.8 (1122)	7.1 (1205)	16.1 (1183)	33.5 (1111)	14.5 (4521)

correlation and causation. 'These people are poor because they have such and such characteristics.' In order to illustrate the fact that genetic correlations cannot explain social structure or poverty, let us imagine a geneticist from Mars who knew how to read both genetic codes and bank accounts. Let us suppose that he found a significant negative correlation between the size of the bank account and some gene B. He might return to Mars to present his discovery of the 'banking gene', unless some terrestrial friend pointed out to him that in South Africa, where the observations were made, the B gene is characteristic of Blacks. Actually, poverty is first and foremost a lack of money.

In the following sections, we shall analyse the indicator of social status which can be considered as most intimately connected to IQ, namely access to education. We shall see that even there, the social class of the parents plays a crucial role.

2. Social discrimination beyond IQ: a study of 9000 Wisconsin high school seniors

As an introduction to our analysis of social heredity in higher education, we present the results of a study published by Sewell and Shah (1967). The authors examined the academic careers of a cohort of Wisconsin high school seniors. A follow-up study was made of a random sample of 10 321 students, seven years after their high school graduation. The information obtained by the authors on 87 per cent of the students included the sex of the subjects, the socio-economic status of their parents, the 'measured intelligence' of the subjects and their educational attainment.

Levels of 'intelligence' were based on scores obtained with the Henmon-Nelson Test of Mental Ability (1942). SES levels were based on a combination of father's occupation, parental educational level and family economic status. The percentage of subjects who graduated from college is presented below, separately for males and females.

The lines of Table 4.1 correspond to the SES level. The columns correspond to the levels on the test (labelled 'intelligence levels' by the authors). Each number gives the percentage of college graduates, within the corresponding SES and test category; the number of subjects within the same category is indicated below in parentheses.

Within a given SES group (and for a given sex) the probability of college graduation shows large concomitant variations with IQ scores. Once again, we remind the reader that this type of variation concerns differences *within* groups, not *between* groups. This first type of variation tells us nothing about social heredity.

For a given sex, and for a given quartile of test scores, the probability of

Table 4.2   *The waste of academic potential between high school and col-*
lege. The figures were derived from the data of Sewell and Shah reproduced
in Table 4.1 (see text)

	Potential no.	Actual no.	'Wasted'
Male college graduates			
Low SES	270	73	197
Lower-middle SES	375	164	211
Upper-middle SES	400	251	149
High SES	466	466	0*
All males	1511	956	555
Female college graduates			
Low SES	296	30	266
Lower-middle SES	372	94	278
Upper-middle SES	414	148	266
High SES	483	396	87
All females	1565	670	895

* By definition.

college graduation shows large variations with the SES category. In order
to analyse this variation, here and throughout the chapter, we have chosen
to base our analysis on a quantity which fulfils both of the following
requirements:

—It has direct relevance to the question asked in the title of this chapter:
   How much *could* we boost access to universities?
—It is relatively insensitive to methodological uncertainties, and in particu-
   lar to uncertainties about genetic differences.

The quantity which we chose to define and analyse is the percentage of
waste, w, defined as

$$w = \frac{\text{no. of potential students} - \text{no. of actual students}}{\text{no. of potential students}} \quad (1)$$

Both the potential and the actual numbers of students can be computed
from the data reproduced in Table 4.1. For each test level, the potential
number of students was estimated by multiplying the number of high
school seniors by the probability of graduation observed for high SES
males. The comparison between the potential number of students estimated in this way and the actual number observed by Sewell and Shah is
presented in Table 4.2 for each sex and SES category.

With the data presented in Table 4.2, we can then use eqn (1) to obtain
the percentages of waste for the three lower quartiles. The percentages of
waste obtained in this manner are shown in Fig. 4.1, for the three lower

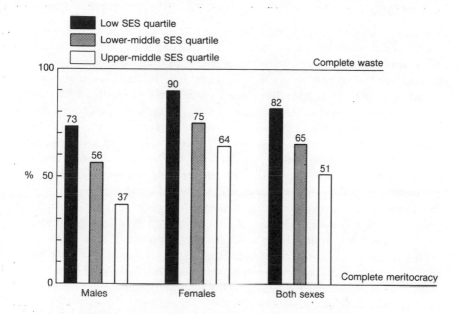

Fig. 4.1 The waste of academic potential between high school and college. The figures were derived from the data of Sewell and Shah reproduced in Table 4.1. The coefficient of waste, w, is one minus the ratio of the number of actual students to the number of potential students (see text).

quartiles. In spite of a series of assumptions, which as we shall show, all tend to reduce the percentage of waste, these percentages are substantial for all but the highest SES group.

One of the arguments used by Eysenck (1973) to scare people away from democracy in education is the claim that this would inevitably produce incompetent students. Let us assume that the acquisition of the bachelor's degree by children of low SES is not hindered by social discrimination. We could then use the probabilities given in the first line of Table 4.1 to estimate the number of bachelor's degrees expected for high SES males. From the figures reported in Table 4.1, one would then predict that, out of 466 high SES males receiving a bachelor's degree, 70 per cent did not 'deserve' it.

As we shall see, the discrepancy between the meritocratic prediction and present reality increases as one goes up the educational ladder. If one claimed that working-class children are currently getting fair treatment, the inevitable conclusion would have to be that graduate schools are producing vast numbers of incompetent doctors, lawyers, etc., who received their professional diplomas solely because of their social origin.

3. The waste of educational potential: the example of France

An analysis of the data of Sewell and Shah allowed us to introduce the parameter which we shall use throughout this chapter as an index of social discrimination in education. This parameter is the percentage of waste among the children whose parents are in the 'lower' half of the SES distribution.

Although IQ scores have been used extensively in several educational systems, there is an almost complete absence of data on the probability of access to various levels of education (and in particular of university education) as a function of IQ scores *and* of social origin. Once again, we note that, while models are built to explain or justify social segregation, the scientific data that would permit a quantitative check on the models are almost totally lacking. For such a check, we will therefore be forced to rely on whatever data are available. In order to do so, we shall use a simplified version of the meritocratic model. This version can be directly confronted with statistics on unequal access to university that are available.

This simplified version of the meritocratic model actually leads to an under-estimate of the waste of educational potential (see Appendix 1). We shall see that, in advanced education, the amount of social discrimination is so large that even this conservative model is sufficient to reveal that discrimination. Specifically, we shall see that (*a*) IQ in the meritocracy does not apply to the real world, (*b*) social discrimination leads to a considerable waste of educational potential, and (*c*) genetic parameters concerning IQ scores are almost irrelevant to the quantitative estimate of that waste.

In this section, we first define a simplified model of 'IQ in the meritocracy' and then apply it to a series of French educational data.

A simplified model of IQ in the meritocracy

The way in which the probability of access to university varies with IQ scores for a given social group is not known. In order to obtain a first approximation of that probability, we shall use a method proposed by de Wolff and Härnqvist (1962). This method is based on the following three assumptions:

1. IQ scores give an estimate of the genetic potential for learning.
2. To each academic level, there corresponds a minimum IQ score needed to reach that level (threshold IQ).
3. All children of the highest SES who score above that threshold reach the corresponding academic level.

Before using this model, we briefly discuss the above assumptions.
Assumption number one means that we ignore the social bias inherent in

IQ tests and in the test situation; we also neglect environmental effects associated with social class. In practice these effects are confounded. For the moment, let us only note that the neglect of these social effects leads one to under-estimate the waste of academic potential.

The second assumption means that an unknown probability distribution is replaced by a step function. The probability is taken to be zero for IQ scores below the threshold and one for scores above that threshold. The data of Sewell and Shah allow us to estimate the effect of that approximation. The analysis presented in Appendix 1 shows that this approximation leads to a substantial under-estimate of academic potential: in the low- and lower-middle SES group, the estimated number of potential diplomas is 687 when the threshold model is used, while the number estimated from the observed probability distribution is 1182; (the actual number of diplomas in these two groups was 361).

While the effect of the first two assumptions can be examined in a quantitative manner by an analysis of published quantitative data, the last assumption is of a different nature. The meaning of that assumption is that, at least for children of high SES, everything is for the best in the best of all possible school systems. Such an assumption can only be challenged by a radical questioning of current educational and social values. Here, let us only suggest that, even for males of the highest SES, current educational systems are probably less than 100 per cent efficient. To the extent that the real efficiency is lower, this is still another source of bias in the direction of underestimating academic potential.

The percentage of waste of educational potential increases as one goes up the educational ladder

Because of a high degree of centralization, and for other cultural reasons, French statistical data on the sociology of education are of exceptional quality. They were also the ones most readily available to us. For these reasons, we start by an analysis of French educational data, from the end of primary school to advanced graduate studies.

The elimination of students of low SES is a cumulative process. The result of this gradual elimination is presented in Table 4.3.

In column one access rates are presented for the children of blue-collar workers; the corresponding rates for children of upper-middle-class parents and for the general population are given in columns two and three (for details, see Appendix 2). Between the sixth grade and advanced graduate studies, the ratio of the probabilities given in column two over that given in column one goes from 1.4 to 34. As we shall see, even the use of socially biased IQ tests does not suffice to account for such inequalities. Although IQ tests do discriminate highly between children of contrasted

Table 4.3   *Unequal access to education in France*

Level of education	Children of blue-collar workers (%)	Children of upper-middle-class parents[a] (%)	All social groups (%)
Secondary school			
Access to 'normal' 6th grade	74	98	82
Access to academic 8th grade	38	95	57
Access to selective 10th grade	5	55	15
University			
Access to university	4.6	58	14
Graduate studies	2.4	52	10
Advanced graduate studies	1.2	41	7

[a] An average of eight per cent of active males in the period considered. For methodological details, see Schiff (1982b) and Appendix 2.

Table 4.4   *Percentage of waste at various levels of education. Children of French blue-collar workers. Comparing probabilities of reaching various levels of education with probabilities estimated from a purely genetic meritocratic model*

Level of education	Rates (%) Observed	Computed	Conservative estimate of percentage of waste
Secondary school			
Access to 'normal' 6th grade	74	85	13
Access to academic 8th grade	38	72	47
Access to selective 10th grade	5	17.6	72
University			
Access to university	4.6	18.7	75
Graduate studies	2.4	14.5	83
Advanced graduate studies	1.2	9.0	87

groups, there remains a large overlap in the distributions of IQ scores, so that these distributions fail to explain social inequalities such as those presented in Table 4.3.

By using the meritocratic model presented above, we can estimate in a quantitative manner the extent to which the academic system is even more unfair to low SES children than IQ tests are. If academic systems had no social discrimination beyond that inherent in IQ tests, the rank within the academic system would be the same as the rank within IQ scales. As was shown in Chapter 2, this is approximately true within primary grades. In primary school, social discrimination and social segregation remain invisible, or at least appear to be unrelated to the school system as such.

In order to compare the facts reported in Table 4.3 with what one would expect if IQ in the meritocracy held true, we have to estimate, at each educational level, what proportion of children of the 'low' SES group have IQ scores above the threshold needed for that educational level. The threshold IQ is computed by equating the proportion of 'high' SES students who succeed in reaching the educational level to the proportion whose score is above the threshold. The calculations therefore proceed according to the following steps.

1. Estimate the mean and σ of IQ scores for children of the high SES group.
2. Compute the threshold IQ, by using the access rate observed for children of the high SES group.
3. Estimate the mean and σ of IQ scores for children of the low SES group.
4. Compute the proportion of children of the low SES group with IQ above the threshold.

The results of the above calculations are presented in Table 4.4. The details of these calculations are presented in Appendix 2.

Out of 1000 children of blue-collar workers, the distribution of IQ scores predicts that 850 should be in the 'normal' sixth grade, instead of the actual 740. The corresponding percentage of waste is $(850-740)/850 = 13$ per cent. In the eighth grade, the expected number of students in the academic track is 720; actually, almost half of these potential students have been placed in a vocational track or have dropped out of school. At the university level, the waste of academic potential reaches 80 per cent.

At the university level, the question of genetic differences between groups becomes irrelevant to the issue of waste

The figures presented in Table 4.4 do not take into account social effects. We therefore proceed to the next step, which is to incorporate in the model a parameter describing the influence of the social class of rearing on mean IQ scores. In order to confront the meritocratic model with social facts, however, one first needs to define 'innate intelligence'. To give an operational meaning to the word 'intelligence', we shall temporarily accept the confusion with IQ. To give an operational meaning to the word 'innate', we must define under what social conditions the children would have to be reared for their IQ scores to be considered as valid measure of their 'true

IQ'. In order to compare the 'true IQ' of two groups of children, we have to assume that, at least in a 'Gedanken Experiment', both groups have been reared under equivalent and optimal conditions.

In order to know the 'true IQ' of a group of children of working-class parents, one would have to answer the question posed by Richardson in 1913. To our knowledge, the most direct answer to that question is provided by the adoption study presented in Chapter 3. Several other observations lead one to predict that, in the absence of social discrimination and in the absence of environmental differences, the IQ gap between the children of blue-collar workers and children of upper-middle-class parents would be reduced by a considerable amount or would disappear. We refer here to authors who have reported IQ scores above the population mean for children whose social origin was below average (Skodak and Skeels 1949; Scarr and Weinberg 1976). We also note that Wheeler (1942) observed that, in an underdeveloped region of the United States, significant economic improvements were followed by a 10-point increase in the mean IQ scores of schoolchildren.

Rather than arguing about the relative importance of nature and nurture in mean IQ differences between contrasted groups of children, we shall show that this issue is largely irrelevant to our analysis of social heredity. We shall represent the relative importance of social effects (test bias *and* social environment) by a parameter s which will be left free to vary between 0 (no social effect) and 1 (maximum social effect).*

Let us call IQ_{low} and IQ_{high} the observed mean IQ of the children of the low SES group and of the high SES group respectively. In the absence of any social effect, when the parameter s is zero, the 'true' or 'adjusted' mean IQ of the low SES group would be the same as the observed one:

$$IQ_a = IQ_{low} \quad (\text{when } s = 0)$$

In the absence of any genetic effect, on the other hand, the adjusted IQ would be the same for the two groups:

$$IQ_a = IQ_{high} = IQ_{low} + (IQ_{high} - IQ_{low}) \quad (\text{when } s = 1)$$

In the intermediate situation, the adjustment is proportional to the parameter s:

$$IQ_a = IQ_{low} + s\,(IQ_{high} - IQ_{low}) \quad (2)$$

Equation (2) means that the distribution of 'true IQ' among the children of blue collar workers is the same as that usually observed, except for an upward shift of $s\,(IQ_{high} - IQ_{low})$. We can then use the simplified merito-

---

* The parameter s is actually one element of a matrix; the parameter used here corresponds to the matrix element s_{nl} (see Appendix 6).

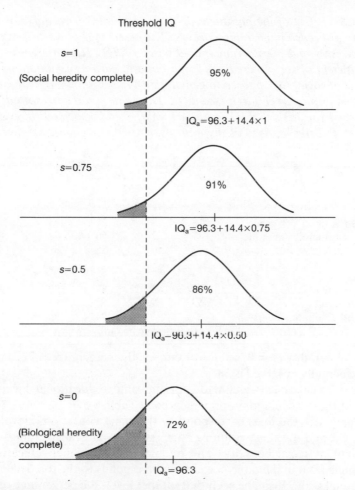

Fig. 4.2 Effect of the parameter s (influence of social class) on the number of potential students for academic 8th grade.

The above diagram concerns French children of blue-collar workers. The white area under the curve gives the proportion of students with a true IQ above the threshold, i.e. the proportion of students expected to enter academic tracks. The proportion actually entering academic tracks in the eighth grade is 38 per cent.

cratic model exactly as before, except for this shift in the distribution. The effect of such a shift on the estimate of the number of potential students is illustrated in Fig. 4.2 in the particular case of access to academic tracks at the eighth grade level in France. When social heredity is complete for IQ scores ($s = 1$, see upper curve of Fig. 4.2), the potential percentage of students is the same as in the high SES group, i.e. 95. In the intermediate case ($s = 0.50$), that percentage is 86. Under the assumption of complete

Table 4.5   *Effect of the parameter* s *on the estimated percentage of waste. Children of French blue-collar workers. The percentage of waste is estimated with a conservative meritocratic model based on IQ. The different values of the coefficient of social heredity* s *correspond to various assumptions about the effect of social (as opposed to genetic) differences on the IQ gap between contrasted groups of children (see text). The value* s = 0 *corresponds to the unrealistic hypothesis that IQ scores are unaffected by social differences; the value* s = 1 *corresponds to the hypothesis of an absence of* mean *genetic differences*

Level of education	Percentage of waste				
	s = 0	s = 0.25	s = 0.5	s = 0.75	s = 1
Secondary school					
Access to 'normal' 6th grade	13	18	21	23	24
Access to academic 8th grade	47	52	56	58	60
Access to selective 10th grade	72	80	85	89	91
University					
Access to university	75	83	87	90	92
Graduate studies	83	89	92	94	95
Advanced graduate studies	87	92	94	96	97

biological heredity ($s = 0$, see lower curve), the percentage is 72. The percentage actually observed is 38.

Similar calculations were made for the other educational levels. The results of these calculations are presented in Table 4.5.

In Table 4.5, the lines correspond to the same educational levels as in Tables 4.3 and 4.4. The columns correspond to increasing values of the coefficient of social heredity. The middle level of higher education has been singled out in the table because it corresponds to the top decile of the educational scale. It can be seen that, at that level, the percentage of waste is rather insensitive to the value of the coefficient of social heredity s. When access to the top decile of educational qualifications is being examined, even the question of heritable genetic differences *between* groups becomes somewhat academic.

THE RESULTS OF TABLE 4.5 CONCERN CHILDREN OF BLUE-COLLAR WORKERS. WE HAVE FOCUSED THE ATTENTION ON AN EDUCATIONAL LEVEL NOW REACHED BY ONLY 10 PER CENT OF THE GENERAL POPULATION. UNDER THESE CIRCUMSTANCES, ASKING IF SOCIAL EFFECTS ACCOUNT FOR 100 PER CENT OR FOR 50 PER CENT OF THE USUAL IQ GAP (OR EVEN FOR 0 PER CENT) IS EQUIVALENT TO ASKING IF, AMONG CAPABLE STUDENTS, THE PERCENTAGE PREVENTED BY SOCIAL EFFECTS FROM REACHING THAT LEVEL IS 95 PER CENT OR 92 PER CENT (OR 'ONLY' 83 PER CENT).

4. Comparing data from 12 OECD countries

The methodology of international comparisons

International comparisons of social inequalities pose methodological problems which are rarely faced.

The first type of problem concerns the definition of the groups that are being compared. In some statistics, the most privileged group is a very broad one, including 20 or even 30 per cent of the active male population; in others, it is extremely narrow and concerns one or two per cent of that population. Thus, in the raw data published by OECD (1971), the high SES group corresponds to 1.7 per cent of the active males in Italy, while it corresponds to 23 per cent of the active males in the United States. Some variations are also observed in the definition of the low SES group. In the case of England, for instance, the low SES group corresponds to 71 per cent of all active males; this very broad definition of the low SES group blurs the contrast between high and low SES groups, especially since the high SES group is also defined in a broad manner (21.5 per cent of active males). The amount of inequality between contrasted groups obviously depends on the way in which these groups have been defined.

The situation is further complicated by the fact that the proportion of highly skilled professions has increased significantly over the last generation. A group of senior executives, for example, which used to include only six per cent of active males may now include 10 per cent of these males.

The solution to these problems consists in defining high and low SES groups by fixed proportions of the active population. We have chosen to define the high SES group by the top decile of a socio-professional scale; the low SES group has been defined by the lower half of that scale. In current statistics, the high SES group corresponds roughly to professions requiring at least a first university degree or some form of graduate education. The low SES group corresponds roughly to urban and rural manual workers.

Because each country has a different way of categorizing social groups, even this ordinal scale does not allow perfect comparisons. Any imperfection in the manner in which social groups have been ranked will decrease the apparent correlation between educational participation and parental status, thus blurring existing contrasts. In the field of education, this remark is especially relevant to US official statistics where students are often grouped by income brackets of their parents rather than by professional categories.

The second type of problem is even more serious, although it stems from the same source, namely geographical and chronological variability. Some way must be found to define an educational level in a manner that is invariant with space and time. An analogy with economic inequalities may serve to illustrate both the nature of the problem and its solution. The question of whether a given social group lives better now than a generation ago, or is better off in this country than in that one is fraught with methodological and conceptual difficulties. On the other hand, the question of relative economic standing within one's own country is relatively straightforward. As was already mentioned, people in the high income group (the top decile) earn five times more than people in the low income group (the bottom half), both in the United States and in France.

Diplomas are subject to the same type of inflation as money. In addition, the only available metric scale, i.e. the mean number of years of education, is grossly inadequate. When assessing inequalities, educational 'wealth' must be defined in relative terms, just like economic wealth. In the case of a diploma, we shall define its relative value, at a given time and in a given country, by its rarity in the general population, i.e. by the inverse of the access rate. In 1970, for example, six per cent of an age cohort received master's degrees in the United States. At that time and in that country, this diploma corresponded to a degree of selectivity of $1/0.06 = 17$. In other words, educational levels will be defined with an ordinal scale analogous to current IQ scales. The comparison of international data on the social stratification of children's IQ scores presented in Appendix 3 will serve as a model for the comparison of other data on social heredity. For the purpose of these comparisons, educational levels will be graded with a scale based on percentages of the general population reaching those levels.

The numerical methods used for the analysis of educational data along the lines just outlined are described in Appendix 4. These numerical methods are essentially based on the use of ordinal scales analogous to IQ scales and on the mathematical continuity of the data. These data are often subject to large uncertainties, as are the standard rates derived from them. Fortunately, the quantity which ultimately interests us, namely the percentage of waste, is fairly insensitive to these methodological uncertainties.

The results of international comparisons

For an analysis of IQ scores, we considered the five publications known to us, where an effort had been made to obtain samples of schoolchildren representative of each social class. The results of the analysis presented in Appendix 3 are summarized below in Table 4.6.

For the high SES group, the mean IQ value varies between 107 and 111, with an unweighted average of 109; for the low SES group, the estimated means are consistently close to the unweighted average of 96. The estimated gap between the standardized groups varies between 10 and 15 IQ

Table 4.6 *Social stratification of IQ scores. Mean IQ scores of contrasted groups of children. The high SES group corresponds to the upper decile of the SES scale, the low SES group to the lower five deciles. For details, see Appendix 3*

		Mean IQ scores		
Source	Country	High SES group	Low SES group	Difference (points)
Terman and Merrill (1937)	USA	108	97	11
Seashore *et al.* (1950)	USA	109	95	14
INED (1950)	France	107	97	10
Scottish Council (1953)	Scotland	111	96	15
INED–INOP (1973)	France	111	96	15
Unweighted mean		109	96	13

points, with an unweighted average of 13 points. Because of the various methodological uncertainties, no significance should be attached to the slight discrepancies between the various estimates of that gap (see Appendix 3).

For educational data, meaningful comparisons between a large number of countries can be obtained from OECD publications. Data concerning group disparities in educational participation in 12 countries are presented in Table 4.7.

The statistics presented in Table 4.7 come from a single compilation (OECD 1971). Other sources were consulted only for the purpose of obtaining supplementary information needed for our analysis. The raw data used are therefore fairly homogeneous, both in terms of dates and of presentation. The level of higher education considered is indicated in the third column of the table; the corresponding access rate in the general population is given in the following column. The high SES groups are defined in column five, by the percentage of fathers of this group in the male active population. In the case of Belgium, the high SES group happens to coincide exactly with the top decile. For other countires, two values were used whenever possible, to permit interpolation. In the case of Denmark, for instance, data are given for two groups; one group includes nine per cent of all fathers, the other includes the top 25 per cent. The less selective group is indicated in parentheses. The access rates for the children of the high SES group are given in column six. Thus, in the example of Denmark, children of the restricted high SES group had an 18 per cent chance of being at the university; the corresponding chance for the less restrictive group was 12 per cent. Similar data are given for the low SES group in

Table 4.7 *Group disparities in educational participation in 12 OECD countries**

Country (1)	Year (2)	Type of education (3)	Rate^a (4)	High group		Low group		Adjusted values	
				%^b (5)	Rates(s)^c (6)	(%)^d (7)	Rate(s)^e (8)	10% group (9)	50% group (10)
Austria	1965	Higher education	5.9	7.4(19)	26(20)	64	.51	24	.17
Belgium	1966	Entering university	9.6	10	31	55	4.0	31	3.6
Denmark	1964	University	4.8	9(25)	18(12)	43(60)	1.1(2.3)	17	1.5
France	1964	Higher education	11	5.4(23)	59(27)	50	1.9	46	1.9
Germany	1964	Higher education	4.5	9.2(28)	16(10)	55	.44	16	.34
Italy	1964	Entering h. educ.	12	15	44	60	3.2	49	2.2
The Netherlands	1964	University	3.2	6.7(19)	20(11)	66	.46	17	.17
Norway	1964	Entering university	7.9	10	26	55	3.4	26	3.1
Sweden	1960	Entering university	10	4.5(24)	69(25)	53	2.7	50	2.4
Switzerland	1959	University	3.0	9.7(26)	16(9.1)	59	.71	16	.51
UK	1960	Entering university	4.2	21	12	71	1.6	16	.73
USA	1958	Bachelor's degree	17	23	39	57	7.9	48	6.8

* Main source of raw data OECD (1971), see also text and Appendix 4.
a Percentage of general population having access to the level of education considered.
b Percentage(s) of fathers of high group(s) in active male population.
c Percentage(s) of children of high group(s) having access to the level of education considered.
d Percentage(s) of fathers of the low group(s) in active male population.
e Percentage(s) of children of low group(s) having access to the level of education considered.

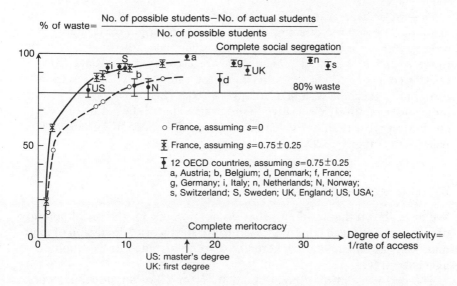

$$\% \text{ of waste} = \frac{\text{No. of possible students} - \text{No. of actual students}}{\text{No. of possible students}}$$

Fig. 4.3 Percentage of waste of academic potential in 12 OECD countries (for children born in the lower half of the population).

columns seven and eight. The rates estimated for the standard high and low SES groups are given in columns nine and ten. The manner in which these estimates were obtained is described in Appendix 4.

From then on, the analysis is relatively straightforward. The same four steps are used as in the preceding section. The IQ distribution in the standard high and low SES groups was computed in Appendix 3 by pooling international data on the influence of parental class on the IQ scores of children. The mean IQ scores of the high and low SES groups turn out to be 109 and 96 respectively.

The position of the threshold IQ with respect to the mean IQ of the high SES group was obtained from a table of the normal distribution, using the rates given in column nine. The rates expected in the low SES group are the percentages of IQ above the threshold, in that group. The distribution of 'true IQ' was derived from that of IQ scores by using eqn (2) in Section 3.

For each value assumed for the parameter s, the percentage of waste was obtained by a comparison between the rates expected for the low SES group and the rate given in column ten; this comparison was made by using eqn (1) in Section 2. The results of this final computation are presented in graphical form in Fig. 4.3.

In Fig. 4.3 the abscissa is the degree of selectivity defined above; the ordinate is the percentage of waste. Three types of results are presented in Fig. 4.3.

The circles represent the French data analysed in Section 3, under the assumption $s = 0$ (no effect of the social class of origin on IQ gaps). The crosses with error bars correspond to the same data, for values of s in the range of 0.5 to 1. These French data are compared with data from 12 OECD countries, using the same range of values for s (full circles with error bars). It can be seen that, for all countries, the percentage of waste is large and is relatively insensitive to the exact value of the parameter s. The conclusion presented for French data at the end of Section 3 seems to hold true for the other OECD countries.

5. Who is afraid of social class?

We have shown that children's IQ's do not account for the social heredity of access to advanced education. Before we start a brief discussion of alternate ways of explaining this heredity, two points need to be emphasized again about IQ.

The first is a statistical point about IQ scores. For an individual whose parents belong to social class s, an IQ score can be expressed as:

$$IQ = 100 + \Delta IQ$$
$$\Delta IQ = \Delta IQ_s + \Delta IQ_i$$

where ΔIQ is the deviation of the individual's IQ score from the population mean (usually 100), ΔIQ_s is the deviation of the group mean from that same population mean, and ΔIQ_i is the deviation of the individual score from the group mean. Let us consider, for instance, two children of upper-middle-class parents and let us assume that the group mean for the children of that class is 110. The social class component ΔIQ_s is 10. If we assume that the individual scores are 105 and 115, the individual deviations ΔIQ_i will be -5 and $+5$ respectively. The component ΔIQ_s is the systematic component, which is related to social heredity, while the individual component ΔIQ_i appears as a random variation with respect to social class.

The second point concerns the contribution of genetics to the meritocratic model. From an ideological point of view, the reference to genetics provides the foundation of the model. From the scientific point of view, however, this reference weakens the model. As we have seen in Sections 3 and 4, when the distinction between genotype and phenotype is introduced, all estimates of the percentage of waste increase. We shall now briefly indicate why the reference to variables other than IQ also weakens the model.

Spearman, the inventor of the famous 'g' factor, was aware of the fact that the reduction of human abilities to one dimension is necessary for a

Fig. 4.4 Eugenic ideals from different points of view. (Cartoons from the *Daily Mirror* quoted by Spearman 1914).

socio-biological view of inequality.* This necessity was illustrated by Spearman (1914) in the cartoon reproduced above in Fig. 4.4.

Quotations from two of the most outspoken proponents of a genetic view of social stratification will serve to introduce our discussion of multiparametric models of social heredity. In the first quotation, Burt (1958) quotes the High Master of a private school:

The parents are themselves imbued with four traditional ideals which they hand on to their posterity: self-discipline, a community spirit, the Christian religion, and a readiness to accept social responsibility even at the sacrifice of material enjoyments – a genuine *noblesse oblige*.

Commenting on this quotation, Burt when writes:

Underlying all these differences in outlook I myself am tempted to suspect an innate and transmissible difference in temperamental stability and character, or in the neurophysiological basis on which such temperamental and moral differences tend to be built up. Tradition may explain much; it can hardly account for all. However, it would be idle to pursue such speculations here in the absence of more adequate data.

---

* Jacquard (1984) has emphasized that differences can be defined in a multidimensional space, while inequalities can only be defined in a one-dimensional space.

When it comes to socio-biology, Burt can certainly claim priority over many authors: in the above, we have the outline of a four parameter model of social heredity. Burt even affords himself the luxury of stating that, for the moment, these are idle speculations.

The second quotation is by Gottesman (1968) who quotes the author of a famous experiment on rats:

It is possible to approach this topic from a slightly different point of view, one closer to home. In a society which provides for social mobility, the varieties of genotypes migrate to different strata or social ecological niches by social selection. In this schema the strata are ordered by the single major variable – money–reward. Tryon (1957), a pioneer in American behavior genetics research, outlined the workings of the model: 'Individuals receiving the same money–reward but for different kinds of ability tend to gravitate to the same social area. The hierarchy of social strata is determined by the hierarchy of money–reward characteristic of all occupations. The abilities requisite for performance in the different occupations depend upon different sensory–motor component, which are in turn determined by different independent polygenic combinations. Most matings occur within strata so that a correlation among abilities is developed not only because there is one general factor underlying achievement in all fields, but because of the selective influence of the common denominator, money–reward, which collects comparable levels of various abilities within the same social strata'. It would appear that social classes too can be profitably* construed as Mendelian populations that have diverged genetically and are continuing to do so.

If a multiparametric model of social heredity based on 'different independent polygenic combinations' is to be taken seriously, some quantitative analysis will have to be done, based on 'adequate data', both for the genetic parameters and for the social facts. Even if social structure at a given time were built on genetic meritocracy, this in itself would not suffice to produce the kind of social heredity presently observed. It is rarely realized that two supplementary ingredients are needed for a meritocratic model of social heredity. The variables making up the 'merit' must not only be innate, they must also be transmissible, *and* the amount of social mobility must be large. In other words, the between-group heritability coefficients of the variables making up 'merit' must all be large.

It seems to us that the burden of proof rests on the inventors of multiparametric models claiming to provide a biological explanation of social heredity. Specifically, until someone uses 'adequate data' to show that the combined effect of additive genes and social mobility is sufficient to compensate for the homogenizing effect of independent assortment of genes, genetic models based on 'money-reward which collects comparable levels

---

* We wonder who profits from this model.

of various abilities within the same social strata' will remain as much of an ideological fantasy as Burt's model, based on the genes for 'self-discipline, a community spirit, the Christian religion and a readiness to accept social responsibility'.

Let us now consider briefly the multiparametric models of social heredity of a non-biological flavour. There is no lack of theories to explain in psychological terms the exclusion of working-class children from academic tracks and from advanced education. Burt's variables (self-discipline, etc.) can be used without assuming a genetic basis to the unequal distribution of these variables among the children of the various social classes. To a large extent, these psychological theories are based on the confusion between correlation and causation or contribute to this confusion. Qualities like motivation are often referred to. For instance, Burt (1958) wrote about the children of the working-classes that 'by the time they are sixteen the attractions of high wages and of cheap entertainment during leisure hours prove stronger than their desire for further knowledge and skill . . . '. This theory of deferred gratification has been used by many authors. It is true that various attitudes are transmitted in part from one generation to the next, so that they appear to contribute to the social heredity, for instance, of academic status. But this is simply a description, not an explanation.

By choosing to describe people in terms of *individual* variables, it is indeed possible to eliminate social class from the picture almost entirely. There is an increasing tendency among some psychologists to use multiple correlations to partial out social class from their description of social heredity. An illustration of this tendency is provided by a quotation concerning education by Miller (1970):

This study has suggested that less attention may well be given in the future to social class per se with regard to school performance. It is a crude variable of limited direct importance in the problem of school achievement.

As we have seen in this chapter, even when IQ is partialled out, the remaining importance of social class is far from 'limited'. How can authors reach the conclusion that social class is of 'limited' importance? The secret lies in the word 'direct'. By using multiple correlations, it is indeed possible to partial out social class almost completely. To show the inadequacy of such an approach, let us examine a fictitious example. Suppose we were to study the correlation between capital and the ownership of a private home. We could correlate this ownership with various indices like ownership of a car, ethnicity, number of bank accounts, etc. By the use of partial correlation, one could then show that the possession of capital *per se* is a 'crude variable of limited direct importance' for the ownership of a private home.

A spectacular illustration of the elimination of social class by the multiplication of individual variables was provided by the Coleman report. This report, published in the United States in 1966, describes the largest educational study ever made. The sample studied was constituted by a rep resentative group of more than 600 000 schoolchildren and students. In Appendix 5, we have reproduced the list of variables used by the authors, as it was published in the second volume of their report. Among the 93 independent variables chosen to describe the subjects of the study, the profession of the parents is conspicuously absent. This absence becomes even more surprising when we note that the profession of the parents was included in the study's questionnaire (e.g. pp. 590, 603, 629).

The correlations between the 10 dependent variables and the 93 independent variables chosen by the authors were published in a volume containing over 500 pages of numbers. From this list of some 50 000 numbers, we can learn, for instance, that, for twelfth graders of Mexican origin, the score obtained on a non-verbal test has a correlation 0.1671 with the numbers of books in the home. For White children who are in first grade in the southern United States, their mathematical performance has a correlation of 0.0979 with the proportion of classmates whose parents own an encyclopaedia. Of this avalanche of numbers, none concerns the social class of the parents, nor the social segregation of schoolchildren between tracks or between schools. Social class is apparently a European myth!

In conclusion, a meritocratic model of social heredity based on IQ had at least the merit of being related to some quantitative data. The distribution of IQ scores is known as a function of the social class of origin, and some attempt has been made towards a genetic analysis of the variations of IQ scores. To extend the meritocratic model to other variables besides IQ, one would first need to obtain the corresponding information for these variables. In addition, one would have to solve the problem posed by one of the fundamental mechanisms of biology, namely the fact that independent genes are reshuffled at each generation by the Mendelian lottery. As to psychological explanations of social heredity based on the familial transmission of individual characteristics, they can be valid only on the individual level. Social heredity, however, is a structural phenomenon, and the replacement of social class by individual variables correlated with it is in effect an attempt to eliminate social class from the description of social reality.

Appendix 1. Methodological discussion of the threshold model

In the threshold model, a step function is used to approximate the probability of access to a given academic status, as a function of IQ. Since existing data do not provide information on this probability distribution, let us examine the effect of using a step function instead of the real distribution. The effect of this approxima-tion must be examined at an educational level where discrimination is high, i.e. at the university level. The data of Sewell and Shah discussed in Section 2 allow such an examination.

We shall compare the potential number of students estimated in two different ways. In the first type of estimate, the probability function is that actually observed for high SES students. This first method of estimation was outlined in Section 2. The second method uses a step function, for the access probability as a function of IQ: the calculation of the potential number of students then proceeds as in Section 3. Since we want to examine the specific bias introduced by a step function, we shall neglect the extra amount of waste introduced by sexual discrimination.

Estimate no. 1

For male high school students, the probability distribution used is that observed for high SES males. For female students, the corresponding probability is that observed for high SES females. The expected numbers of college graduates are 507 for low SES students (males and females) and 675 for students of lower-middle SES.

Estimate no. 2

The calculations proceed in four steps. First we find the mean IQ of the high SES group. For this purpose, we can use the fraction of scores in the upper half of the distribution. This fraction is 1523/2238 − 68 per cent. The mean score of the group is therefore situated at 0.47σ above the mean of the whole cohort. Defining this lat-ter mean to be 100 and assuming a σ of 14 within each SES quartile, we find for the high SES quartile a mean of 106.6. We then compute the threshold. When the two sexes are considered together, the probability of college graduation is 38.5 per cent, corresponding to a threshold $0.29\ \sigma$ above the mean of the high SES group. Hence the value of the threshold IQ: $106.6 + 0.29 \times 14 = 110.7$.

For the third step, we turn to the two lower quartiles. For the low SES group, the proportion of scores in the upper half of the distribution is 34.5 per cent (grouping males and females). This means that the conventional score of 100 is at $0.40\ \sigma$ above the mean of the distribution. Hence, the mean score for the students of the lower SES quartile: $100 - 0.40 \times 14 = 94.4$. In a similar manner, the mean IQ of the lower-middle group is found to be 98.1.

In the last step, we compute the proportion of scores above the threshold, in each of the two lower quartiles. For the low SES group, the mean score is situated 16.3 IQ points ($1.16\ \sigma$) below the threshold; the proportion of scores above the threshold is 12.3 per cent. For the lower-middle group, the proportion of scores above the threshold is 18.4 per cent.

For each of the two groups, we can now compare the number of potential students derived from the threshold model with the number derived from the actual probability distribution. This comparison is presented in Table 4.8.

The numbers presented in Table 4.8 show that the use of a step function to approximate the probability of access as a function of IQ scores leads to a

Table 4.8 *Bias introduced by the use of a step function in the meritocratic model. The number of college graduates expected from the threshold model is compared to the number expected by using u more realistic probability dis tribution*

	Number of college graduates		
	Expected from threshold model	Expected from real probability distribution	Actually observed
Low SES	255	507	103
Lower-middle SES	432	675	258
Total: lower half SES	687	1182	361

Table 4.9 *Variation with time of the proportion of children belonging to the high SES group and corresponding variation of mean IQ scores*

Children who were in the 6th grade in the year	High SES children represented (% of age group)	Mean IQ score of high SES children[a]	On the average, these children were
1966	6.3	112.3	Advanced graduate students in 1978
1968	6.5	112.2	Graduate students in 1978
1971	7.3	111.8	Entering university in 1978
1972	7.6	111.7	In 10th grade in 1976
1974	8.1	111.5	In 8th grade in 1976

[a] In Chapter 3, IQ scores were expressed in the original scale of the INED study (population mean = 99.2). For the sake of international comparisons, scores in Chapter 4 have been adjusted to a scale centred around 100 (see Appendix 3).

substantial underestimate in the number of potential students of working-class origin. For students whose parents belong to the lower half of the SES scale, the number of college graduates expected from the threshold model is 687; when the real probability distribution is used, the expected number is almost twice as large (1182).

Appendix 2. Unequal access to education: a report on some French data (see Section 3).

An analysis of French educational and demographic data has been published elsewhere (Schiff 1982*b*). The data presented here come from that source.

The low SES group is composed of children of blue-collar workers. Using data from three successive censuses (1962, 1968, 1975), we estimated that these children represent 45 per cent of their age group. The high SES group is composed of children of senior executives and professionals. Between 1966 and 1974, the proportion of men who were in that professional category increased by 30 per cent (from 7.2 to

Table 4.10 *Number of students in the general population and in the high and low SES groups, at various levels of education*

	Number of students in		
Education level	General population	High SES group	Low SES group
6th grade remedial and slow learner's track, 1974[a]	154 000	1230	98 500
8th grade academic track, 1976[b]	508 600	68 000	151 300
8th grade non academic track, 1976[b]	202 400	3650	97 100
10th grade math. majors, 1976[d]	130 700	37 000	19 000
Entering university, 1978[d]	112 700	35 100	17 100
Graduate students, 1978[e]	312 600	111 700	34 900
Advanced graduate students, 1978[f]	117 500	43 600	9000

[a] Raw data from Ministère de l'Education (1976).
[b] Raw data from Ministère de l'Education (1978 and 1979a).
[c] Mathematics majors (*Seconde C*); raw data from same source as b.
[d] *Bacheliers* entering universities in 1976; *grandes écoles* and technological institutes not included; raw data from Ministère de l'Education (1979b).
[e] *Deuxième cycle*; raw data from the same source as d.
[f] *Troisième cycle*; raw data from the same source as d.

Table 4.11 *Demographic data concerning the general population, the high and the low SES groups*

Social group, date and age level	All groups	High SES group	Low SES group
1974: 6th grade	845 000	68 400	380 000
1976: 8th grade[a]	885 600	71 700	398 000
1976: 10th grade[a]	880 300	66 800	396 000
1978: entering university[b]	830 000	60 800	373 000
1978: graduate students[c]	3296 000	215 200	1484 000
1978: advanced grad. stud.[d]	1670 000	105 000	752 000

[a] Assuming the same mean duration of studies = 1.048 years as the high SES group in the eighth grade.
[b] One year cohort.
[c] Four year cohort.
[d] Two year cohort.

9.3 per cent of active males in the age bracket 35–44). The corresponding increase in the proportion of children of an age cohort who had high SES fathers is shown in column two of Table 4.9. As the group of fathers becomes less selected, their maximum possible IQ decreases slightly. The corresponding decrease in the mean IQ of their children was estimated by assuming a constant regression between the IQ of fathers and the IQ of children within the high SES group (column three of Table 4.9).

The number of students in the various levels of education is presented in Table

4.10, for the general population and for high and low SES children. The demographic data corresponding to the same age group are presented in Table 4.11.

The rates presented in the text in Table 4.3 were obtained by dividing the number of students (Table 4.10) by the number of children in the corresponding age cohort (Table 4.11).

We now have all the data needed to estimate the percentage of waste for children of blue-collar workers at various levels of the French educational system. To illustrate the way in which the results presented in Table 4.4 were obtained, let us consider the highest level of education. The calculation proceeds in four steps:

Step 1: For the high SES group, the scores are distributed normally, with a mean of 112.3* and a σ of 13.6.

Step 2: The access rate of the children of the high SES group is 41.4 per cent. According to a table of the normal distribution, this corresponds to a threshold of 0.22σ above the mean of the group. Therefore, the value of the threshold is 112.3 + $0.22 \times 13.6 = 115.3$.

Step 3: For the low SES group, the scores are distributed normally, with a mean of 97.1 and a σ of 13.6.

Step 4: The threshold is located at $115.3 - 97.1 = 18.2$ points above the mean of the distribution of the low SES group. This distance corresponds to $18.2/13.6 = 1.34 \ \sigma$. The percentage of children of the low SES group with IQ scores above the threshold is therefore nine per cent.

The results of the above calculations are presented in Table 4.4, for each of the six educational levels considered.

Appendix 3. Social stratification of children's IQ scores: methodology of international comparisons (see Table 4.6, Section 4)

An analysis of the social heredity essentially amounts to a comparison of the ranking within two ordinal scales. When the social stratification of children's IQ scores is examined, the ranking of the children by IQ tests is compared with the ranking of the fathers in some occupational scale. For the purpose of international comparisons, some sort of standardized scale is needed for each type of hierarchy. Standardized IQ scores provide such a scale. In this scale, the correspondence between percentiles and scores is such that the scores are normally distributed with a mean of 100 and a σ of 15.

In the last 50 years, very few authors have published data on the distribution of IQ scores within representative samples of various social groups of children. Only five such publications were known to us.† These publications were listed in Table 4.6. In order to compare the results obtained by different authors, these results

---

* In the general population, the mean ECNI score is 99.2 (see Chapter 3). Throughout this chapter all IQ scores have been expressed in a standardized scale (mean 100, $\sigma = 15$).

† The standardization data of the revised version of the WISC published by Kaufman and Doppelt (1976) were not known to us at the time of writing.

have been expressed in a standard way (mean 100 and $\sigma = 15$). The results of this standardization are given in Table 4.12.

The next step of the comparison consists in estimating the mean score for standardized high and low social groups. The standardized high SES group has been chosen to correspond to the top decile of the occupational scale, while the low SES group corresponds to the lower half of that scale.

The social groups have been defined by percentiles on a supposedly hierarchical scale of occupations. These percentages can be expressed in terms of standard scores, by using a table of the normal distribution. With a table of *truncated* normal distributions (Falconer 1981), the mean score of the top decile is found to be 126.3, while the mean score of the lower half is found to be 88.0. For each high and low occupational group actually observed, the percentages can be similarly transformed into socio-professional scores and one can compute the regression of mean children's (IQ) scores on mean father's (socio-professional) scores. Using the same regression values, one can then estimate the mean IQ score for standard high and low SES groups of children. The results of these estimates are presented in Table 4.13 and were summarized in Table 4.6.

Appendix 4. Unequal access to education: methodology of international comparisons

The results presented in Fig. 4.3 were obtained by analysing the most complete set of educational and demographical data known to us. The educational data used are reproduced in Table 4.14.
The three steps of the analysis are:

(*a*)   The estimate of access rates for the general population
(*b*)   The estimate of access rates for contrasted groups
(*c*)   The estimate of access rates for standard high and low social groups

(a) The estimate of access rates for the general population

Let N_s be the number of students and N_p the corresponding number in the general population with the same age distribution. The simplest case is when students are being counted at a given point in the curriculum (entering students or recipients of a diploma). The reference population N_p is then defined as people of a given age (19 for new students) at the time the students are being counted.

When students of all levels are being counted, the calculation proceeds as follows. First one determines the fraction f of the student population in the age bracket 19–24; this fraction turns out to be generally around 60 per cent. The number of students in that age bracket is then $f \times N_s$. The access rate within that conventional age bracket is then:

$$r = (f \times N_s)/N_{19\text{–}24}$$

where $N_{19\text{–}24}$ is the number of people in the age bracket 19–24.

The values of N and the access rates derived from them for 12 OECD countries

Table 4.12   Mean IQ scores for various social groups of children expressed in a standardized scale

Social group	% of active males in population	% of children in sample	Mean IQ score	σ
Test No. 1: Stanford-Binet[a]				
Professional	3.1	4.2	111.8	13.5
Semi-professional, managerial	5.2	7.3	106.1	12.9
Clerical, skilled trades, retail bus.	15.0	25.5	102.7	14.2
Semi-skilled occs., minor cler., bus.	30.6	31.0	100.7	13.9
Farmers	15.3	15.0	91.1	13.5
Slightly skilled trades	11.3	9.6	97.3	12.8
Day labourers (urban and rural)	19.5	7.2	93.9	13.2
Total	100.0	(No. = 1731)	99.8	15.0
Test No. 2: WISC[b]				
Professional, semi-professional	5.9	8.0	110.3	13.3
Proprietors, managers, officials	10.6	11.6	106.2	12.4
Clerical, sales, kindred workers	13.9	12.7	105.2	11.1
Craftsmen, foremen, kindred workers	15.6	17.9	101.3	12.4
Farmers, farm managers	14.0	10.1	97.4	14.0
Operatives, kindred workers	18.8	16.5	99.1	12.2
Domestic, protective, other services wkrs	6.0	5.5	97.0	12.5
Farm labourers, foremen, labourers	14.6	13.8	94.2	12.8
Occupation not reported	0.7	1.4	99.5	15.2
Feeble-minded	–	2.5	56.6	9.5
Total	100.0	(No. = 2200)	100.0	15.0
Test No. 3: Echelle de Benedetto[c]				
Intellectual, professionals		1.7	112.2	13.5
Executives, business		9.5	105.6	13.6
Employees, urban area		19.2	104.0	13.7
Employees, rural area		5.1	100.5	14.7
Workers, urban area		22.8	100.0	14.2

Social group	% of active males in population	% of children in sample	Mean IQ score	σ
Workers, rural area		11.1	96.3	14.5
Farmers		17.5	94.5	14.8
Unknown, retired		13.1	–	–
Total		(No. = 95 237)	100.0	15.0
Test No. 4: Scottish Mental Survey[d]				
Professional, large employers		3.3	114.0	11.7
Small employers		4.8	105.5	13.7
Salaried employees		3.6	110.2	12.5
Non-manual wage earners		8.3	106.4	12.8
Skilled manual wage earners		35.9	100.4	14.5
Semi-skilled manual wage earners		18.1	96.7	14.4
Unskilled manual wage earners		17.3	94.7	14.7
Farmers		2.0	99.5	14.6
Agricultural workers		6.6	95.8	15.0
Total		(No. = 7129)	100.0	15.0
Test No. 5: Echelle Collective de Niveau Intellectuel[a]				
Junior executives industrialists, professionals		15.0	109.7	13.8
Small business and artisans		8.7	103.8	13.9
Employees		11.3	102.6	13.7
Skilled workers, one foreman		19.0	99.6	13.5
Unskilled workers		23.4	95.6	13.5
Farmers and agricultural workers		16.3	96.4	13.2
Professional unknown		6.3	93.9	14.8
Total		(No. = 120 000)	100.0	15.0

[a] Terman and Merrill (1937).
[b] Seashore *et al.* (1950).
[c] INED (1950).
[d] Scottish Council (1953).
[e] INED–INOP (1973).

Table 4.13(a) *Estimating mean IQ scores for standard high SES group. The high SES group corresponds to the upper decile (mean SES score 126.3)*

Test no.	SES percentile	Mean SES score	Children's mean IQ	r^a	Estimated IQ score, high SES group
1	8.3	127.6	108.2	0.30	107.8
2	16.5	122.6	107.9	0.35	109.2
3	11.2	125.5	106.6	0.26	106.8
4	6.9	128.9	112.0	0.41	110.9
5	15.0	123.3	109.7	0.42	110.9
			Unweighted average		109.1

^{a} r = regression.

Table 4.13(b) *Estimating mean IQ scores for standard low SES group. The low SES group corresponds to the lower half of the occupational scale. The mean score of the low SES group was obtained from the mean score of the upper half. The mean scores of the two halves are symmetrical with respect to the score 100 (e.g. 103 and 97)*

Test no.	SES percentile	Mean SES score	Children's mean IQ	r^a	IQ upper half of SES	IQ lower half of SES
1	53.9	111.0	102.7	0.24	102.9	97.1
2	46.0	112.9	104.9	0.38	104.6	95.4
3	35.5	115.7	104.3	0.27	103.3	96.7
4	55.9	110.6	103.2	0.30	103.6	96.4
5	35.0	115.9	105.9	0.37	104.5	95.5
			Unweighted average			96.2

^{a} r = regression.

are presented in Table 4.15. The number of students (column 4) is followed by the source used (column 5); the same is true for the reference population given in column 6. Both the number of students N_s and the reference population N_p are expressed in units of thousands. The access rate in the general population is given in the last column of Table 4.15.

The sources used are three OECD publications (OECD 1967, 1974, 1975b) supplemented by a UNESCO document (1967).

(b) The estimate of access rates for contrasted groups

The raw data published by OECD that were reproduced in Table 4.14 are percentages indicating the way in which the various social groups are represented in the student population (left part of Table 4.14) and in the active male population (right part of Table 4.14). The correspondence between the groups labelled A, B, C, D,

Table 4.14 *Distribution of students and of male active population by social categories*[a]

Country	Year S = students M = manpower	Students by categories[b]					Male active population[b]				
		A	B	C	D	E	A	B	C	D	E
Austria	S.1965; M.1961	32.4	31.8	2.4	14.9	5.5	7.4	11.8	9.8	6.7	63.7
Belgium	S.1966; M.1961	32.3	18.3	5.3	15.7	22.8	10.0	10.6	7.9	13.8	55.1
Denmark	S.1964; M.1960	32.9	27.0	11.1	18.2	10.1	9	16	15	17	43
France	S.1964; M.1964	30.2	27.1	5.5	15.2	9.0	5.4	17.3	13.7	9.8	50.1
Germany	S.1964; M.1964	32.8	30.3	30.2		5.3	9.2	18.5		14.8	54.7
Italy	S.1964; M.1964	11.6	39.9	24.9		15.4	1.7	13.0		25.7	59.6
The Netherlands	S.1964; M.1964	42.4	26.5	5.6	14.4	9.4	6.7	12.7	6.1	8.0	66.2
Norway	S.1964; M.1960	33.6	11.1	12.0	–	23.9	10.4	9.1	24.0	–	55.4
Sweden	S.1960; M.1960	31.1	29.5	9.2	11.9	14.3	4.5	20.0	15.1	7.4	53.0
Switzerland	S.1959; M.1960	52.5	24.3	4.8	–	13.8	9.7	16.1	15.0	–	59.1
UK	S.1960; M.1961	62.9	9.9	–	–	27.2	21.5	7.0	–	–	71.5
USA	S.1958; M.1958	52.4	9.6	10.6	–	26.6	22.9	12.8	6.9	–	57.4

[a] Source: OECD (1971, p. 56).
[b] A, upper stratum; B, middle stratum; C, farmers; D, other independents; E, lower stratum (workers).

Table 4.15 *Access rates to a given level of higher education in 12 OECD countries*

Country (1)	Year (2)	Level[a] (3)	Students		Reference population		Access Rates (%) (8)
			No. (000) (4)	Source (5)	No. (000) (6)	Source (7)	
Austria	1965	H	50.3	OECD (1974)	499.2/0.58	OECD (1975b)	5.9
Belgium	1966	eU	14.0	OECD (1975b)	145.2	OECD (1975b)	9.6
Denmark	1964	U	26.3	OECD (1974)	339/0.62	OECD (1975b)	4.8
France	1964	H	476	OECD (1974)	2748/0.61	OECD (1967, 1975b)	10.6
Germany	1964	H	330	OECD (1974)	4534/0.62	OECD (1975b)	4.5
Italy	1964	eH	96.3	OECD (1975b)	768	OECD (1975b)	12.5
The Netherlands	1964	U	59.7	OECD (1974)	910/0.49	OECD (1967, 1975b)	3.2
Norway	1964	eU	4.8	OECD (1975b)	60.4	OECD (1975b)	7.9
Sweden	1960	eU	9.7	OECD (1975b)	97	OECD (1967)	10.0
Switzerland	1959	U	19.2	OECD (1974)	397/0.63	{UNESCO (1967) / OECD (1974, 1975b)	3.0
UK	1960	U	23.3	OECD (1967)	553	OECD (1967)	4.2[b]
USA	1958	Bachelor's degree	366	OECD (1967)	2144	OECD (1967)	17.1

[a] H, higher education; U, university; e, entering students.
[b] Access rate of new entrants in 1960.

Table 4.16 *Correspondence between the social groups of Table 4.14 and the high and low SES groups of Table 4.7*

Country	High SES groups(s)	Low SES group(s)
Austria	A (A+B)	E
Belgium	A	E
Denmark	A (A+B)	E (E+D)
France	A (A+B)	E
Germany	A (A+B)	E
Italy	(A+B)	E
The Netherlands	A (A+B)	E
Norway	A	E
Sweden	A (A+B)	E
Switzerland	A (A+B)	E
UK	A	E
USA	A	E

and E in Table 4.14 and the high and low social groups of Table 4.7 is given in Table 4.16.

For any social group, let f_p be the proportion of active males of that group among all active males and let f_s be the proportion of students of that group among all students. The access rate for the group is given by

$$r \times f_s/f_p$$

where r is the access rate for the general population.

The rates thus derived from the data of Table 4.14 were presented in the text in Table 4.7. The rates of the high group appeared in column 6 of that table while the rates of the low group appeared in column 8 of the same table.

(c) The estimate of access rates for standard high and low groups

As in Appendix 3, we are using the correspondence between two ordinal scales. The first scale indicates the hierarchy of the fathers' professions. The second scale indicates the hierarchy of the academic status of the children. In both scales, the correspondence between percentiles and scores is the same as in the IQ scale. Using these scales, the calculations proceed in three steps:

(*a*) An SES score is computed for each group (100 for the general population, 126.3 for the high 10 per cent group, 88.0 for the low 50 per cent group, etc.)

(*b*) For each group, the rate of access to university is converted into an 'academic quotient'. If we consider US data, for instance, the rate of access of the general population to the bachelor's degree was 17.1 per cent in 1958. At that time, the 'academic quotient' of 100 was therefore 0.95 standard deviation below the threshold 'academic quotient'. In the high group the access rate was 39.1 per cent so that the corresponding score was 0.28 standard deviation below the same threshold.

(*c*) Finally, linear regression is used between the SES scores and the academic

scores. The SES scores of the standard high and low groups are then converted into academic scores. The comparison of these academic scores with
the threshold score computed in (*b*) then yields the required access rates

It should be noted that SES scores and academic scores are defined only for
groups, not for individuals. It should also be noted that these scores are introduced
simply as computational devices to facilitate extrapolations and interpolations of
percentages.

Appendix 5. List of the variables used in the Coleman Report

Variable number	Dependent	Variable name
1	1	Non-verbal score
2	2	General information: test 1
3	3	" " test 2
4	4	" " test 3
5	5	" " test 4
6	6	" " test 5
7	7	General information: *Total*
8	8	Verbal score
9	9	Reading comprehension
10	10	Mathematics achievement
	Student	
11	1	Reading material in home
12	2	Items in home
13	3	Parents' education
14	4	Siblings (positive = few)
15	5	Parents' educational desires
16	6	Parents' interest
17	7	Structural integrity of home
18	8	Changing schools
19	9	Foreign language in home
20	10	Urbanism of background or migration
21	11	Control of environment
22	12	Self concept
23	13	Interest in school and reading
24	14	Homework (grades 12, 9, 6)
		Head start (grade 1)
25	15	Pre-school
	School environment	
26	1	Number of x grade students
27	2	Non-verbal mean score
28	3	Verbal mean score

29	4	Proportion Negro in grade
30	5	" White in grade
31	6	" Mexican-American in grade
32	7	" Puerto Rican in grade
33	8	" Indian in grade
34	9	" Oriental in grade
35	10	" other in grade
36	11	Average White in class last year
37	12	Average White through school
38	13	Proportion definite plans for college
39	14	" mother attend college
40	15	" mother wishes excellence
41	16	" own encyclopaedia
42	17	" college prep curric.
43	18	" read over 16 books
44	19	" member debate club
45	20	Average number science courses
46	21	" " language courses
47	22	" " math courses
48	23	Average time with counsellor
49	24	Proportion teachers expect to be best
50	25	Proportion no chance for successful life
51	26	Proportion want to be best in class
52	27	Average hours homework
	Teacher averages	
53	1	Perception of student quality
54	2	Perception of school quality
55	3	Teachers SES level
56	4	Experience
57	5	Localism
58	6	Quality of college attended
59	7	Degree received
60	8	Professionalism
61	9	Attitude toward integration
62	10	Preference for middle-class students
63	11	Preference for White students
64	12	Verbal score
65	13	Variation in proportion of White students taught
66	14	Sex: proportion male
67	15	Race: proportion White
68	16	Type of certification
69	17	Average salary
70	18	Number of absences
71	19	Attended institution for disadvantaged
72	20	Attended NSF institute

	Principal and Superintendent	
73	1	Pupils per teacher
74	2	Proportion makeshift rooms
75	3	Number of specialized rooms
76	4	Science lab. facilities (usable only in grades 12 and 9)
77	5	Volumes per student
78	6	Extra-curricular activities (usable only in grades 12 and 9)
79	7	Separate classes for special students
80	8	Comprehensiveness of curriculum (usable only in grades 12 and 9)
81	9	Correctional and service personnel
82	10	Student transfers
83	11	Number of types of testing
84	12	Movement between tracks (usable only in grades 12 and 9)
85	13	Accreditation index
	Teacher averages	
86	14	Days in session
87	15	Age of texts
88	16	Part-day attendance
89	17	Teacher turn over
90	18	Guidance counsellors (usable only in grades 12 and 9)
91	19	Attendance
92	20	College attendance (usable only in grades 12 and 9)
93	21	Teachers' college for principal
94	22	Salary
95	23	School location
96	24	Length of academic day
97	25	Tracking (usable only in grades 12 and 9)
98	26	Accelerated curriculum
99	27	Promotion of slow learners
100	28	Attitude toward integration
101	29	Per pupil instructional expenditure
102	30	School board elected
103	31	Teachers' examination

Appendix 6. Note on the parametrization of social effects (Section 3)

The parameter s introduced in Section 3 is defined here in a more general way. Let us consider a hierarchical set of social groups 1, 2, . . . , n, and a given trait. The mean phenotypic value P_{ij} observed for the children of a given group depends on the genotypic pool of the parents (here characterized by the social rank, i) and also on the environment provided by the group where the children are reared (here characterized by the social rank, j). Since the birth group is generally the same as the rearing group, one usually knows only the diagonal elements P_{ii}. When the rearing group differs from the birth group, one obtains off diagonal elements.

The information concerning social heredity is contained in a matrix s_{ij} of coefficients which relate the off diagonal elements of the phenotypic mean to the diagonal elements:

$$P_{ij} = P_{ii} + s_{ij} (P_{jj} - P_{ii}) = (1\text{-}s_{ij}) P_{ii} + s_{ij} P_{jj} \tag{1}$$

For a given trait within a given social system, if all off diagonal elements of the s matrix are nil, the reproduction of social inequalities will be said to be entirely dependent on genotypic differences. If all off diagonal elements are unity, it will be said to be entirely dependent on social differences.

Hogben (1933) has stressed the fallacy of a simplistic partitioning of the causes of variations, and this point has been made several times since (e.g. Feldman and Lewontin 1975). To illustrate this point in the case of social heredity, let us consider the bottom group n and the top group 1 and assume that we have

$$P_{n1} = P_{1n} = P_{11}$$

The s matrix is completely asymmetrical ($s_{n1} = 1$ and $s_{1n} = 0$). In this extreme case, the traditional question about 'the relative importance of nature and nurture' loses all significance, i.e. the high phenotypic value could be attributed entirely to the change in social conditions in the first case and entirely to the genotype in the second.

Part III
Relevant and irrelevant technical issues

In the first part of the book, we examined the social and ideological context of the IQ controversy. In the second part, we presented original work directly relevant to the issue of social heredity. In this last part, we present an overview of the main technical points about the genetics of IQ scores, with an emphasis on the relevance or lack of relevance of these technical points to the issue of social heredity. We hope that this overview will be a useful intro-duction to the vast literature on the subject, including recent overviews or cri-tical articles about the heritability of IQ (e.g. Block and Dworkin 1976; Eysenck 1979; Eysenck and Kamin 1981; Feldman and Lewontin 1975; Flynn 1980; Gould 1981; Halsey 1977; Kamin 1974; Layzer 1974; Loehlin, Lindzey, and Spuhler 1975; Scarr 1981; Taylor 1980).

The most important point of our overview is probably that made by Hog-ben in 1933 when he wrote in the Journal of Genetics *that 'a balance sheet of nature and nurture, if it has any significance in the light of modern experi-mental concepts, does not entitle us to set limits to changes which might be produced by regulating the social or physical environment of a human popu-lation.'*

5. Twelve errors about genetics and their social consequences

One of the most striking features of the literature and discussions of human behavioural genetics, and especially of human intelligence, is the degree to which a supposedly 'scientific' field is permeated with basic conceptual and experimental errors. Indeed, as we will show, much of the discussion of the biology of intelligence would simply evaporate if fundamental biological and statistical notions were applied to the genetics of human behaviour with the same degree of rigour and logic that is standard in, say, the study of milk yield in cattle or body weight in mice.

These errors are of three sorts, although there is no very sharp dividing line among them. First, there are general conceptual errors that are widespread among social scientists and even biologists when they are not thinking carefully about their subject. Examples are the confusion between genotype and phenotype, a distinction on which all of developmental and population genetics is grounded, or the confusion between the causes of differences among individuals and the causes of the differences between groups. Secondly, there are technical errors of experimental design, measurement, and data analysis, so that familial resemblances and differences are confused with genetic similarities and differences, which may or may not contribute to the similarity and difference among family members. Thirdly, there are what can only be described as *mystification* rather than simply 'errors', because they involve the repeated use of words and concepts that are universally understood among scientists to have an opposite significance to that claimed by writers on IQ, but which serve these writers as polemical devices. Examples are the use of phenomena of regression and the normality of the distribution of IQ scores as supposed demonstration of the biological basis of scores, rather than the true significance of regression and normality, which is exactly the opposite.

We do not claim that we are the first to notice and warn against these various errors. On the contrary, there have been repeated cautions in the last 80 years that have been ignored repeatedly. As early as 1903, Karl Pearson warned against confusing familial correlations with biological causation. Speaking of correlation between parents and offspring, he wrote:

The law of ancestral heredity in its most general form is not a biological hypothesis at all, it is simply the statement of a fundamental theorem in the statistical theory of multiple correlation applied to a particular type of statistics. . . .

The law of ancestral heredity as founded on the theory of multiple correlation involves no *biological** theory of regression.

Galton observed that positions of social and intellectual eminence tend to run in families and concluded that these positions must be based on some hereditary factor. One century later, the same confusion persists despite repeated warnings. As Scarr and Weinberg (1977*a*) have observed, 'a word by the wise is sometimes lost'. Sometimes, too, it is deliberately thrown away.

1. Error 1: Genotype and phenotype

Lying at the heart of the confusion about intelligence and heredity is a fundamental misunderstanding about the relationship of organisms and their life activities to the genes that those organisms have inherited from their parents. It is the confusion between *genotype* and *phenotype*. The genotype to which an organism belongs is specified by the DNA molecules and other molecules and cellular structures that are present in the fertilized egg and whose form is essentially isolated from the influence of any variations in the external world. The phenotype of an organism, at a given moment in its life history, is specified by the complete set of morphological, physiological, and behavioural characters manifested by the organism. While the genotype is fixed at fertilization, the phenotype is changing throughout the lifetime of the individual organism. That is, the organism is the outcome of a process of development. The characteristic of such a developmental process is that what the organism will become at the next instant of time depends both upon its current state and upon the environment that impinges upon the developing system during the developmental interval. But the current state of the organism is, in time, a consequence of both the genes possessed by the organism and of the sequence of previous environments. The individual living being is then, at every moment the consequence of a unique interaction between its genotype and the history of the environments in which it has found itself. A wild-type *Drosophila* that passes its immature stages at a temperature of 25 °C will develop an eye with about 800 cells, while at 15 °C it would have developed more than 1000. Moreover, the order of environments is critical. If a *Drosophila* is given a temperature shock of 37 °C during its pupal stage, the pattern of wing veins will be altered, but not if the shock is given earlier or later in development.

The relationship between genotype, environment, and organism is encapsulated in the concept of the *norm of reaction*. The norm of reaction of a genotype is the correspondence between the different possible phenotypes that may develop and the different environments that will result in those phenotypes. The norm of reaction is then a mapping function that

---

* Emphasis in original

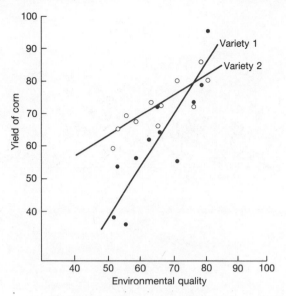

Fig. 5.1 Examples of norms of reaction. Yield of grain in two genotypes of maize in environments of different qualities. From Suzuki *et al.* (1981).

transforms the set of environments into the set of phenotypes. Typically it is shown as a curve relating the value of some environmental variable, say, temperature, to the phenotype that will result, say size. Each genotype has its own unique norm of reaction which is, in general, of a different shape than those for other genotypes. These norms of reaction may cross each other so that in one environment adults of genotype A will be larger than those of genotype B, but at a different environment the sizes will be reversed. An example of such a relation for yield in corn is shown in Fig. 5.1.

Another illustration of the norm of reaction is given in the experiment shown in Fig. 5.2. Seven individual plants of a Californian plant, *Achillea*, were collected from a natural population and each plant was cut into three pieces. One piece of each plant was regrown at sea-level, (Fig. 5.2(*a*)), one at 1400 metres elevation (Fig. 5.2(*b*)), and one at 3050 metres (Fig. 5.2(*c*)). The three plants that grew from each piece of an original plant are all genetically identical, while the seven original plants are, of course, of different genotypes. For comparison the three identical triplets from each plant are shown one under the other in the figure. As the picture shows, the tallest plant at sea-level was the shortest at medium elevation and did not even flower there, while the next to the shortest plant at sea-level was next to the tallest at the high elevation. The order of phenotypic sizes of the seven genotypes is inconsistent from altitude to altitude. None

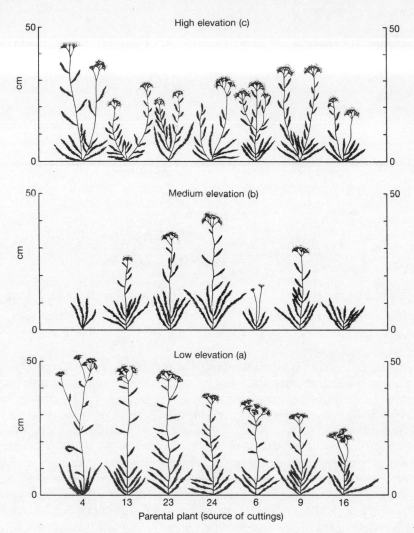

Fig. 5.2 The impossibility of ordering genotypes by ordering phenotypes. Norms of reaction to elevation for seven different *Achillea* plants (seven different genotypes). A cutting from each plant was grown at low, medium, and high elevations. The cuttings from the same original plant are shown one under the other (Carnegie Institute of Washington).

is consistently tallest or shortest and there is no altitude that is unambiguously the best for all genotypes.

A second feature of development is that it depends not only on genotype and environment at some moment, but on small random perturbations at the cellular and molecular level that are not ordinarily thought of as environmental changes. The importance of these perturbations can be seen in the left–right asymmetry of individual organisms. If the number of eye cells in the left and right eyes of a single *Drosophila* are counted, it will be found that they differ between sides, although in the average there is no tendency of *Drosophila* to be 'right-eyed' or 'left-eyed'. A *Drosophila* adult, about the size of the point of a lead pencil develops in the laboratory while being attached to the vertical side of a glass culture bottle. No sensible notion of environment would allow that the environments of the left and right side of the developing fly are different, and the genes of the left and right halves of the fly are the same. Yet a considerable asymmetry results such that the variation from left to right side is as great as the variation between individual flies. In like manner, the location of every hair on our bodies is not determined by genes and environment alone, but depends upon certain random cell movements and divisions during embryonic life. The same indeterminacy is also true for the billions of neural connections in our central nervous system. How important such randomly influenced connections may be in our behaviour is not known. None of the authors of this book can play the violin like Isaac Stern and it is entirely possible that no matter how rigorous our training, we might never have reached that level of ability because at birth our neuronal connections were different from his. That does not mean, however, that those neuronal differences were coded in our genes or a consequence of intra-uterine nutrition. They may be entirely accidental. 'Inborn' is not to be confused with 'genetic'.

The fact that an organism is the consequence of a constant interaction between genes, environment, and accident means that the relationship between genotype and organism is not one-to-one, but many-to-many. For each genotype there are many possible phenotypic outcomes and for any particular phenotype, there are many possible genotypes that may underlie it. It is precisely this many–many relationship that makes genetic analysis of most phenotypes so difficult if not impossible.

When we turn from phenotypes included in the morphology of organisms to a description of their behaviour, a new level of complexity arises. Behaviour is not just another phenotype because, by its very nature it is a process rather than an object. Genes are concrete physical objects. They participate in a process of development that has, as one of its consequences, the production of another concrete physical object, the organism; or rather, a sequence of physical objects, the organism at each moment of time. Behaviour, and in particular intelligence, is not a physical object or a concrete thing that occupies space. It cannot be located, seen, or weighed, nor is it a physical property like colour or mass. It is, in fact, a description of some aspect of a process engaged in by organisms, and while it depends upon the physical state of the organism, it is not simply an extension of it. The reification of intelligence as a thing, inside of human beings, that exist sometimes in 'fluid', sometimes in 'crystallized' form, encourages the belief that there can be a gene or genes 'for' intelligence. Genes do not make eyes or brains, which are the outcome of developmental processes. Still less do they make 'intelligence' which is the name for a process itself.

In summary, the phenotype is *not* a 'first approximation' to the genotype. In many cases is provides hardly any information at all about genotype. In particular, the idea that a ranking of phenotypes corresponds, even approximately, to a ranking of intrinsic 'genetic value' is incorrect, as Fig. 5.2 showed. What is true for plants is *a fortiori* true of that most flexible of all phenotypes, human behaviour.

2. Error 2: Malleability and heritability

The concept of the norm of reaction makes clear why differences between individuals may be highly heritable, yet the trait being considered may be highly malleable as a result of environmental change. Yield in corn is both heritable and malleable. By 'heritable' is meant that genetic differences between strains result in different norms of reaction as shown in Fig. 5.1. That is, in any given environment, there is a genetically caused difference in phenotype between the strains, and this difference, variety 1 having a lower yield than variety 2, persists over a range of environments. Nevertheless, size in both strains changes with environment, such that the heritable trait is also malleable. Indeed the malleability is such that in better environments the phenotype difference between genotype 1 and genotype 2 is reversed. Traits are heritable to the degree that phenotypic differences exist between genotypes over a range of environment. Traits are malleable to the degree that phenotype changes with environment. As the figure shows, there is no necessary connection between the two properties.

That the confusion between heritability and lack of malleability is a vital source of misunderstanding and of false claims about social policy becomes clear when we consider the rhetorical question that served as the title for A.R. Jensen's famous article (1969): 'How much can we boost IQ and scholastic achievement?' Jensen's answer was 'not much', because IQ is said to be highly heritable! Had Jensen not made that basic error, his entire article could never have come into being.

3. Error 3: Group and individual differences

Claims about the importance of genes in producing IQ differences have not been left simply as explanations of variations among individuals. The real issue has always been revealed in the extension of the explanation to group differences. As we showed in Chapter 1, the mental testing movement from its beginnings in America and Britain has been concerned with differ-

ences between social classes, ethnic groups, and races. While early eugeni-
cists and ideologues of race simply asserted that differences in IQ performance between ethnic groups and social classes were biological, without
attempting to build a technical case for that prejudice, more recent writers
have used studies of the heritability of IQ to make similar claims. A.R.
Jensen's chief interest lay in differences between Blacks and Whites while
Burt, Eysenck, and Herrnstein have been preoccupied with social class.
But whether it is race or class the argument has been the same: Because IQ
is highly heritable, differences in performance between groups are also to
be explained genetically and are, incidentally, unchangeable since heritable means not malleable. Exactly the same point of view is contained
implicitly in Loehlin *et al.'s Race differences in intelligence* (1975) since
most of the book is devoted to the question of the heritability of IQ.

The error here is a confusion of totally different sets of causes. There is
neither a logical nor empirical connection between the causes of individual
differences and the causes of group differences. Indeed, over a long-range
evolutionary perspective, because evolution occurs by the conversion of
variation between individuals within populations into variation between
groups, with a consequent loss of variation within groups, there is actually
an inverse relationship between within- and between-group variation.

Differences in phenotype between individual organisms arise both
because there are different genotypes in a population and because different
individual organisms develop in different environments. Differences in
average phenotype between groups also arise from genetic and environmental differences, but at a different level. A genetic difference between
groups is a difference in the *frequency distribution* of genotypes between
the groups and is not related to the amount of genetic variation within the
group. So, two groups may be completely homogeneous genetically, so
there is no genetic variation among individuals *within* groups, yet the genotype common to all members of one group may be different from the genotype of the second group. In this case there is no heritable variation
between individuals within groups, yet considerable genetic difference
between groups. Conversely, both groups may be very heterogeneous
genetically, yet the groups will be indistinguishable from each other if the
array of genotypes is the same in each. One should not confuse average differences with individual differences.

A similar distinction applies to environmental sources of variation within
and between groups. The amount of variation that exist from family to
family, and from individual life history to individual life history, gives us no
information on how much or how little difference exist between the
environments of groups as a whole. Skin colour is to a large extent heritable, and there is a good deal of genetic variation among White New
Yorkers in skin colour partly as a consequence of genetic differences

among their Mediterranean, Central European and Northern European ancestors. But the skin colour of white New Yorkers is, as a group, lighter than that of their richer relatives who spend the winter in Miami Beach and that difference is entirely environmental. Whether working-class children and Blacks owe their lower average performance on IQ tests to social discrimination cannot be determined on the basis of the heritability of IQ performance within these groups, because discrimination against Blacks or the children of workers when compared with middle-class White children is not a variable *within* these groups, only between them.

The distinction between the causes of variation between groups and the causes of variation within groups has been clarified repeatedly in the past. Halsey (1958), for example, pointed out that a heritability as large as 0.8 for IQ scores would permit a completely social explanation of differences in average IQ scores between children of various social groups.

Genetic variation among individuals is the basis for evolutionary divergence between populations. As a result of natural selection or of chance survival of some genotypes, a few genotypes in a population become very common while others become rare or disappear. The consequence is that variation within the populations decreases. If the populations are living in different environments and are isolated from each other, different genotypes will be enriched in different populations, so that the loss in variation within populations corresponds to an increased difference between population. Conversely, if there is migration between populations, they will remain genetically very similar to each other, but there will also be the maintenance of genetic variation within each group because of the different selective pressures operating in different localities. In general, in evolution those forces that decrease the variation within groups increase the variation between groups and vice versa. Thus, if we expect to see any relation at all between genetic differences between individuals and groups it will be an inverse one, and not the direct correspondence supposed by Jensen, Eysenck, and others.

4. Error 4: Familiality and heritability

The study of genetics is the study of relatives. Mendel formulated the laws of genetics by considering similarity and differences between parents and offspring, and between sibs. Thus, to study the role of genetics in influencing a trait one must study the phenotypic similarity between organisms of a known degree of biological relationship. Unfortunately, for many organisms and for many traits, phenotypic similarity between relatives arises from two sources. Relatives carry many of the same genes, but they are also likely to have experienced similar developmental environments. To turn observations about phenotypic similarity between relatives, *famili-*

ality, into results about genotypic similarity, *heritability*, it is necessary to break the environmental tie between relatives. In experimental organisms it is relatively easy. Two seeds from the same plant can be planted in different soils, two mice from the same litter can be given to different foster mothers. Of course even in such cases there remain the common environmental effects of a common seed capsule and a common uterus that are rather more difficult to get around.

The problem in studying human beings is that family environmental effects are unusually strong, especially in early psycho-social development, while at the same time moral and practical considerations make it particularly unlikely that biological sibs will be raised in totally unrelated environments. As a consequence, familial resemblance which is a consequence of both genetic and environmental similarities cannot be distinguished from genetic resemblance. Despite the problem, people who study human behaviour persist in confusing familiality with heritability and offer as evidence for the heritability of IQ that offspring resemble their parents or their sibs. As late as 1975, there appeared in *Behavior Genetics*, the leading journal on the subject, an article estimating the heritability of IQ among Canadian children simply from the resemblance of children's IQ's to those of their parents by whom they were raised (Williams 1975). Even worse, the same journal published a review of 'sibling resemblance in mental ability' with the following conclusion (Paul 1980):

. . . collectively the sibling correlations they have yielded are highly consistent with the polygenic hypothesis and the conclusion that genetic factors are the major source of individual differences in intelligence.

Finally, one of the editors himself ended a short communication in *Behavior Genetics* with the following sentence (Spuhler and Vandenberg 1980):

Most noteworthy is that these estimates for parent–offspring resemblance in the family studies, taken as a whole, strongly indicate intermediate values for heritability of specific cognitive abilities.

This represents a total confusion between an observation, familiality, and an explanation of its cause, heritability, which is the question at issue. Nor is the familial resemblance an 'estimate' or an 'approximation' to the heritability. These two words are often used to imply that the result, although not perfect, is at least somewhere in the vicinity of the right answer. In fact, observed family resemblance is neither an estimate nor an approximation to heritability. In the absence of knowledge about how family environment affects IQ scores, familiality contains no information at all about heritability.

5. Error 5: Broad and narrow heritability

The word 'heritability' is used interchangeably in a technical and an every-day sense, which has the effect of mystifying the subject. In an everyday sense to say that a characteristic is highly heritable is to imply that genes are powerful in their effect and that one will look very much like ones parents. In this sense having two legs, one mouth, and 10 fingers is highly heritable. In the technical sense, however, heritability has an exact (or rather two exact) statistical meanings. The total phenotypic variation for some trait in a population can be assigned to two sources. The first is the variation between the mean phenotypes of different genotypes, when each genotype is averaged over all the environments in which it develops. The variance of these mean phenotypes among the genotypes is called the gene-tic variance, σ_G^2. The remainder of the total phenotypic variance, σ_T^2, is a consequence of interaction between the different genotypes and the vary-ing environment. It is sometimes assigned completely to 'environmental' variance, σ_E^2, so that

$$\sigma_T^2 = \sigma_G^2 + \sigma_E^2, \text{ tautologically.}$$

Sometimes, however, it is explicitly recognized that there are genotype–environment interactions so that the bookkeeping appears as

$$\sigma_T^2 = \sigma_G^2 + \sigma_E^2 + \sigma_{GE}^2$$

In either case, the heritability, H^2, of a trait is defined as the proportion of the total phenotypic variance that is contained in σ_G^2. That is

$$H^2 = \sigma_G^2 / \sigma_T^2$$

To distinguish H^2 from a related statistical concept, it is sometimes called 'heritability in the broad sense'.

The genetic variance, σ_G^2, itself can be broken down into two main com-ponents, the additive genetic variance, σ_A^2, and the remainder σ_I^2.

$$\sigma_G^2 = \sigma_A^2 + \sigma_I^2$$

Because of the phenomenon of dominance and because of interaction among genes affecting a character, there is a non-linear relationship between the phenotype of a genotypic class and the number of alleles favourable to the trait that characterize that genotype. The additive genetic variance is that portion of all the genetic variance associated with the linear trend of phenotype with the number of favourable alleles.

Using $\sigma_A{}^2$, another heritability statistic h^2, *heritability in the narrow sense*, is defined as

$$h^2 = \sigma_A{}^2/\sigma_T{}^2$$

which is clearly always smaller than or equal to H^2. The importance of h^2 is that it is a prediction of how rapidly a population will evolve under natural or artificial selection. Traits with large h^2 respond rapidly to selection, those with small h^2 respond slowly. One of the consequences of selection is that $\sigma_A{}^2$, and therefore, h^2 decrease, finally becoming zero, leaving only the other part of the genotype variance, $\sigma_I{}^2$. Thus, after long-term selection h^2 will be zero or nearly so, while H^2 may still be substantial.

The importance of the contrast between h^2 and H^2 is that the former has a clear place in population genetic theory, being the prediction of progress under selection, while the latter has no place at all. A knowledge of H^2 does not allow us to make any prediction of the result of selection, as we showed above, nor does it say anything about phenotypic malleability. It is, in fact, a useless parameter. The fact that so much attention has been given in behavioural genetics to its estimation arises from two sources. First, there is the confusion between heritability and malleability and secondly the desire to get some kind of a number, no matter what its lack of meaning, to provide a semblance of the scientific. H^2 has value only as a polemical tool. It tells us nothing interesting about nature. This was recognized by the founder of heritability studies, who, over 30 years ago, called it 'an unfortunate shortcut' (Fisher 1951).

6. Error 6: Correlation and equality

Much is made in the IQ literature of claims that adopted children have a correlation in their IQ's with their biological parents, but not with their adoptive parents. Quite aside from the validity of the data on which these claims are based, their interpretation has been deformed. It is claimed that such a result shows that genes determine IQ. In fact, replacing the word 'determine' with 'influence', such a claim would be true, provided the experiment were carefully controlled, no mean problem in itself. What is not usually discussed is the fact that adopted children, even though they may correlate *individually* with their biological parents more than with their adoptive parents, are, in fact, more similar as *a group* to the adoptive parents than to their biological ones. The apparent contradiction between these two assertions arises because correlation is confused (often deliberately) with identity. The two are not at all the same. A high correlation between two sets of values means only that an increase or decrease in one is matched by an increase or decrease in the other. The absolute value of

Table 5.1 *Hypothetical data on the correlation between IQ scores of adoptees and IQ scores of their biological and adoptive parents. This fictitious example illustrates the point that the correlation of individuals contains no information on the causes of group differences*

Children	Biological parents	Adoptive parents
100	93	108
101	94	100
102	95	106
103	96	112
104	97	101
106	99	104
108	101	111
110	103	102
111	104	110
112	105	103
Mean = 105.7	*Mean* = 98.7	*Mean* = 105.7

the two sets may be quite different. Consider Table 5.1 which gives hypothetical but plausible IQ scores for a group of adopted children, their biological parents and their adoptive parents. In this example, the children have a perfect correlation ($r = +1.0$) with their biological parents. Each increase of one unit in parental IQ is exactly matched by an increase of one unit in the child's IQ. On the other hand there is essentially no correlation between the children and their adoptive parents because very high IQ adoptive parents seem no more likely to have their adopted children at the top of their group than at the bottom. In fact, the adoptive couple with the highest IQ score (IQ = 112) has one of the lower scoring children (IQ = 103). We would then conclude, correctly that genes play a role in influencing IQ. However, as a group, the children all have higher IQ's than their biological parents and their mean IQ is seven points higher, equal to that of their adoptive families. Correlation is not identity. Once again we see that there is no contradiction between heritability of a trait, as evidenced by correlation, and malleability as evidenced by the large rise in IQ scores consequent upon adoption.

7. Error 7: Normality as a biological phenomenon

IQ scores are normally distributed with a mean of 100 and a standard deviation of 15. The fact that the scores have a normal distribution has been claimed to be evidence that something real and biological is being measured. After all, why else would IQ scores have the same form of distribution as biological variables like height and weight? The problem with this reasoning is that it completely inverts the actual causation. As it happens, many, if not most variables measured in populations of objects are normally distributed. The number of grains of sand in repeated spoonsful from the beach are normally distributed, as are the weights of the bricks in an apartment house and the number of letters on the pages of this book. To bring the matter closer to home, suppose we give a multiple choice IQ test with four choices per question and 100 questions to the school children of Detroit, Michigan, but let us make the test in Turkish. Assuming that the children will be well enough disciplined to sit through such nonsense, they will get about 25 out of the 100 questions right by chance alone. Some will, again by chance, get a few more, some a few less. The test scores will be normally distributed and if we award four points for every correct answer, the mean score will be 100 and the standard deviation 17. Not bad for an IQ test. Far from being evidence of some underlying biological cause, normality shows that the measurement is subject to a large number of small uncorrelated random errors. Normality is a good indicator of *lack* of underlying order, not its presence, and it is no accident that the normal distribution was originally called in statistics, 'the error function'.

8. Error 8: Regression as a biological phenomenon

The most egregious misrepresentation of the meaning of a statistics of the literature of IQ testing is Eysenck's claim that the phenomenon of regression is powerful evidence of the heritability of IQ (Eysenck 1971, pp. 67–8):

This regression to the mean is a phenomenon well known in genetics, and characteristic of traits markedly influenced by genetic causes; environment would favour the children of the higher professional fathers, and disfavour those of unskilled working-class fathers, tending to make the difference between them even greater than that observed between their fathers. Clearly this is not what happens; *regression presents strong evidence for genetic determination of IQ differences.**

This claim is a concatenation of a reversal of meaning with a historical confusion to produce a totally incorrect conclusion.

We owe the original concept of regression to Francis Galton. He observed that if the height of children (after reaching adulthood) were plotted against the mean heights of their parents, the points formed a straight line as one might expect, but that the slope of the line was less than unity. That is, very tall parents had children who were closer to the mean of the entire population than the parents themselves, as did very short parents. The tendency of children's height to be closer to the mean of the population than the heights of their parents Galton called 'regression to the

---

* Emphasis added.

mean'. This regression meant, of course, that whatever causes were operating to make the parent's height, were operating imperfectly in the children. In the limit, suppose that the causes of parent's heights were
completely at random with respect to the causes of children's heights. Then
the average height of children of tall parents would be exactly the same as
the average height of children of short parents. The regression to the mean
would be complete. So, the phenomenon of regression is a consequence of
the *lack* of influence of parents on offspring. Galton originally hoped to
understand the laws of heredity from studying the phenomenon of regression, but he failed because the relation between parents and children arises
from both genetic and environmental causes. By a curious and unfortunate
historical inversion, the word regression in statistics has now come to be
used to describe the slope of the line itself so that a regression coefficient of
zero in present usage correspond to complete regression in Galton's original sense. The point is, however, that whether one takes regression in its
original Galtonian sense, or in its modern sense, it says nothing about
genetics. If children resemble their parents (low regression in Galton's
original sense) this is simply the observation of familiality, not heritability.
If there is strong regression in Galton's sense (the sense in which Eysenck
takes it), this is evidence that parents genes and the family environment
have *little* effect on children. The phenomenon of regression toward the
mean, like the character of normality of a distribution, far from being evidence of biological regularity, arises from random events in the determination of the measurement. All phenomena that are imperfectly related to
each other show regression. The rainfall in April of a given year is imperfectly correlated with the total rainfall for that year. If we plot the total
year's rainfall against April rainfall, we will find that very wet years do
have somewhat wetter Aprils than dry years, but not as wet as we would
have predicted from the total precipitation. April rainfalls regress toward
the mean, but we do not imagine that there are genes for rain.

As pointed out earlier, the distinction between a statistical law and a biological one was made by Pearson 80 years ago. Yet Eysenck (1971,
pp. 67–8; 1973, p. 9, 103–5; 1981, pp. 62–4), Jensen (1972, p. 165) and a
few others still confuse statistics with genetics. As stated by Mackenzie
(1980), 'the repeated misuse of an elementary statistical concept, by psychologists who are highly trained in statistics, is a matter of some concern'.

9. Error 9: Correlation and causation

It is tempting to conclude that two variables that vary in parallel do so
because of common causation, but it is a temptation that must be resisted.
In past years gasoline prices have risen fairly steadily, while at the same
time Halley's comet has been getting closer and closer to the Earth. Even

the most devoted astrologer would not suggest any causal connection between them. Independent processes in time or accidental coincidences of place are frequent sources of correlation in the absence of common cause.

Even when correlated variables are indeed causally related, the form of the causal connection may be extremely complex and indirect. IQ scores are indeed correlated with income, but it certainly does not follow as claimed by the ideologues of meritocracy that high IQ causes high income. It is at least plausible that the positive correlation between IQ score and income arises from a third cause common to both, namely the social class of origin. The children of high status, high income parents will acquire the culture and maturation necessary to good performance on IQ tests, while through social heredity they will eventually get access to better education and better jobs. That is, two variables like IQ performance and income may be correlated because they both flow from a common cause, rather than one being the direct result of the other. Chains of correlation may be yet more complex such that A and B influence C which influences D, while at the same time D is directly influenced by A, and so on. So, for example, parents education influences parents income, which influences child's education, which in turn influences child's IQ score, while at the same time the parents education will directly influence the child's test performance.

The problem in all cases of complex interacting causes is to distinguish those correlations that are evidence of direct causation from those that arise from complex chains of antecedent conditions. The usual method in statistics is the technique of partial correlation. This consists, essentially, in calculating the correlation between two variables, while holding other possibly relevant variables constant. When this technique is applied to IQ and to economic status, the ability to perform well on IQ tests turn out not to be a significant cause of social and economic success, even though the two variables are significantly correlated. The correlation between IQ and eventual success becomes very low if parents social status is held constant, while conversely, the correlation between parents status and childrens eventual status is barely affected by holding IQ constant (Bowles and Nelson 1974). That is, the best predictor of eventual socio-economic success is parents social status, while IQ by itself, is a poor predictor. The naïve meritocratic argument is that mental performance is the *cause* but an examination of the chains of causation and correlation shows that both high IQ and social success are consequences of a system of social heredity of status and economic power.

10. Error 10: Individual variance hides social class

An extremely powerful tool in arguing for a particular model of causation is to choose judiciously the categories into which objects are grouped for analysis. If, in the analysis of variation in IQ scores, one simply assigns children to social status categories by, say, occupational status of the male parent, then a significant fraction of the variation in IQ score will turn out to be associated with the child's social class. Suppose, however, in addition to social status so defined, one also scores the children for place of residence, school attended, number of days of school absence, ethnic origin, and family size. Then the analysis of IQ scores will show that social status no longer accounts for much of the variation which is taken up a bit by each of the many variables. The reason that social class has disappeared as an important variable is that all of the new categories introduced are themselves determiners or consequences of social class and so absorb the variation originally appearing in that variable. By dividing social class into a large number of its partial attributes the variable of social class *per se* has been diluted. This is exactly what has been done in the analysis of IQ to 'prove' that social class, *per se*, is not a cause of performance. The general point is that there is no 'objective' way to 'discover' from the data which variable are most important in causation. Rather, the identification of variables is itself an act of imposing an *a priori* structure of explanation within which the statistical analysis correlations must operate. If one's *a priori* social analysis presumes that school success is a consequence of a conjunction of individual idiosynpatic qualities, the data can be made to support that view by categorizing the population according to that set of qualities. If, on the other hand, social class is the fundamental analytical concept being used, of which the other categories are only reflections, the data analysis will bear out the importance of that variable.

The point made here concerns social class as a variable, independantly of its possible genetic correlates. Whether social class is correlated to genetic IQ differences is a different question altogether. As was shown in chapter 4, this other question is essentially irrelevant to the issue of social heredity.

11. Error 11: The 'laws' of the market as 'natural laws'

Much of the claimed social relevance of IQ testing rests on implicit or explicit suppositions about human nature. One of the early leaders of the mental test movement (Thorndike 1916) wrote that 'In the actual race of life, which is not to get ahead, but to get ahead of somebody, the chief determining factor is heredity'. This aphorism of Thorndike's epitomizes the social theory of the mental testing movement. Material and psychic rewards are limited. Human beings are in constant competition to achieve these rewards, and since there is not enough to go around, there will be winners and losers. The purpose of the IQ test is to identify the potential winners, presumably so that society will not waste its precious resources on those whose abilities are insufficient.

It is difficult to quarrel with a description of the society in which we live as being characterized by hierarchy, by intense competition to achieve a limited number of high status places, by the 'race to get ahead of somebody', even if it is only to be hired for a job on an assembly line. The mystification introduced by the social theory of Thorndike and his successors is the claim that this social organization is an inevitable manifestation of human biology, that the war of all against all is a natural law.

An inverse form of this confusion between historically contingent social organization and natural law is the claim that the limited number of high status positions is a *consequence* of the limited supply of natural ability. According to this view, laid out, for example, by Herrnstein in *IQ in the meritocracy* (1973), society rewards those abilities that are in short supply. Physicians make a lot of money because there are so few people with the ability to be doctors that they can demand and receive a high price for their rare intellectual metal. This argument wilfully ignores the fact that the supply of physicians is regulated entirely by the number of medical schools and the size of their classes, which are kept deliberately small in order not to flood the market with doctors. Anyone who has sat on medical school admissions committees knows that there are several equally 'qualified' applicants for each one that is admitted and thus final admission is largely a form of lottery. There is, in fact, no evidence at all that the numbers of physicians, lawyers, tool and die makers, violinists, salespeople, and unemployed are in a way determined by the supply of natural talent to fill these roles. On the contrary, the historical record shows exactly the reverse to be true, equally for the numbers of surgeons and the number of barbers.

12. Error 12: If it is new and complicated it must be true

Partly through self-delusion, and partly through a deliberate attempt to mystify the innocent, some of those who have written about the genetics of IQ have tried to make the story more believable by making it more complicated. This process consists essentially in introducing a complex mathematical model involving many variables and parameters and finding the set of parameters that best fits the data. These techniques have two effects. First, each method is 'new and improved'. Older, simple-minded genetic models are dismissed as insufficiently sophisticated, whereas the newer statistical techniques are said to be more powerful and true-to-life. Secondly, the models are statistically or mathematically complicated and so for that reason alone seem deeper and more 'scientific' (e.g. Eysenck 1979, p. 3).

To understand what such models can do, we must remind ourselves of the structure of the data. Individual people of different degrees of relationship and environmental commonality are compared, and the correlation (or differences) in their IQ scores are put in correspondence with their closeness of biological and environmental relationships. At one end are identical twins raised together who, because they share the same genes and (supposedly) a very similar environment have very similar IQ scores. At the other extreme is a sample of unrelated persons raised apart, a sample for the general population, who will show no correlation in IQ scores, provided the sample is taken correctly. Between these two extremes are pairs of persons of intermediate relationships. There are not many intermediate values available: sibs, first degree relatives reared together, twins raised apart, and unrelated persons raised together. Whatever theory one makes, from a completely genetical to a completely social theory, one predicts a decreasing similarity between persons as their degree of relationship decreases. That is *all* theories predict that IQ correlation will be somewhere near the upper limit of 1.0 for identical twins raised together, will decrease through intermediate degrees of relationship and will be 0.0 for unrelated persons raised apart. To distinguish one theory from another then amounts to distinguishing one curve that decreases from around 1.0 to 0.0 from another one that does the same thing, but with a somewhat different detailed shape.

There are two problems with trying to distinguish hypotheses by fitting one or another of such lines to the data. First, the data themselves have a very large variation from study to study. If one takes the observed correlations of IQ in various studies, say from the summary given by Erlenmeyer-Kimling and Jarvik, most actual data are, in fact, more variable than the variation among the hypotheses that are to be distinguished. The second problem is summarized in the well known statisticians aphorism 'Give me three parameters and I will draw an elephant; give me four and I will make it walk'. That is, with a sufficient number of undetermined parameters to be estimated from a limited supply of data *any* hypothesis can be validated because curves of almost any shape can be generated.

An example of this sort of mystification is an explicit mathematical model of Eaves (1973) that is claimed to show an excellent fit to the observed data on IQ correlations for relatives separated by various numbers of generations. The predicted correlation of IQ scores, r_n, of relatives separated by $n + 1$ generations from their common ancestor is given by:

$$r_n = c_1 c_2 \left(\frac{1 + A}{2}\right)^n + \tfrac{1}{2}(n + 1)\, A\, (n - 1)\, c_2\, (1 - c_2).$$

where c_1 is heritability in the broad sense, c_2 is the fraction of the genetic variance that is additive, and A is the genotypic correlation between mates. Evaluation of these quantities requires separate estimates of environmental variation within and between families, an estimate of genotypic assortative mating (even though nothing is known about the genetics of the trait!) and an estimate of additive and non-additive components of genetic variance. Since no data exist for the separate estimates, all that could be done was to fit the entire three parameter equation to the data to draw the elephant. The reader may note that the equation has exactly the general form discussed above, namely that the predicted correlation falls off exponentially with relationship, with a slope that is a complicated expression of three unknown parameters.

Other complicated methods look very different, but are essentially the same. Thus, path coefficient theories that attempt to estimate the influence of a dozen variables of the genotype and environment on each other and on IQ must make use of a collection of heterogeneous studies of relative and foster families, gathered over many years, by many investigators using different tests and different populations. It is absurd to think that the numbers that come from such models have any meaning.

13. The social implications

The conceptual errors that have been propagated in the field of IQ studies come together to press home a single major theme. They form a kind of syllogism as follows:

1. We live in a world of limited resources in which there will always be a race to get ahead of others (error 11).
2. IQ tests measure something that is the cause of success in the race (error 9).
3. IQ has a high heritability (error 4).
4. IQ is thus, fixed and not malleable (error 2),
   from which it follows that:
5. Differences between social class and races are heritable and unchangeable (errors 2, 3, and 9).

It is, of course, the last line of the 'syllogism' that is the bottom line of the social accounting. The message is that we are essentially fixed both in the form of our social organization and in the roles that we and our children will play in that social structure. Therefore, social policy that attempts to change either the structure or the assignment of groups to it is misdirected, a waste of time, and even harmful because it raises hopes that are bound to be dashed. It is essentially an argument for the inevitability and justice of the status quo. It is fairly obvious who the argument serves.

Appendix. Textbooks

There is no better way to grasp the general attitudes and deep assumptions current in a field than to look at its textbooks. They are not simply technical treatises that provide objective knowledge sufficient to make a new generation of scholars mechanically competent at their trade. In what they emphasize, leave out, discuss and then minimize as unessential or misinterpret, textbooks create the shape of a field for students by telling them what to believe and by directing their attention toward some issues and away from others. In addition to their didactic function of defining a field for a coming cohort, they consolidate and legitimize the attitudes and practices of the current scholarly community. In the very writing down and publishing of an overview of a field, scholars reinforce their own theory and practice. Textbooks then tell us which bits of objective knowledge and modes of interpretation are given serious consideration by practitioners, and which have come to be ignored or submerged in general practice. So, for example, as we will discuss in more detail below, many textbooks of genetics up to about 1950 placed emphasis on the relation between genotype, environment, and phenotype (e.g. Sinnott *et al*. 1950), but beginning in the 1950s with the rise of molecular genetics, DNA became the sole determiner of phenotype. It is not that facts have been discovered or new interpretations found to have much greater explanatory power (indeed, the opposite is true) but that they have, for various reasons, gone out of fashion. These older facts and concepts universally agreed to be correct, often contradict the fashionable view, showing it to be false. So they are ignored and denied and thus pass out of the collective consciousness of the field. They become skeletons in the intellectual closet, evidence of the wilful murder of the truth, that is ignored or suppressed by all the interested parties.

To illustrate how various errors about intelligence and heredity become propagated and even respectable, we have carried out an analysis of the treatment of genotype and phenotype, quantitative genetics, and intelligence in 11 textbooks (Cavalli-Sforza and Bodmer 1971; Falconer 1981; Fuller and Thompson 1960; Kempthorne 1957; Penrose 1963; Spiess 1977; Srb *et al*. 1965; Stern 1973; Sutton 1965; Wittinghill 1965; Wright 1968). These were virtually all written by prominent research scientists in various fields of genetics, including some of the most eminent scientists of the day. They include textbooks of general genetics, population genetics, human genetics, and quantitative genetics. In level, they run from texts for beginning college students, including non-specialists, to an extremely mathematical text for advanced graduate students. While hardly exhaustive, they seem a fair representation of what is being presented as the central and essential knowledge in genetic textbooks pertinent to an understanding of heredity in relation to intelligence.

When examined in the light of classical knowledge in genetics, development, and statistics, the texts have some remarkable features.

1. The universality of genetic causation

All of the books take the proper sphere of genetics to be the way in which genes are transmitted, how they work, and of what they are constructed. No matter what the *character*, the emphasis is on the gene so that the student gets the definite impression that genes are the primary causal agents in all characters. The possibility that important human variation is not genetically based is simply not considered. Thus, Stern (1973, p. 1) writes:

The study of human inheritance is concerned with the existence of 'inborn' characteristics of human beings: physical and mental, normal and abnormal . . . it is largely a study of hereditary similarities and differences among human beings. It is concerned with the causes of these similarities and differences and the way in which they are transmitted from generation to generation.

At first sight, it seems reasonable that a genetics text should be concerned with genetic differences. But a moment's further thought convinces us that the demonstration that some characters have *no* genetic variation is just as relevant for genetics. In its broadest sense the problem of genetics is to understand how genes enter into the causation of organisms, and this must *necessarily* include an understanding of when they do not. Textbooks of genetics take it as an undiscussed *a priori* that all characters are influenced directly by genes, although some may also be influenced by environment. Cavalli-Sforza and Bodmer write that: 'characters such as anthropometrics and IQ, which must represent the sum of a large number of separate effects, *both genetic and environmental*, should be normally distributed' [emphasis added], and that in general: *Phenotypic variation in a quantitative character is the result of a combination of genetic and environmental effects*' [emphasis in the original], and: 'Most traits of social importance are *determined* by a large number of genes and strongly *influenced* by environmental factors' [emphasis added].

2. The neglect of development

Not one of the 11 books examined contained a reference to the norm of reaction, nor did any have a chapter devoted to what is known about the relation between genotype, environment, and phenotype. The general textbooks did have chapters on developmental genetics, but these were devoted exclusively to a discussion of how *genes* affect development or even cause it. Genes are regarded as the causes of organisms, although environment may sometimes modulate the genetic effect. In other words, the authors fail to emphasize the essential lack of symmetry between genes and environment or rather between genes and development. So Falconer writes: 'The property of "variable expression" assumes great importance and might be raised to the status of another premiss: that the expression of the genotype in the phenotype is modifiable by non-genetic causes'. One wonders what the reaction of geneticists would be to the symmetrical statement, 'that the expression of the environment in the phenotype is modifiable by genetic causes'! The only discussion that comes close to hinting at the norm of reaction is on pp. 521–2 of Cavalli-Sforza and Bodmer under the rubric '*Interactions between the genotype and environmental factors may be very important for the interpretation of quantitative inheritance*'. It should be pointed out, however, that in a later book on human genetics and evolution, Bodmer and Cavalli-Sforza give considerably more attention to the interaction between genotype and environment and include several examples of norms of reaction.

3. An attempt to assign a relative 'importance' to genes and environment in 'determining' traits

The fact that one can perform an analysis of variance and thus separate out, tautologically, a genetic and an environmental component of variance, although neither component, in fact, isolates causes of variation leads even the most sophisticated textbook writers, despite their own caution against it, to talk about the relative weight to be attached to genes and environment. This partition is sometimes even applied to individuals!

From these two studies it appears that the causes which lead a person to only one criminal offense are less dependent on his genotype – and more on non-genetic 'chance' – than those which make him a chronic criminal. (Stern, p. 723)

. . . Environment does not predominate in the causation of schizophrenia . . . (Cavalli-Sforza and Bodmer, p. 623)

An interesting study taking a somewhat different tack . . . has also tended to favor the importance of hereditary over environmental factors. (Fuller and Thompson, p. 195)

In the first place the resemblance in intelligence appears to depend in most populations more on hereditary than environmental or experiential factors. (Fuller and Thompson, p. 198)

4. A confusion between 'intelligence' and IQ

Most books use the words interchangeably as if the performance in an IQ test were intelligence. Others are more explicit in asking the question whether IQ tests measure something called intelligence. Fuller and Thompson accept the reification of the 'g' factor by Spearman saying that 'if two traits or abilities vary together, they have something in common'. This confusion between correlation and common cause has been analysed above as error number 9. Srb *et al.* simply state that 'the best and most usable measures of intelligence so far available are the IQ (*intelligence quotient*) ratings devised by psychologists' (p. 521). Even the very circumspect and sophisticated Cavalli-Sforza and Bodmer refer to such tests as 'measures of intelligence' (p. 548). It follows that reification of intelligence as an internal, intinsic property or capacity of the organism is frequent. Stern speaks of 'the endowment of persons' (pp. 770, 776). Srb *et al.* (p. 521) say that:

While I.Q.'s are not considered wholly reliable or all-inclusive measures of 'innate' intelligence, they represent a fairly reproducible estimate of capacity for some kinds of rational behavior.

5. Heritability estimates are assumed to indicate how changeable or malleable a trait is

This complete error in the understanding of the meaning of heritability, despite repeated disavowals on the part of many authors (including A. Jensen!) is universal with the exception of Cavalli-Sforza and Bodmer, who alone of all authors deny any such relationship. Thus:

the author speculates on the basis of heritability estimates that possibly good art students are born whereas mathematicians, engineers, and statisticians are made by training. If true this conclusion is an important one. (Fuller and Thompson, p. 202) they (heritability estimates) may be useful as indicators of the effects to be expected from various types of intervention programs. (Spiess, p. 228)

in the case of human population, estimates of heritability (and non-heritability) are useful as indicators of the traits that are most likely to respond to environmental manipulation. (Sutton, p. 358)

6. Models of various degrees of complexity are taken seriously even though the assumptions are violated

Textbooks seem to be engaged more in playing a game of fixed rules rather than in attempting to assess the contingent truth about quantitative characters. Stern, for example, gives serious consideration to an absurd and untestable model for the inheritance of IQ involving a single locus with a major dominant allele for 'mediocrity' and six modifier loci each with two alleles. He also discusses the possibility that IQ has not declined because a single over-dominant gene has resulted in an equilibrium, even though Bajema had shown ten years before (work quoted by Stern!) that there is no negative correlation between IQ and fertility. Spiess uses an estimate of heritability from twin studies that depends crucially on MZ and DZ twins having the same degree of environmental similarity. Kempthorne uses extremely complex models for estimation of variance components when the assumption of environmental correlation are clearly violated. In general textbooks give the impression of grasping at any data that can be plugged into equations and models to exemplify them. Genetics is then turned from a study of the real and contingent world into a branch of mathematics without any roots in material reality.

6. Genetic studies of IQ scores: asking irrelevant questions

The social scientist is trained to think that he does not know all the answers. The social scientist is not trained to realize that he does not know all the questions. And that is why his social influence is not unfailingly constructive. (L.J. Cronbach 1975)

In this chapter, we shall attempt to give the reader a general view of the genetic studies of IQ scores. Rather than presenting a catalogue of these studies, which might be obsolete soon after being published, we shall try to provide a general framework for the evaluation of such studies. As was emphasized in the introduction to this book, the way in which a question is formulated should not be taken for granted. Specifically, we shall examine the discrepancies between the limited questions which genetic studies of IQ scores *could* answer and the broader questions which have been associated with such studies.

Our goal in writing this chapter has been to provide the reader with a key to the literature on nature–nurture and IQ. By focusing on general principles rather than on any particular study, we hope to help the reader in her or his assessment not only of the current literature but also of future studies and reviews. Such an assessment should include both technical and social considerations. For this assessment, the clarifications presented in the previous chapter will turn out to prove of crucial importance.

As a leading thread through the maze of publications, we shall propose the following approach: concentrate on the questions rather than on the answers. In other words, we shall try to clarify what the various questions have been, rather than argue about the extent to which these questions have been answered. We shall first situate the genetic analysis of IQ scores within the more general area of genetics and point out the intrinsic difficulties of a genetic study of human behaviour. We shall then concentrate our attention on the phenomena revealed by an analysis of IQ scores rather than on the models that have been proposed to account for these phenomena.

According to Mendel's theory, it is not traits that are transmitted from one generation to the next but 'factors', which were later called genes. Even in the simplest case, a trait is associated with two factors, one coming from each parent. This two-factor theory elegantly explains through a single mechanism two apparently contradictory facts: the resemblance and the difference observed between parents and offspring. In the classic example of Mendel's peas, a cross between two similarly looking individuals can lead to offspring similar to the two parents; it can also lead to individuals unlike both parents.

We now know that genes are located on chromosomes, which indeed come in pairs, one provided by each parent. The understanding of the molecular structure of the genes was an important step towards the analysis of the chain of causality from the genes to some traits.

In short, the purpose of genetic research has been: (*a*) to establish the existence of genetic variability and to study this variability in various environments, (*b*) to understand the mechanisms of genetic transmission, and (*c*) to understand the chain of causes from genotype to phenotype.

How does human behavioural genetics, specifically the genetic study of IQ scores fit into this general scheme? Very poorly indeed. For several reasons, even the first part of that scheme has not yet been successful.

The first reason is our inability to make experiments, i.e. to manipulate human matings. In order to disentangle genetic factors from environmental ones, behaviour geneticists have had to rely on some rare natural events. Under favourable circumstances, adoption may provide such natural events, where the biological heritage is transmitted by one set of parents while the cultural heritage is independently transmitted by another.

The second reason is as follows. At the beginning of the century, when people were still intrigued by the elegant simplicity of Mendel's laws about recessive and dominant genes, attempts were made to find a gene for mental retardation, using the method of pedigree analysis. Except in the case of some rare diseases, no single gene could be associated with mental retardation. *A priori*, the failure to observe Mendelian ratios in the analysis of families can be attributed to any one of the following causes:

—There is no genetic variation.
—There is some genetic variation, but without any one to one correspondence between genotypes and phenotypes, in particular because of environmental variations.
—Whatever genetic variation is present is due to more than one locus.

The third hypothesis was proposed by Fisher in 1918. Although this possibility is usually the only one that is considered, it should be pointed out that it is only one of three possible hypotheses. In principle, that hypothesis can be tested. In order to do so, one would need to observe and analyse pairs of individuals that vary in their degree of similarity, both in terms of biological relationships and in terms of environmental relationships.

In reality, the genetic analysis of IQ scores has been plagued by three facts:

1. The numerical values reported for correlations between kins have been inconsistent, to say the least.

2. Most reviewers have compiled these correlations in a biased way (see appendix). These biased correlations have then been used in an uncritical manner. McAskie and Clarke (1976) have remarked that 'even Jencks' most sophisticated attempt failed to match an elaborate mathematical analysis with a commensurate attention to the nature of the data'.

3. The number of unknown parameters, both genetic and environmental, exceeds the number of independent observations. In fact, the most serious reason for the failure of the genetic analysis of IQ scores is our inability to control or evaluate in any quantitative manner the effect of environment. The term environment itself is somewhat inappropriate to the human situation. The terms social, cultural, and psychological *processes* would be more precise. In order to infer genetic differences, the effects of these processes must be eliminated by careful matching of what we shall call for short the environment. But this is more easily said than done.

Practically all builders of quantitative models imagine that they are keeping an open mind because they introduce both environmental and genetic parameters in a symmetric way into their model. But this built-in symmetry is precisely what makes the models unrealistic. Genetic parameters concern genotypes, i.e. static objects defined at conception. The environmental parameters, on the other hand, are supposed to represent environmental processes, i.e. an ordered sequence of events in time.

In order to detect an effect of one kind (genetic or 'environmental') one needs to control or evaluate completely the effects of the other kind. Thus, to isolate an 'environmental' effect, one needs to compare individuals of identical genotypes (true twins) or groups of individuals where the mean genotypic values have been equalized by randomization. To detect a genetic effect, on the other hand, is much more difficult because we generally do not know how to match environmental processes. This lack of symmetry between the detection of 'environmental' effects and the detection of genetic effects has been emphasized elsewhere, using the example of schizophrenia (Cassou *et al.* 1980; Schiff *et al.* 1981*a*).

As we shall see presently, the inability and unwillingness to cope with this third fact has characterized most of the research on the 'nature and nurture of intelligence' ever since it was initiated by Galton. Most research workers in that field have only paid lip service to one of the fundamental facts of life, namely the distinction between phenotype and genotype. This distinction has often been disregarded precisely in the area where it is most significant: namely human behaviour.

Even if the research workers had been willing to face this difficulty, it would have remained insurmountable in most cases. How are we to judge whether two 'environments' are indeed equivalent? The history of each human being is even more diversified than his genes, so that it is nearly impossible to match individual environments or to evaluate the effect of whatever differences in environments must be present.

There is actually one environmental variable that can be estimated with a fair degree of accuracy, so that its influence could have been studied. This variable is social class, a most unpopular one among behaviour geneticists. We will see that observations directly relevant to the issue of social heredity are remarkably scarce.

In our opinion, the traditional question of how environmental factors combine with genetic ones is based on an erroneous picture of human reality. In its most naïve form, the question is still being posed in the news media and in everyday conversations. Anyone working in the field is constantly being asked: 'Now tell me, is intelligence determined by heredity or by environment?'

There have been many technical refinements on this naïve question. The first refinement consists in pointing out that the question concerns variations of a trait around some average value rather than the trait itself. A second refinement consists in asking for the 'relative weight of nature and nurture' in these variations. A third refinement consists in recognizing that these two causes of variations do not act independently. A fourth refinement consists in recognizing the distinction between genetic variability and genetic transmission, i.e. between heritability in the broad sense and heritability in the narrow sense.

The essential point, however, is elsewhere. Despite all the refinements, the usual approach to the genetic analysis of IQ scores remains qualitatively inadequate and not simply imperfect. The reason for this inadequacy is the following.

If we may use a geometrical analogy, it is as if the builders of parametric models of IQ scores had decided to project a multi-dimensional universe onto a single axis called nature–nurture. One could hardly expect a one dimensional model to describe a multi-dimensional universe. We shall see that the situation is even worse: the models cannot even adequately account for a projection of the real world onto the single axis of nature–nurture.

In the present chapter, we shall examine some phenomena of the real world and their projections onto the nature–nurture axis. The three types of phenomena we shall examine are:

1. Individual variability
2. Familial transmission
3. Social heredity.

1. Individual variability

At the beginning of biological evolution, cells reproduced by simple division, one mother cell turning into two identical daughters. The rare variations produced by mutations were at a great disadvantage and could only survive if they happened to correspond to some large selective advantage. Later on, sexual reproduction developed as an efficient mechanism for maintaining genetic diversity. When two germinal cells contribute to the making of a new organism, the mutated form of a gene can be propagated along with the original form.

From a biological point of view, variability is the stuff of which genetics is made. Even if a trait were completely determined by a single gene locus, the corresponding gene could not be identified by the usual methods of genetic and molecular analysis unless it came in at least two varieties, whose transmission could be studied from one generation to the next. Another case when genetic analysis is impossible is when the genetic variation is masked by environmental variations.

To some extent, the expression 'individual variability' is tautological. An individual can only be identified as such if there is at least one unique feature or combination of features that is specific of that individual. Every human being, including members of a pair of monozygotic twins, thinks of herself or himself as unique. This is not simply a subjective feeling; it is based on the reality of a unique personal history.

However, the extent to which individual differences are perceived is largely subjective and culturally determined, as are the consequences that are drawn from the perceived differences. In some situations, the colour of your skin may have no more importance than the shape of your ears. In others, it may practically determine your place in society. To illustrate the relativity of our perception of individual differences, the following incident that occurred in the library of an American university may be of some interest. A woman of Asiatic origin was checking the library cards at the entrance of the library. A professor who had gone out of the library and come back was asked to show his library card. Slightly irritated at being asked his card for the second time, he asked the woman: 'Don't you recognize me? I showed you my card an hour ago'. She smiled at him and said: 'To you, all Asians look alike; to us, all White people look alike'.*

In order to give meaning to the exploration of genetic variations of IQ scores, one must first ask several questions, and obtain satisfactory answers. For the purpose of illustration, let us choose an example where the genetic determination of the variations is not in doubt, namely the case

---

* This event was reported to the first author by his wife. After this chapter had been written, he was amused to learn from Lewontin that he had previously reported a similar incident involving his own wife (Lewontin 1982).

of blood types. Suppose we combined the various blood types into a single number and used the value of this number to define a physical hierarchy between individuals. One could do this in a large number of ways, by assigning arbitrary scores to each of the blood groups (for instance: for the ABO group $O = 0$, $A = 1$, $B = 2$, $AB = 3$; for rhesus group $Rh^+ = 0$, $Rh^-= 1$ etc.). One could then define a blood quotient. By suitable choices of the individual scores, this quotient could be made to have a normal distribution, with a mean of 100 and a standard deviation of 15. This quotient would have a heritability in the broad sense of 100 per cent. Since the different human 'races' have rather different distributions in the various blood groups, it would be easy to define the scale of blood quotients in such a way that, on the average, White people had the highest blood quotient. In a society built around blood groups, validation studies would show the high predictive power of blood quotients.

One could object that a comparison with individual height would have been more relevant. However, the fact that a ranking can be defined is not a sufficient explanation of why that ranking has to be used to reward and punish individuals. Also, the comparison of IQ with height is misleading, because the metric properties of heights are natural, while those of IQ scores are entirely artificial. Whatever units are being used, heights can validly be added. If two men are five feet tall and one stands on top of the other, they can reach to a ten foot height. There is no corresponding operation for IQ scores. The association of two people with a score of 100 will not lead to performances that correspond to a score of 200 (whatever that score may mean).

The French geneticist Albert Jacquard (1984) has emphasized the fundamental distinction between difference and inequality. Two points are worth stressing concerning that distinction. From a purely mathematical point of view, differences between two individuals can be defined in a space with any number of dimensions (height, sex, number of teeth, age, etc.). Ranking, on the other hand, can only be defined in one dimension. In order to define a hierarchy between individuals, we therefore have to agree to a reductionist approach, where one trait is singled out for comparing individuals. The second point is that, even if we do rank individuals according to a trait like IQ score, there is no logical reason to use that same trait to define ranking *in another dimension* like wealth and income, or 'human worth', or even 'intelligence'.

The arbitrary nature of the IQ scale is rarely realized. Even if we took for granted the ranking of individuals that is built into any one-dimensional scale, the numerical values of scores and their distribution would still be arbitrary. The usual scores are defined by a correspondence with percentiles such that the distribution of scores is normal. By modifying the rules of this correspondence, one could obtain any distribution one liked.

If we thought of individual differences between humans in biological terms on an evolutionary scale, these differences would appear insignificant. On the scale of evolution between species, the difference between an IQ score of 96 and a score of 109 is microscopic. What is remarkable is the fact that it is precisely those people who can hardly see the difference between a rat and a man and who glibly extrapolate from one species to the next who give the greatest attention to these individual differences.

Genetic studies of IQ scores can provide no answer to questions about the significance of individual differences and about the consequences of these differences. The only questions that genetic studies of individual differences could possibly answer are

(a) Can we demonstrate the effect of genetic variability on the phenotype which we have defined as IQ score?

(b) Taking for granted the scale used for IQ scores and the society we live in, what fraction of the variance in IQ scores within a given group can be correlated to genetic variance?

If they were known, answers to the above questions would be of no biological, psychological, historical or social importance. Their relevance is purely ideological. Actually, these answers are not really known. As we are writing this chapter, in 1983, a hundred years after Galton published his book *Inquiries into human faculty and its development* (1883), answers to the above inconsequential questions are still widely controversial.

Without going into any detail, let us outline the principal methods that have been used in an attempt to analyse individual differences in IQ scores in terms of genetic variability (the study of genetic transmission will be outlined in the next section).

The most widely used method of analysing IQ scores has been to examine pairs of individuals with different sorts of relationships, both biological and psychological. A recent summary of such data is reproduced below, as it was presented in a recent review article (Plomin and de Fries, 1980). In this section and in the following, we shall examine the type of data presented in Fig. 6.1.

Plomin and de Fries present their figure in the following manner:

For didactic purposes, the new correlational data are summarized in terms of average absolute differences in Figure 1. It is possible to convert correlations into average differences if the standard deviation is known and if the variable is normally distributed. The relationship between correlations (r) and absolute average differences ($\bar{z}$) is: $\bar{z} = 1.13 \, \sigma \sqrt{1-r}$. Thus, for pairs of randomly selected individuals for whom the correlation is zero, the average IQ difference is 17 given a standard deviation of 15 for IQ.

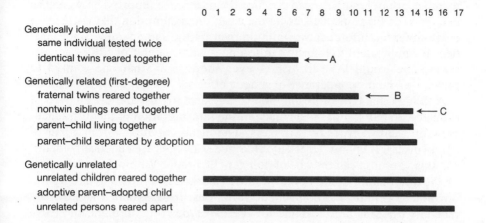

Fig. 6.1   Recent summary of IQ data expressed as average absolute differences in IQ points. The graph and the commentary are reproduced from Plomin and de Fries (1980). The arrows marked A, B, and C have been added by us.

Although the presentation chosen by the reviewers is unusual, it has two advantages. First of all, with such a presentation, it is easier to get an idea of the size of the various effects and the various uncertainties. Secondly, this form of presentation is closer to the observations that are being reported; the correlations *r* are *derived* from the variations in IQ scores. For instance, an absolute average difference of 10 IQ points corresponds to a correlation of 0.65; an average absolute difference of 17 points corresponds to a correlation of 0. To compare different types of pairs, we shall compare their average absolute differences. To avoid talking about differences between differences, we shall talk of differences between variations.

To a lay person, the most compelling proof of the existence of a genetic variability in IQ scores is the observation of pairs of siblings both living with their parents. Mothers will often say: 'I have raised them in the same way, and yet, see how different they are'. Actually, this parental intuition concerns temperament rather than IQ scores. More to the point, how can we know whether environmental differences between two siblings have a negligible effect?

To discuss the origin of variations between children of the same parents, let us consider the pairs marked B and C in Fig. 6.1 These two types of pairs correspond to identical genetic variations. Notice however the difference between ordinary pairs of sibs (marked C) and pairs of fraternal twins (marked B). Since the genetic variations are equal, this difference can only correspond to non-genetic causes. The small differences of being born together or not is sufficient to produce the difference reported between the two types of sib pairs. This being the case, the assumption that there is no environmental difference worth noting within the same family is not veri fied. If one wanted to interpret differences within a pair of sibs in genetic terms, one would have to *assume* even more than what one wanted to prove, i.e. the preponderance of genetic effects.

Although this type of assumption is not currently used in the analysis of ordinary sib pairs, it has been made in the interpretation of the differences between the two types of twin pairs. The mean variation within a pair of MZ twins is 6 IQ points (marked A). Since MZ twins are genetically identical, this variation can only be of non genetic origin. Within DZ twin pairs, on the other hand, the 10 point variation (marked B) is attributed to a combination of genetic and non genetic variations. If we *assume* that environmental variations are the same for the two types of twin pairs, the extra variation of DZ twins as compared to MZ twins can be attributed to the genetic variation within DZ pairs. But this is wishful thinking, just as in the case of sibs. Since Galton, the analysis of variations within pairs of related individuals has been vitiated by the idea that, if we don't think about environment, it will hardly bother us.

Before we turn to other kinds of pairs, we need to examine another type of cause for the lowering or raising of variations within certain types of pairs. By this we mean artefacts in the empirical observations and in the way they have been compiled by reviewers. Even in the physical sciences, the authority of previous observations or of theoretical expectations have sometimes led to an accumulation of biased observations. In the last century, for instance, the measurement of the speed of light has been subjected to such systematic biases. More recently, the number of human chromosomes was consistently reported to be 48; now, all observers report that number to be 46. An example of what Adair (1969) has called a 'bandwagon effect' is reproduced in Fig. 6.2.

The data used in the genetic analysis of IQ scores are subject to the same type of systematic biases. Let us look at the most common type of data, i.e. the correlations in IQ scores reported between various types of first degree relatives. In Table 6.1, we report three sets of such correlations. The first two sets were presented by Jensen (1969); the last set was presented by Plomin and de Fries (1980). In the first column we find correlations expected under the assumption of complete genetic determination in some theoretical model. In the second column we find corresponding empirical data. The agreement between the two sets of numbers is remarkable. A completely new set of data was compiled by Plomin and de Fries. The numbers reproduced in the third column were obtained in studies performed after 1969, i.e. after Jensen's review. The comparison between the three sets of correlations is a testimony of the power of biases in obser-

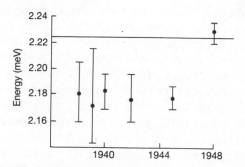

Fig. 6.2 The 'bandwagon effect' on the estimate of a physical quantity.
Measured value of the binding energy of the deuteron plotted against the time of
publication of the result. The solid line represents the currently accepted value.
(From Adair 1969).

Table 6.1 *Correlation of IQ scores reported for first degree relatives*

	Theoretical values computed by Jensen[a]	Empirical values compiled by Jensen[b]	New empirical values compiled by Plomin and de Fries
Children of the same parents			
DZ pairs of different sex	0.50	0.49	0.62[c]
DZ pairs of the same sex	0.54	0.56	0.62[c]
Ordinary siblings	0.52	0.55	0.34[d]
Parent child			
Parent (as adult) and child	0.49	0.50	0.35[e]

[a] Assuming assortative mating and partial dominance.

[b] Median values.

[c] Based on two extensive new studies; a value of 0.61 was obtained by Loehlin and Nichols (1976) from 18 twin studies with sample size greater than 25.

[d] Weighted average correlation for four recent studies.

[e] Weighted average correlation for five recent studies.

vations and/or in compilations. Evidence of artefacts due solely to
reviewers are presented in the appendix.

We are now ready to consider the study of separated twins. The effect of
environmental variance can be isolated either by matching genetic variance
or by eliminating it. The elimination of genetic variance in an individual
pair can only be achieved with monozygotic twins. The ordinary situation
where twins are reared in the same family is not very informative, since
there is also very little environmental variation, and of a very special sort.
Only twins reared apart can allow us to make an estimate of significant
environmental differences between individuals (the differences between

groups will be considered in the third section). In the general population, the variance observed within pairs of individuals picked at random stems from both genetic and environmental variance. Under appropriate circum stances, pairs of identical twins could allow one to isolate the environmental components of the variance within pairs of individuals.

Let us imagine an ideal experiment on separated twins, each member of a pair being placed at birth in an environment uncorrelated to his family of origin. The total variance in the population of twins would be a sum of the genetic variance (between pairs of twins) and of the environmental variance (within pairs of twins). By subtracting the variance within pairs from the total variance, one would obtain an estimate of the genetic variance. When this is done with pairs of monozygotic twins observed in real studies of separated twins (as opposed to ideal or imaginary studies) the environmental variance is grossly underestimated. In real studies, there have been three types of artefacts, each one equivalent to a spurious genetic effect.

The first source of bias stems from the correlation between the families raising the twins of a given pair. As has been stressed by Kamin (1974), the families were often related to the twins and to one another. The social and geographical proximity of these families is often striking (for a table of all twin pairs reared 'apart', see Schiff *et al.* 1981*b*, pp. 94–5). A second artefact comes from the improper age standardization of the tests used. The similarity in age within a pair of twins introduces a spurious correlation between the IQ scores. The third and most important source of bias comes from the manner in which the subjects have been ascertained and chosen. The samples have been very biased indeed. On the one hand, the subjects were self selected. On the other hand, the pairs who did not consider themselves to be identical twins were eliminated by the investigators, *without being tested*. Here is another example of the importance of the distinction between genotypes and phenotypes. When one is trying to compare fraternal twins to monozygotic twins, the use of subjective judgement to distinguish the types of pairs is reasonably reliable, although slightly biased. In the case of separated twins, this procedure insures the exclusion of dissimilar twins. Photographs of identical twins who look identical in spite of the separation have been widely publicized. But no conclusion can be drawn from these pictures since the pairs were required to look alike in order to participate in the study. In view of the above biases, it is difficult to predict how the within pair variance of monozygotic twins placed in random families would compare to the total variance.

Before we end this section on individual variation, one more type of study needs to be mentioned, namely the study of the effect of inbreeding. Inbreeding corresponds to the mating between relatives. The most common cases that have been studied are those of second degree relatives (marriage between cousins) and of first degree relatives (cases of incest).

The offspring of cousins have been of interest to human geneticists studying rare diseases for the following reason. In the population at large some rare unfavourable genes are present. These genes only manifest themselves when they happen to be passed on by both parents at the same time. Such coincidences occur much more frequently when the parents are related. Hence, it has been a standard practice of human geneticists to look at the offspring of cousins to identify rare recessive genes.

This procedure has sometimes been extended to IQ scores. An average loss of one or two points has been reported for the children of cousin marriages. The genetic interpretation of the observation, however, is doubly ambiguous. On the one hand, it may be indicative of the presence of genes which play no significant role in the offspring of ordinary matings because they are both recessive and rare. On the other hand, the effect observed could be entirely due to psychological factors. The fact of inbreeding is not simply a genetic phenomenon, it is also a psychological one.

In conclusion, not only do genetic studies fail to answer any of the crucial questions concerning individual variability, but they lead to a genetic interpretation of that variability only to the extent that one is willing to neglect the possibility of psychological effects. As was emphasized by Newman *et al.* (1937) 'the soundness of the estimate rests on the correctness of the assumptions'.

2. Familial transmission

Children resemble their parents and children of the same family resemble each other. In the case of behaviour, the interpretation of these resemblances is totally ambiguous. This ambiguity has been formulated in a humorous way by the authors of an adoption study of schizophrenia (Wender *et al.* 1968):

Inspecting these data, we are in a position analogous to that of a naïve observer who has found an increased prevalence of red hair and talking Chinese, respectively, in the relatives of redheaded and Chinese-speaking probands; without further knowledge, this observer could not ascertain the mechanism of transmission of these characteristics.

The systematic study of the resemblance between relatives was initiated by Galton. In the preface of a book describing this type of research, he wrote (Galton 1869):

I began by thinking over the dispositions and achievements of my contemporaries at school, at college, and in after life, and was surprised to find how frequently ability seemed to go by descent.

Later in the book, Galton expresses his impatience at the idea that ability might be acquired by training. As a proof of the natural character of ability, he mentions the fact that each man soon hits his own natural limits.

It is clear from his writings that Galton did not distinguish between four different concepts:

Concept 1 The familial transmission of a trait.
Concept 2 The biological mechanisms that might influence that transmission.
Concept 3 The innate character of a trait.
Concept 4 The degree to which a trait can be changed by training.

In other words, Galton confused familiality with narrow heritability, with broad heritability, with heritability between groups and with a lack of educability. These confusions are still common. From a social point of view, the analysis of family transmission has been used to denigrate the 'lower races' and the 'inferior' groups. It has also been used to advocate eugenic proposals for the preservation of the 'élite' and to support conservative social and educational policies.

The first American version of the Binet test contained the following comments (Terman 1916, cited by Kamin 1974):

. . . in the near future intelligence tests will bring tens of thousands of these high-grade defectives under the surveillance and protection of society. This will ultimately result in curtailing the reproduction of feeble-mindedness and in the elimination of an enormous amount of crime, pauperism, and industrial inefficiency. It is hardly necessary to emphasize that the high-grade cases, of the type now so frequently overlooked, are precisely the ones whose guardianship it is most important for the State to assume.

In the 1920s, IQ tests were used to advocate restrictions on the immigration of 'inferior races', both in England (Pearson and Moul, 1925) and in the United States (Yerkes 1921).

The results of IQ tests have also been used to develop a modern version of the fear of the 'yellow peril'. The 'inferior groups', so the argument ran, were outbreeding the better ones. Typical of this IQ scare is a statement by one of the leading psychometricians. In his book, *The fight for our national intelligence*, R.B. Cattell (1937) wrote:

We have to bear in mind that a real deterioration of our race is going on here and now, day by day, hour by hour . . . An organizing headquarters for grappling with this enormous, spreading evil already exists in the Eugenics Society: let us hope one will soon arise in the Government of our country.

Meanwhile, another government was taking action to combat the 'deterioration of our race'. It is interesting to note that Nazi eugenists did not seem overly concerned with IQ tests. In the 1940 issue of a scientific journal, for instance, Konrad Lorenz advocated the following procedure for eugenic selection (quoted by Eisenberg 1972):

The racial idea as the basis of our state has already accomplished much in this respect . . . The most effective race-preserving measure is . . . the greatest support of the natural defenses. We must – and should – rely on the healthy feelings of our Best and charge them with the selection which will determine the prosperity or the decay of our people.

After the 1940s, eugenics seemed to go out of fashion, and the *Annals of Eugenics* quietly changed its title to *Annals of Human Genetics*. More recently, the *Eugenics Quarterly* changed its title to *Social Biology*. With a few notable exceptions, eugenic ideology became covert rather than overt. Three of these exceptions are worth noting here.

In an invited paper presented at the Third International Congress of Human Genetics, a Nobel laureate made a proposal for positive eugenic action through artificial insemination (Muller 1966). Another laureate proposed the sterilization of low IQ men (Shockley, as quoted in *Science* 1980). McKusick's proposal for giving prolific university professors tax privileges was mentioned in Chapter 2.

Herrnstein's statements about the 'Specter of Meritocracy' and about a future where 'the tendency to be unemployed may run in the genes of a family about as certainly as the IQ does now' can be considered as an updated version of the eugenicist's IQ scare. Like other authors quoted, Herrnstein did not seem to be aware of the distinction between the various types of heritability coefficients.

In 1969, exactly 100 years after the publication of Galton's book quoted above, Jensen appeared to be confusing broad heritability (with an alleged value of 0.8), with narrow heritability and with heritability between groups. With Jensen, the concern over the inferior specimens of mankind turned from eugenics to education. He appeared to confuse heritability with a lack of educability.

Not only did the authors mentioned above apear to make some fundamental errors in their use of genetic concepts, but they also failed to distinguish between scientific questions and social ones. Discussions about our species involve questions of values as well as questions of facts. Nevertheless, let us see briefly what facts have been uncovered by a century of research on the familial transmission of 'ability'.

The majority of studies of familial transmission have consisted simply in an estimate of the resemblances between relatives in ordinary families (as opposed to adoptive ones). Most of these studies concern the resemblance between parents and offspring or between siblings. The results of these extensive efforts have been disappointing. They show that Mendel's ratios do not apply, they also show that the resemblance between relatives decreases as the degree of relationship decreases. The first result shows that IQ scores do not correspond to a single gene locus; or if they do, the genetic effects are masked by the environmental ones. The second result is consistent with a polyfactorial genetic transmission as well as with a cultural one.

In a recent review of 'familial studies of intelligence', Bouchard and McGue (1981) reported no less than 43 correlation values for parent–offspring resemblance and 69 values for sibling resemblance. Thus, on the average one 'familial study of intelligence' has been published every year since Galton's book on hereditary genius. Since these studies provide essentially no genetic information, one can wonder why society has paid scientists to repeat essentially the same observation for so long.

Historically, the first approach to genetic transmission was indirect. This indirect approach consists of studying the resemblance between unrelated individuals living in similar environments. Five studies reported correlations much lower for adoptive families than for ordinary families (Burks 1928; Leahy 1935; Fisch et al. 1976; Scarr and Weinberg 1978; Horn et al. 1979). Two other studies reported correlations as high as in ordinary families (Freeman et al. 1928; Skodak 1950). Sims (1931) reported a sizeable correlation between unrelated children matched for various environmental variables (but living in *different* families).

Apart from the methodological problems involved, the interpretation of these studies in genetic terms poses the same type of dilemmas as the studies already reviewed. Let us assume that the variation within adoptive families really was one or two points higher than in ordinary families. Should the corresponding extra variance be attributed to the increase in genetic variation or to some increase in psychological variation? Let us note that this hypothetical increase in psychological variance would be smaller than the observed environmental effect manifested by the comparison between sibs and fraternal twins (see Fig. 6.1).

By studying unrelated individuals living in similar environments, the authors just quoted tried to estimate the amount of cultural transmission. Anyone interested in the *genetic* transmission of a trait, however, must do what geneticists have been doing since Mendel: observe how offspring resemble their parents, in a manner that is not masked by environmental effects. In the case of IQ scores, this entails a study of the resemblance between parents and children abandoned at an early age and placed early in an adoptive family uncorrelated to the biological one. Alternatively, one could study the resemblance between sibs placed in uncorrelated environments.

In his extensive analysis of correlation data, Jencks (1972) reports on sibs reared apart in the following way:

In light of the fact that siblings reared apart are far more common than identical twins, and the fact that the correlations among siblings reared apart tell us nearly as much as the correlations among twins reared apart, it is both surprising and unfortunate that we do not have better data on such siblings. The two American studies are almost useless for our purposes. Freeman et al., in 'Influence of Environment', worked with a sample which included some children who were not separated until the age of 6. Hildreth's sample, described in 'The Resemblance of Siblings', shows a very restricted range of test scores. Burt gives no details on his English sample, but many of the separations may well have been quite late. In light of these difficulties, we have not tried to analyze this data.

We shall follow Jencks in his last statement, but would like to clarify the first one. Indeed, separated siblings must be far more common than separated monozygotic twins. But monozygotic twins tell us nothing about genetic transmission. Even when reared apart, monozygotic twins always have the same sex, and yet sex is not heritable (narrow heritability zero).

In this connection, it is worth noting the title chosen by Burt (1966) to report on his twin study: 'The genetic determination of differences in intelligence: a study of monozygotic twins reared together and apart'. Contrary to what that title implies, the observation of identical twins cannot provide direct information on the effect of genetic differences, since there is no genetic difference within an MZ pair. At best, MZ pairs can provide information on *non-genetic differences*. In short, the correlation among sibs reared apart would not tell us 'nearly as much as the correlation among (identical) twins reared apart'; they would tell us something completely different: instead of analysing non-genetic differences, one would be analysing genetic transmission.

Data directly relevant to genetic transmission have been reported in three studies (Snygg 1938; Skodak and Skeels 1949; Horn et al. 1979). Correlations were reported between the IQ scores of biological mothers and the scores of their children who had been placed in foster or adoptive homes. In no study were the fathers tested.

In the first study, the correlation of IQ scores estimated from 312 mother–child pairs was reported to be 0.13. In the second, the correlation based on 63 pairs was reported to be 0.38 or 0.44, depending on the test used. In the third study, the authors reported on 345 pairs. Using a complex mathematical analysis, the authors obtained a correlation of 0.31. When they used a different and more direct approach, however, the genetic effect disappeared. Horn et al. (1979) write:

Insofar as the method is applicable at all, however, it suggests a heritability of
IQ that is close to zero – the two groups of children show little or no difference
in average IQ. This result is inconsistent with that of a correlational analysis, to
be reported below, so that a second look at the assumptions underlying it is in
order. Two major possibilities suggest themselves. One is there may be little
difference in the genetic potential of the adoptive and biological parents. The
other is that the assumptions about equality of children's environments may be
wrong.

The 'two major possibilities' which Horn *et al.* (1979) considered in trying to resolve an apparent contradiction did not include the possibility that
the error could lie with the complex approach rather than with the simple
one. If genetic models do not work, blame the environment.

In this section on familial transmission, we have considered the three
possible approaches. In the first one, namely the study of ordinary families,
the genetic and cultural transmission are entirely confounded. In the
second approach, namely the study of unrelated individuals living
together, the authors tried to analyse cultural transmission. The only direct
estimate of genetic transmission comes from the third type of study: the
analysis of the resemblance between biological mothers and their adopted
children.

The data on familial transmission corresponding to the three approaches
discussed above have been summarized in Fig. 6.3. As was done in
Fig. 6.1, we have plotted here the absolute difference in IQ points
obtained in each of the three approaches. The central part of the figure corresponds to the usual family studies, where the genetic transmission is confounded with the cultural one. In the top part are presented the values
reported in the only three studies having attempted to isolate genetic transmission. In the bottom part are presented the values reported by the
studies having attempted to isolate cultural transmission.

Let us first consider the studies designed to isolate the effect of cultural
transmission. In one study (11) the intra-pair variance is as small as for DZ
twins reared together. In three studies, this variance is the same for unrelated persons reared together as for first degree relatives reared together
(8, 12, 7). These results would point to a purely environmental hypothesis.
In one study, on the contrary (13), the intra-pair variance is as large for
adopted sibs living together as for unrelated people living apart, as would
be expected from a purely genetic hypothesis. Results consistent with all
intermediate hypothesis have also been reported (6, 9, 10, 13, 14). These
results are clearly inconclusive. As pointed out above, they would be inconclusive even if they were all consistent with one of the results reported in
study 13. Such results could be interpreted in genetic terms only through the
usual faulty logic of neglecting possible environmental differences. The difference in intra-pair variation when genetic variation is the same (the dif-

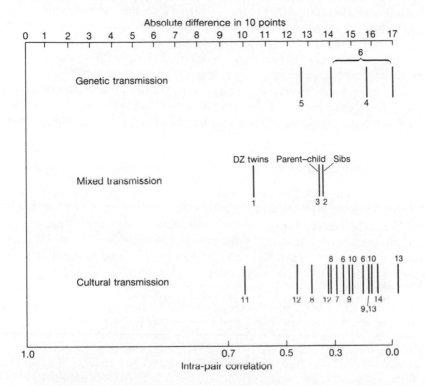

Fig. 6.3 Familial transmission. Mean absolute variation in IO scores within pairs. The data are presented as average IQ differences within pairs of individuals. These are closer to the direct observations than the more usual correlation values, which are derived from these differences. The data are inconsistent and inconclusive (see text).

Sources: 1, 2, 3, Plomin and de Fries (1980); 4, Snygg (1938); 5, Skodak and Skeels (1949); 6, Horn *et al.* (1979); 7, Sims (1931); 8, Freeman *et al.* (1928); 9, Burks (1928); 10, Leahy (1935); 11, Skodak (1950); 12, Scarr and Weinberg (1977*b*); 13, Scarr and Weinberg (1978); 14, Fisch *et al.* (1976)

ference between 1 and 2) should serve as a reminder against this faulty logic.

Let us now consider the studies designed to isolate the effect of genetic transmission. Although only four values have been reported, these are inconsistent with one another, and therefore inconclusive. The result reported in study 5 is consistent with a genetic hypothesis, as is one of the results reported in study 6; the other result reported in study 6 is consistent with a purely environmental hypothesis; the result reported in study 4 is also consistent with an evironmental hypothesis.

The fact that the study reporting the highest value for genetic transmission (Skodak and Skeels, 1949) is also the one reporting large effects for a change in environment should serve as a reminder of the limited social relevance of heritability coefficients.

After one century of research on familial transmission, the scientific results are inconclusive to say the least. The issue raised by the major authors have been eugenic action and educational policy. The questions raised by eugenics are social and ethical rather than scientific. As to educability, it has no factual connections with heritability, only ideological ones.

3. Social heredity

At the beginning of Chapter 2, data were presented on the correlation of the social class of parents with the intellectual status of their children. This correlation is equally large, whether this status is defined by the relative ranking in primary school or by the relative ranking on IQ tests. Without any supporting data, Terman et al. (1917) were quick to attribute this correlation to the quality of parental genes:

That the children of the superior social classes do better in the tests is almost certainly due primarily to superior original endowment. This conclusion is supported by five supplementary lines of evidence: (a) the teachers' rankings of the children according to intelligence, (b) the age–grade progress of the children, (c) the quality of the school work, (d) the comparison of older and younger children as regards the influence of social environment, (e) the study of individual cases of bright and dull children in the same family.

We leave it to the reader to decide which of the 12 errors listed in the previous chapter Terman et al. did not make.

We shall now examine how the correlation of the social class of parents with the IQ scores of their children has been analysed in genetic and non-genetic terms. As we have done in the case of individual variability and familial transmission, we must first emphasize that this type of analysis begs the essential questions. In the case of social heredity, the reproduction of social inequality from one generation to the next is not limited to IQ scores. The social class of parents also correlates with unequal access to education, to employment, to housing, to health care, to food, and to money, to name only a few of the important facts of social heredity.

The relevance of the social heredity of IQ scores to the issue of unequal access to education has been examined in detail in Chapter 4. When unequal access to higher education is expressed in terms of educational waste, the analysis of the social heredity of IQ scores in genetic and non-genetic terms becomes essentially irrelevant. One could of course choose to assume that upper-middle-class parents transmit to their children not only genes for higher IQ scores but also genes favouring behaviours relevant to education. As was pointed out in Chapter 4, this would be pure fantasy, for lack of relevant data. The remarkable fact is that, with very few exceptions, adoption studies have concentrated on the variable furthest removed from social status, namely IQ scores. Authors of adoption studies have shown little interest in the influence of social class on the educational status of adoptees, to say nothing of their professional and financial status. In that context, the study of Skeels (1966) is an outstanding exception; in that study adopted children who had started life with developmental quotients in the sixties had become self-supporting adults leading a normal family life.

Let us imagine for a moment that we did know the environmental and genetic components of the correlation of the social class of parents with the IQ scores of their children. This would give us no information whatsoever on the following questions:

(a) Why are wealth and income distributed the way they are?
(b) In present societies, what is the influence of the social class of parents on the economic status of their children?

For whatever they are worth, let us now examine the studies where authors have tried to analyse the influence of the social class of parents on the IQ scores of their children.

From Galton to Eysenck, the facts of social heredity have been given a biological interpretation, based on the studies reviewed in the preceding sections. Even if these studies did provide valid estimates of the heritability of IQ (broad and narrow), these estimates would be of no relevance to the differences between groups of children of contrasted social origins. As has been emphasized several times in this book, differences *between* groups could be due to social effects, even if differences *within* groups were completely correlated with genetic differences. In fact, no author to our knowledge has dared to use heritability coefficients to answer Richardson's question about the effect of a change of social class in a quantitative manner. This is not surprising, since it cannot be done. What is more surprising is the scarcity of studies on the social heredity of IQ scores.

On the environmental side, a study of the effect of the social class of rearing would require the comparison between children of identical or equivalent genotypes reared in contrasted social classes. To illustrate the irrelevance of existing twin studies for the analysis of social heredity, we have examined the contrast in social class reported in studies of separated twins. This contrast has been compared to the contrast in social class reported in the adoption study described in Chapter 3. As can be seen from Table 6.2 this adoption study contains at least 10 times more information

Table 6.2 *Number of contrasted pairs in four published studies on 'separated' twins*[a]

	Newman *et al.* (1937) Shields (1962) Juel-Nielsen (1965)	Burt (1966)
Number of pairs	68	53
Number of pairs raised in families unrelated to one another	30	53 (?)
Of which were placed for adoption prior to 6 months	4	53 (?)
And where the contrast in socio-professional categories is as large as in the adoption study of Schiff *et al.*	0	1 (?)

[a] Details for individual pairs are presented in Schiff *et al.* (1981*b*, pp. 94–5).

on social heredity than all studies of separated twins put together, including Burt's hypothetical study.

On the genetic side, the design would have to be the reverse one. One would need to study children born in contrasted social classes but reared in equivalent environments. We have often pointed out how difficult it is to match environments. It could be done, however, by studying pairs of adoptees of contrasted social origin reared in the same adoptive family. In such a study, one would have to make sure that the adoptive parents are blind to the contrast and that the order of birth is random with respect to the two groups compared. No such study has been reported. Let us now examine briefly what studies have been reported on the influence of social class, either by rearing or by birth.

From the environmental point of view, the IQ scores of adoptive children have been correlated to the occupation of adoptive parents. Low correlations have been reported, both by Burks (1928) and by Leahy (1935). Kamin (1974) has pointed out that the groups of adoptive families were rather homogeneous. In a recent study by Duyme (1981), where the adoptive families were less restricted in range, academic status at age 15 correlated significantly with social class.

In the analysis of environmental variations, two related issues occur repeatedly. The first point is that authors pretending to look for an environmental effect have consistently failed to use an experimental design that would give them the best chance of observing that effect. In the particular case of social class, it should be remembered that the *combined* genetic and non-genetic effects of social class only add up to 20 per cent of the total variance of IQ scores. To have any hope of isolating the effect of social class, one would need to compare the effects of contrasted social conditions. The second point is related to the first one. When the environmental variance that one is trying to study is only 10 to 20 per cent of the total variance, the way in which this total variance is parametrized becomes crucial. Any discrepancy between the real world and the model used can mask the effect one is trying to estimate. In their studies, Burks and Leahy have compared correlations within adoptive families to correlations within ordinary families. In order to interpret the results of such comparisons, it is necessary:

(a) To match the two types of families more accurately than the authors have been able to do.

(b) To make sure that the intercorrelations between the various factors influencing IQ scores are the same in the two types of families.

To illustrate that last point, let us consider an imaginary but not implausible example. Let us imagine that, in ordinary families, the environmental effects of social class were mediated by a single variable: the intensity of the desire to have children. According to our hypothetical model, the number of unwanted children, and hence the number of lower IQ scores, would be higher in the working class. In adoptive families, there are no unwanted children and hence there would be no effect of social class. In this hypothetical case, this would in no way signify that the correlation with social class observed in ordinary families could be interpreted in genetic terms.

An extremely indirect way of analysing the effect of social class was proposed and used by Scarr (1971). Her approach is a good illustration of the importance of the two points made above. In her article, Scarr presented two models of the effect of social class, an environmental model and a genetic one. According to the first model, the broad heritability estimated by the usual comparison between DZ and MZ pairs of twins should decrease with the SES of the parents. According to the genetic model, this heritability should not vary with social class. As it turns out, the observations reported by Scarr, later confirmed by Fischbein (1980), are in agreement with the predictions of her environmental model. The interpretation of these observations, however, is so dependent on the assumptions of her model, that it is completely ambiguous.

A few authors have designed their study so as to be able to observe non genetic effects directly. Instead of using an analysis of variance, i.e. instead of using correlations, these authors have reported the effect of some social changes on the average score of a group. The effect of adoption by White middle-class families has been shown to lead to significant increases in average IQ scores by Skodak and Skeels (1949), by Scarr and Weinberg (1976) and by Schiff et al. (1978). The remarkable fact is that the last study is the only one in which authors have attempted to evaluate the effect of

Table 6.3   *Correlations reported between SES of biological parents and IQ scores of children not reared by them*

Source	Correlation values reported
Burks (1928)	0.07
Lawrence (1931)	0.21 for boys; 0.26 for girls
Munsinger (1975b)	0.674 for White sample
	0.770 for Mexican-American sample

social class rather than the effect of family environment. In the study of Skodak and Skeels, the social class of origin was not controlled. In the study of Scarr and Weinberg, the effect of race is confounded with that of social class.

From the genetic point of view, three authors reported correlation values between the SES of biological parents and IQ scores of children reared outside their biological families. The correlations reported are reproduced above in Table 6.3.

Let us consider each of these results in turn. Since it is never quoted, we reproduce below Burks' report on the correlation between the occupation of biological fathers and the IQ of their adopted children (Burks 1928, p. 249).

First, the occupations of all the true fathers of our foster children for whom we had adequate information were assigned Barr ratings by Mr. Kurtz and myself. Similar ratings were also assigned to the occupations of the foster fathers as listed *at the time application for a child was filed* with the placement agencies. Not all the occupations of fathers and foster fathers in our group were represented by the 100 occupations listed on the Barr Scale, but estimated Barr Scale values were assigned to the occupations not represented on the scale. The objectivity of the ratings was good; 29 random pairs of independent ratings of true fathers by Mr. Kurtz and myself correlated .92 ± .02, and 47 random pairs of our independent ratings of foster fathers' occupations (at time of applying for foster child) correlated .91 ± .02. But the correlations that were found between Barr ratings of the children's true fathers and certain other variables were exceedingly low. They may be summarized thus:

Barr ratings of true fathers	r	P.E.	N
With Barr ratings of foster father	−0.02	0.07	86
With Whittier rating of foster home (at time of our investigation)	0.01	0.07	· 91
With culture rating of foster home (at time of our investigation)	−0.04	0.07	83
With child's I.Q. (at time of our investigation)	0.07	0.07	91

It should also be noted that, although Leahy (1935) presented information on the social status of the biological parents in several tables, she failed to report on the correlation of that status with the IQ of the adopted children.

Lawrence (1931) reported correlations between the average social class of parents and the IQ scores of children reared in an institution. The children had been abandoned before the age of one year and placed in foster homes until they entered primary school. The average age of the children was 12.5 years at the time of the study. Two methodological problems render the correlations reported by Lawrence hard to interpret. First, nothing is known about the foster homes and the possibility of selective placement. The second problem is the extremely poor standardization of the two tests used. The two graphs below are reproduced from Lawrence's (1931) report (Fig. 6.4). These two graphs throw doubts on the genetic interpretation of the correlation reported.

The final 'proof' of the potency of genes associated with social class was provided in 1975 by Munsinger. The reader may remember that, in 1973, Kamin had exposed Burt's work. Apparently, Munsinger presented data of a quality unequalled by any previous adoption study. SES information was given for the two biological parents as well as for the two adoptive parents. The raw data presented by Munsinger (1975b) are reproduced in Table 6.4, as they appeared in *Behavior Genetics*.

The reader may notice that, out of 82 pairs of mates, 48 have the same SES *rank*. This is not surprising. What is surprising is the fact that, in the 34 pairs where the parents differ in SES the difference is always precisely two. Clearly, the SES ratings have been manipulated in such a way that their average value $\bar{X}$ happens to be an integer 82 times out of 82. Two years after the study had been published, when asked about this strange fact by Kamin (1977a), Munsinger (1977) answered 'I cannot report precisely how the original parental intellectual level ratings were generated because they were not done by me personally'. To end this brief summary we can only agree with Kamin (1977b), when he concludes:

When a scientist indicates that he 'cannot report precisely' how his data were obtained, he has nothing to report – and less than nothing if the data fall into 'unusual distributions'.

To summarize this section on social heredity, we can recall the following facts:

1. The social heredity of IQ scores is essentially irrelevant to the various issues concerning the heredity of social status. In particular, it provides no information on the heredity of poverty.
2. The genetic study of individual variations (broad heritability) and of familial transmission (narrow heritability) provides no information

Table 6.4   *Raw data reported by Munsinger (1975b)*

Table IA   *Raw Data for White Families in This Study*

	Biological parents					Adopting parents					
Code	Mother's age	Father's age	Mother's SES	Father's SES	X̄	Mother's age	Father's age	Mother's SES	Father's SES	Father's SES	X̄	Child's IQ rank
01	30	28	4	4	4	32	33	3	3	3	5
02	21	20	3	3	3	29	32	4	6	5	3
03	19	22	2	4	3	28	32	1	1	1	7
04	19	25	3	3	3	22	23	3	5	4	3
05	21	21	2	4	3	25	30	4	4	4	1
06	16	19	5	5	5	29	31	3	1	2	6
07	24	25	4	2	3	29	36	1	1	1	3
08	19	26	3	3	3	33	33	1	1	1	5
09	19	19	2	4	3	38	40	3	1	2	4
10	16	19	3	3	3	33	33	2	4	3	1
11	25	24	4	4	4	23	23	4	4	4	4
12	19	21	2	4	3	30	34	1	1	1	3
13	20	22	4	4	4	26	25	3	3	3	7
14	19	18	2	4	3	37	40	3	5	4	5
15	22	22	3	5	4	34	34	3	5	4	6
16	25	26	2	2	2	34	34	1	1	1	1
17	14	20	4	4	4	32	36	3	1	2	4
18	21	21	3	5	4	29	29	2	4	3	6
19	26	32	2	2	2	30	33	3	5	4	1
20	16	19	3	3	3	27	32	2	2	2	1
21	17	18	3	5	4	36	37	1	3	2	5

Table IB *Raw Data for Mexican-American Families in This Study*

| | Biological parents | | | | | Adopting parents | | | | | |
| | Mother's age | Father's age | Mother's SES | Father's SES | X̄ | Mother's age | Father's age | Mother's SES | Father's SES | X̄ | Child's IQ rank |
Code											
01	27	30	3	3	3	27	29	3	3	3	3
02	38	31	4	4	4	31	31	3	3	3	4
03	19	22	5	3	4	31	43	2	4	3	5
04	15	16	4	4	4	39	40	1	1	1	5
05	17	23	4	2	3	36	43	3	1	2	1
06	31	23	3	3	3	32	33	3	3	3	2
07	17	16	4	4	4	35	33	2	2	2	5
08	22	22	5	3	4	41	45	2	2	2	5
09	32	37	3	3	3	29	35	5	3	4	2
10	15	17	4	2	3	25	29	1	3	2	2
11	16	17	4	4	4	30	35	3	1	2	5
12	17	19	2	2	2	26	32	4	4	4	1
13	15	20	4	4	4	39	44	2	4	3	5
14	32	42	2	2	2	35	37	4	4	4	3
15	15	17	4	2	3	26	34	4	4	4	4
16	17	17	2	2	2	33	35	1	1	1	3
17	18	22	5	3	4	34	36	3	3	3	5
18	18	20	2	2	2	41	46	4	2	3	2
19	19	25	3	3	3	30	30	4	4	4	4
20	21	23	5	3	4	34	42	4	4	4	4

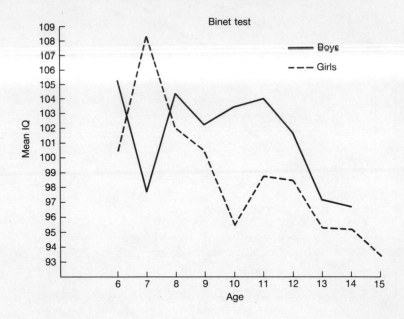

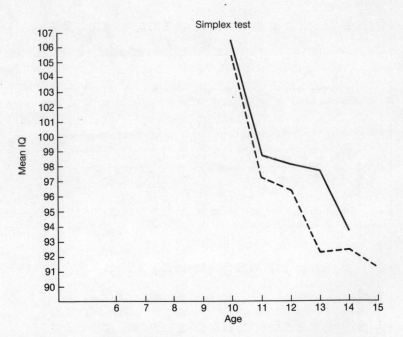

Fig. 6.4 Effect of age on IQ as reported by Lawrence (1931). (From *British Journal of Psychology, Monogr. Suppl.* **16**)

on the transmission of differences between groups defined as social heredity.

3. On the genetic side of social heredity, two positive results are plagued by gross methodological uncertainties. One negative result is never quoted.

4. On the non-genetic side, the results have been mostly indirect and contradictory. Also their interpretation is completely dependent on arbitrary assumptions.

5. Direct observations of non-genetic effects give positive results; however, only one of these observations is directly relevant to the issue of social heredity.

6. None of the heritability coefficients provide information on educability. If it corresponded to observed facts, the opening phrase of Jensen's article ('Compensatory education has been attempted, it has failed'), would only describe the permanence of class and race bias, not of genes.

In other words, the authors of genetic studies and the reviewers of these studies have become obsessed with IQ scores and have gone to great lengths to avoid facing the facts related to social class.

4. Separated twins strike out again

The latest study of MZ twins brought up 'apart' is a twin study directed by Bouchard. As a way of ending this chapter as well as the book, we present here a short analysis of an early report on that study published in 1980. This report seems to us to epitomize some of the confusion we have been analysing. The report was not a scientific publication by Bouchard but a journalistic report by the editorial staff of *Science* magazine.

The report concerns the first nine pairs of identical twins of the study; at the time of the report, 11 additional pairs were due to be included in the study. For three of the nine pairs, the report lists a number of amazing coincidences:

Bridget and Dorothy
. . . the manicured hand of each bore seven rings. Each also wore two bracelets on one wrist and a watch and a bracelet on the other . . . They named their sons Richard Andrew and Andrew Richard, respectively, and their daughters Catherine Louise and Karen Louise.

Jim Springer and Jim Lewis
Both liked math and did not like spelling in school. Both had law enforcement

training and worked part time as deputy sheriffs. Both vacationed in Florida, both drove Chevrolets . . . Both had dogs named Toy. Both married and divorced women named Linda and had second marriages with women named Betty. They named their sons James Allan and James Alan respectively. Both like mechanical drawing and carpentry. They have almost identical drinking and smoking patterns. Both chew their fingernails down to the nubs.

Oskar and Jack
Both were wearing wire-rimmed glasses and mustaches, both sported two-pocket shirts with epaulets. They share idiosyncracies galore: they like spicy foods and sweet liqueurs, are absent minded, have a habit of falling asleep in front of the television, think it's funny to sneeze in a crowd of strangers, flush the toilet before using it, store rubber bands on their wrists, read magazines from back to front, dip buttered toast in their coffee. Oskar is domineering toward women and yells at his wife, which Jack did before he was separated.

The report contains the inevitable pictures of similarly looking twins. It also mentions some medical and temperamental similarities. About IQ, the only quantitative data concerns a pair with a 24 point difference; however, the report also contains the following statement: 'the scores of identical twins on many psychological and ability tests are closer than would be expected for the same person taking the same test twice'.

From the above information, the reader may think that we are simply describing a piece of sensational journalism. Four facts, however, reveal the real significance of the report.

1. The only headline within the report is a quote from the investigators: ' . . . native ability will show . . . over a broad range of backgrounds'.

2. Included in the above report is a one page article on a 'Bank for Nobel sperm', mentioning the eugenic plans of Nobel laureate Herrman Muller. It also mentions Shockley's plans:

In an address to the American Psychological Association, for instance, he proposed that the government pay $1000 for every IQ point below 100 to welfare clients willing to submit to sterilization. This, he said, would shrink welfare rolls within a generation.

3. The report mentions that the Minnesota twin study 'finally got some money from the National Science Foundation'.

4. The above report, with the encapsulated article on sperm bank appeared in a leading journal of the scientific establishment (*Science* **207**, pp. 1323–8).

Appendix. The reliability of secondary sources

In his book, Kamin (1974) devoted a whole chapter to the question of secondary sources. Reviewers and authors of textbooks have often made the following errors:

Table 6.5 *Examples of biased reporting of results by reviewers*

	Results reported by			
	Erlenmer-Kimling and Jarvik (1963)[d]	Jensen (1969)	Jencks (1972, App. A)	Vandenberg (1971)
Results favouring a genetic model				
Skodak and Skeels (1949)[a]	No	Yes	Yes	Yes
Burks (1928)	Yes	Yes	Yes	Yes
Leahy (1935)	Yes	Yes	Yes	No
Results favouring an environmental model				
Skodak and Skeels (1949)[b]	No	No	No	No
Snygg (1938)	No	No	No	No
Sims (1931)	Yes	No	No	No
Burks (1928)[c]	No	No	No	No
Skodak (1950)	No	No	Yes	No

[a] Correlation between biological mother and adopted child.
[b] Increase in mean IQ scores associated with adoption.
[c] Correlation between SES of biological father and IQ scores of adoptees = 0.07.
[d] See footnote, page 24.

(*a*) Draw conclusions from weak or irrelevant data.
(*b*) Omit studies that do not fit their expectations.
(*c*) A few have even invented or propagated non-existent data.

The first type of errors has been analysed in the text. Here are the main examples of significant omissions. Among the studies of genetic transmission, the study of Snygg (1938) has been omitted by most reviewers (and by most builders of genetic models). The correlation report by Burks (1928) between the social class of the biological fathers of adoptees and the IO scores of these adoptees is 0.07 ± 0.1. This result has been universally ignored. From the environmental point of view, two studies reporting a sizeable correlation have also been omitted frequently. In Table 6.5 we present a summary of the way in which recent reviews have reported on these results. The most remarkable omission is the selective reporting on the study of Skodak and Skeels (1949).

Here are two examples of reporting of non-existent data. In the first example, this improvement is implicit. On page 110 of his book *The inequality of man*, Eysenck wrote in 1973:

The actual facts are very clear-cut, and bear out the deductions from our model. *On the whole**, children separated from their parents early in life, and tested as adolescents or *as adults**, have IQs which correlate with those of *their natural parents** to almost the same extent as would be the case had they been brought up by their biological parents.

---

* Emphasis added.

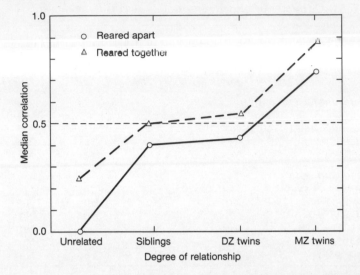

Fig. 6.5   Erroneous graph reproduced by Jensen (1969) without ackowledgement of source. This graph contains data on non-existent studies of DZ twins reared apart.

The facts reported in the scientific literature as of 1973, however, were quite different:

(*a*)   IQ scores were reported only for biological *mothers*, not for *parents*, since fathers were not tested.

(*b*)   The adopted subjects were not tested as *adults*, but only as children (Snygg) or as adolescents (Skodak and Skeels).

(*c*)   On the one hand, Eysenck implies that there are many adoption studies of biological transmission, on the other hand, he only refers to the results of Skodak and Skeels.

In his book, Kamin (1974) reports a few examples of actual fabrication of data. In his 1969 article, Jensen published the graph reproduced as Fig. 6.5.
Contrary to what that graph indicates, there exists no report on studies of dizygotic twins reared apart. This graph was reproduced in a review article published by Scarr in 1975 and reprinted in 1981. Actually, this graph was originally published by Heber *et al.* (1968) and reproduced by Jensen without acknowledgment of the source.

To place Jensen's 'technical errors' in their social perspective, let us note that he was the principal expert consulted by the US Senate, Select Committee on Equal Educational Opportunity: his contribution represented half of the approximately 800 pages published by the Committee (US Senate 1972).

7. Summary and conclusions

In this book, we have presented a critical view of IQ scores and of their genetic analysis. After a short summary of the book, we shall conclude with a few suggestions concerning the epistemological and political choices that anyone dealing with human behaviour is confronted with.

Summary

In Part I, we presented the main facts concerning the relationship between social class and IQ scores.

Chapter 1 provided a historical perspective on biological determinism and on the social use of IQ tests. This historical perspective challenges the notion that the latest discoveries in molecular biology or even the latest brand of computer analysis (Eysenck 1979) might provide a new approach to the issue of social inequality. When placed in this perspective, biological theories of social inequality and of social heredity appear as alternatives to the disturbing thought that our society may not be living up to its democratic ideals.

In Chapter 2, we presented the main facts and discussed the main issues concerning IQ scores. In particular we stressed (*a*) the correlation with the social class of origin and the close analogy between the social heredity of IQ scores and the social heredity of school failure in primary grades, (*b*) the reluctance of authors to consider social class and the double talk about the distinction between IQ and intelligence, (*c*) the reification of IQ scores and the use of the analysis of variance to mask the effect of social class, and (*d*) the confusion between facts and values in the validation of IQ tests.

In our opinion, the most striking fact of the whole IQ story is the contrast between the use of IQ to account for social heredity and the deliberate or unaware avoidance of a direct analysis of that heredity. The two studies presented in Part II illustrate that contrast.

Chapter 3 described a study of children of manual workers adopted early by upper-middle-class families. As is the case in all studies of environmental effects, the methodology of this study does not allow one to reach any conclusion about the possibility of genetic differences. Instead, the results demonstrate the importance of the social contribution to the school and psychometric failures of working-class children. To the rhetorical question 'How much *could* we boost scholastic achievement and IQ scores?', one can confidently answer 'Enough to eliminate the bulk of the failures currently observed'.

Chapter 4 dealt with the question of unequal access to university. When access to the top decile of the educational ladder is considered, the probability of access varies by a factor greater than 10, depending on the social class of the parents. The analysis of educational data was based on the meritocratic model. According to this model, the level of education that a student is capable of reaching is dependent on an innate quality closely related to IQ scores. The model is conservative, both in its implicit values and in its assumptions about human learning. Nevertheless, it suffices to demonstrate the following: (*a*) the percentage of 'waste' due to social discrimination increases as one goes up the educational ladder, and (*b*) at the university level, the question of genetic differences between groups becomes irrelevant to the issue of 'waste'.

In Part III, we presented an overview of the genetic analysis of IQ scores, first from a theoretical viewpoint, then through a systematic analysis of available studies. This overview confirms the fact that scientific efforts have been inversely proportional to their social relevance.

Chapter 5 analysed twelve errors about genetics and their social consequences. Error 1 consists in thinking that the ranking of phenotypes can provide some approximation to a ranking of genotypes. Error 2 is the confusion between heritability and lack of malleability or lack of educability. Error 3 is the confusion between the causes of individual differences and the causes of group differences. Error 4 consists in using familiality as an indication of genetic transmission. Error 5 consists in confusing correlation with equality. Error 6 is the confusion between genetic variability (broad heritability) and genetic transmission (narrow heritability). Errors 7 and 8 are based on the confusion between a statistical law (normality or regression to the mean) and a biological law. Error 9 is the confusion between correlation and causation. Error 10 consists in using an analysis of variance to evaluate the importance of social class. Error 11 is the confusion between observations of a status quo and some 'natural' law. Error 12 consists in relying on complex multiparametric models to compensate for the inadequacy of the raw data and the inadequacy of the theory underlying the analysis.

Chapter 6 provided an overall view of the genetic studies of IQ scores. These studies were classified according to two dimensions. The first dimension concerns the type of phenomenon being analysed (individual variations, familial transmission, social heredity). The second dimension is the extent to which the study can provide information on genetic processes. In most studies, genetic and environmental processes are confounded; in some studies, environmental processes are studied and used as indirect indications of genetic processes; in some rare studies, attempts have been made to isolate genetic processes directly. The reference to these two dimensions shows that practically all studies are irrelevant to the genetic

theory of social heredity. In addition, the studies are often methodologically inadequate, to say the least.

In trying to summarize biological myths about unequal schooling, we can
evoke the French playwriter Molière. In one of his plays, he portrays a
young woman who pretends to have lost the ability to speak, in order to
resist a marriage imposed by her father. The alarmed father calls a pseudo-
doctor named Sganarelle, who displays his ignorance by locating the heart
of his patient on her right side and insisting that this is the latest word in
medical science ('But we have changed all that'). After a confused speeech
about body fluids, Sganarelle ends the consultation by telling the father
'Now this is precisely what makes your daughter dumb'.

In a similar manner, some people now invoke the science of biology to
explain differential access to education among children of the various
classes of society. Had he been writing today, Molière might have described their arguments as follows:

Now this IQ I am talking about, whose very name demonstrates that it measures
intelligence, is distributed according to a law that we mathematicians call normal
law; moreover, the sons resemble their fathers, because the coefficient of regression is equal to the coefficient of correlation, that latter being the name that we statistical experts use to designate the common part of the variance; hence the sons of
the poor will be poor; now this variance, which was analysed by Sir Cyril Burt
according to the polygenic model developed by Fisher turns out to be undeniably of
a genetic nature, since two twins reared apart both wear seven rings, so that we
geneticists have come to the conclusion that the phenotype, which causes the male
ape to be superior to the female one, is confounded with the genotype, itself
located in DNA, which we biochemists call desoxyribonucleic acid. Now this is precisely why Johnny cannot read.

2. Conclusions

Two related issues have been intertwined in this book. On the one hand,
we have examined the relevance of genetic studies of IQ scores to the issue
of education and social class. On the other hand, we have illustrated how a
significant fraction of the scientific establishment has handled this issue in
what appeared to be an inappropriate way.

Eisenberg (1972) has dealt with related issues in an article titled 'The
human nature of human nature'. The concept of species is a key concept of
biology and yet it is hardly used by those who consider *Homo sapiens* as an
elaborate rat or as a naked ape. Some scientists do not like to consider the
issue of the specificity of *Homo sapiens* because they do not know how. So
they analyse DNA chains and show that our DNA chains only differ by one
or two per cent from those of neighbouring species or they try to see how
many 'words' they can teach an ape. Or they construct models of social

inequality based on observations of genetic differences between 'maze-dull' and 'maze-bright' rats.

The psychometric approach to human intelligence misses at least one important qualitative feature of human intelligence, namely the capacity to ask questions, to oneself and to others. The biological significance of this capacity for the survival of our species was stressed in a humorous way by a Harvard mathematician in a song where he had Werner von Braun state 'Don't ask me where the rockets fall, that's not my department' (Tom Lehrer 1965).

The biological deterministic approach to human behavior misses another specific feature of *Homo sapiens*. In part the human animal constructs itself, both individually and socially. It is *Homo sapiens* who decides, consciously or unconsciously, how his society is organized or whether he will annihilate his species.

When it comes to the question of freedom and determinism of their own behaviour, most workers within academia seem to us to be under two contradictory illusions. The first is the illusion of complete academic freedom: there is a denial or lack of awareness of social and economic pressures influencing scientific workers. The second illusion is the opposite one: it is the illusion of complete helplessness, as if one's behaviour were completely *determined* by external processes, rather than simply *influenced* by these processes. Most scientists fail to recognize that the type of question they ask and the type they choose to ignore derive both from social pressure and from a personal choice.

For a scientist dealing with human behaviour, the crucial choice seems to us to be the following. Either we choose to help others to adapt to the existing society or we choose to help them change that society. This choice is not simply a political choice but also an epistemologic one.

Most scientists have been taught to believe that there is a contradiction between knowing reality and getting involved with that reality. We believe that in the specific case of socially significant behaviour, this is scientifically unsound because some essential element of the reality of social processes will forever escape those who refuse to participate in them.

If this belief is correct, the amount of knowledge about child behaviour accumulated among schoolteachers is greater and of a different sort than that accumulated by academic psychologists. Even more instructive than participating in educational processes is the fact of trying to change them. By attempting to change a process, we put our assumptions about that process to a very stringent test.

The idea that scientists may not possess the most important part of the existing knowledge about human behaviour, specifically about human intelligence, may not be very popular among PhD's in psychology. But those who believe that they have a monopoly on something may not be the best judges of the legitimacy of that monopoly.

When we consider stars or atoms as objects of knowledge, the mere observation of these objects requires highly specialized instruments. Both the facts and the theory about these facts are available only to specialists. In contra-distinction, the direct observation of human mental processes is potentially available to four billion observers. The scientific authority granted to a few concerning the functioning of the human mind may then be largely usurped.

Seen in a positive way, this would mean that everybody, including scientists, would gain by an exchange of knowledge between those people who try to interpret the world of human affairs and those who try to change it.

References

Adair, R. K. (1969). *Concepts in physics*. Academic Press, New York.

Albee, C. (1971). The evaluation, judgment, placement process. In *Placement of children in special classes for the retarded*, pp. 5–28. The President's Committee on Mental Retardation, Washington, D.C.

Anastasi, A. (1982). *Psychological testing* (5th edn). Macmillan, New York. (2nd edn, 1961).

Bajema, C. J. (1963). Estimation of the direction and intensity of natural selection in relation to human intelligence by means of the intrinsic rate of natural increase. *Eugenics Quarterly* **10**, 175–87.

Bayley, N. (1970). Development of mental abilities. In *Carmichael's manual of child psychology* (ed. P. H. Mussen), pp. 1163–1209. Wiley and Sons, New York.

Block, N. J. and Dworkin, G. (1976). *The IQ controversy: critical readings*. Random House, New York.

Bloom, B. S. (1964). *Stability and change in human characteristics*. Wiley and Sons, New York.

Bouchard, T. J. and McGue, M. (1981). Familial studies of intelligence: a review. *Science* **212**, 1055–9.

Bowles, S. and Gintis, H. (1973). I.Q. in the U.S. class structure. *A Warner Module Publication*, Reprint 296, pp. 1–27 (reprinted from *Social Policy* **3**, nos 4 and 5).

Bowles, S. and Nelson, V. I. (1974). The 'Inheritance of IQ' and the Intergenerational Reproduction of Economic Inequality. *The Review of Economics and Statistics* **56**, 39–51.

Bradford, E. J. G. (1937). The relation of intelligence to varying birth-rate in different social grades. *British Journal of Educational Psychology* **7**, 229–45.

Burks, B. S. (1928). The relative influence of nature and nurture upon mental development; a comparative study of foster parent–foster child resemblance and true parent–true child resemblance. *Yearbook of the National Society for the Study of Education* **27**(I), 219–316.

Buros, O. K. (1978). *Mental measurements yearbook* (8th edn). Gryphon Press, Highlands Park, New Jersey.

Burt, C. (1909). Experimental tests of general intelligence. *British Journal of Psychology* **3**, 94–177.

Burt, C. (1946). Intelligence and fertility. The effect of the differential birthrate on inborn mental characteristics. *Occasional papers on eugenics*, no. 2.

Burt, C. (1958). The inheritance of mental ability. *Amer. Psychologist* **13**, 1–15.

Burt, C. (1966). The genetic determination of differences in intelligence: a study of monozygotic twins reared together and apart. *British Journal of Psychology* **57**, 137–53.

Carter, C. O. (1954). Differential fertility and intelligence. *Bulletin of the World Federation of Mental Health* **6**, 101–3.

Cassou, B., Schiff, M., and Stewart, J. (1980). Génétique et Schizophrénie: réévaluation d'un consensus. *Pschychiatrie de l'enfant* **23**, 87–201.

Cattell, R. B. (1937). *The fight for our national intelligence*. P. S. King and Son, London.

Cattell, R. B. (1974). *Test de facteur 'g'*. Editions du Centre de Psychologie Appliquée, Paris.

Cavalli-Sforza, L. L. and Bodmer, W. F. (1971). *The genetics of human populations*. W. H. Freeman, San Francisco.

CERC (Centre d'Etude des Revenus et des Coûts) (1977). *Les revenus des Français*. Albatros, Paris.

Chiland, C. (1971). *L'enfant de six ans et son avenir: étude psychopathologique*. PUF, Paris.

Coleman, J. S. *et al.* (1966). *Equality of educational opportunity*. US Department of Health, Education and Welfare, US Government Printing Office, Washington D.C.

Connolly, K. (1980). Introduction. In *A balance sheet on Burt* (ed. H. Beloff). *Bulletin of the British Psychological Society* **33**, sup. i.

Cronbach, L. J. (1975). Five decades of public controversy over mental testing. *American Psychologist* **30**, 1–14.

Dennis, W. (1942). The performance of Hopi children on the Goodenough Draw-a-Man Test. *J. Comp. Psychol.* **34**, 341–8.

Dennis, W. (1966). Goodenough scores, art experience, and modernization. *Journal of Social Psychology* **68**, 211–28.

Dumaret, A. C. (1979). Développement intellectuel et scolaire de frères et soeurs élevés en milieux sociaux différents. Analyse comparative de la descendance de 28 femmes d'origine sociale défavorisée. *Thèse de psychologie appliquée pour le doctorat du 3e cycle*. Université Paris V.

Dumaret, A. C. (1985). IQ, scholastic performance and behaviour of sibs raised in contrasting environments. *Journal of Child Psychology and Psychiatry* **26**, 553–80.

Duyme, M. (1981). *Les enfants abandonnés: rôle des familles adoptives et des assistantes maternelles*. Editions du CNRS, Paris.

Eaves, L. J. (1973). Assortative mating and intelligence: an analysis of pedigree data. *Heredity* **30**, 199–210.

Eisenberg, L. (1972). The *human* nature of human nature. *Science* **176**, 123–8.

Erlenmeyer-Kimling, L. and Jarvik, L. F. (1963). Genetics and intelligence: a review. *Science* **142**, 1477–9.

Eysenck, H. J. (1971). *Race, intelligence and education*. Temple Smith, London.

Eysenck, H. J. (1973). *The inequality of man*. Temple Smith, London.

Eysenck, H. J. (1979). *The structure and measurement of intelligence*. Springer Verlag, Berlin, Heidelberg, New York.

Eysenck, H. J. versus Kamin, L. (1981). *The intelligence controversy*. John Wiley, New York.

Falconer, D. S. (1981). *Introduction to quantitative genetics* (2nd edn). Longman, London and New York.

Feldman, M. W. and Lewontin, R. C. (1975). The heritability hang-up. *Science* **190**, 1163–8.

Fisch, R. O., Bilek, M. K., Deinard, A. S. and Pi-Nian, C. (1976). Growth, behavioral, and psychologic measurements of adopted children. *Journal of Pediatrics* **89**, 494–500.

Fischbein, S. (1980). IQ and social class. *Intelligence* **4**, 51–63.

Fisher, R. A. (1918). The correlation between relatives on the supposition of Mendelian inheritance. *Transactions of the Royal Society of Edinburgh* **52**, 399–433.

Fisher, R. A. (1930). *The genetical theory of natural selection*. Clarendon Press, Oxford.

Fisher, R. A. (1951). Limits to intensive production in animals, *British Agricultural Bulletin* **4**, 217–18.

Flynn, J. R. (1980). *Race, IQ and Jensen*. Routledge and Kegan Paul, London.

Freeman, F. N., Holzinger, K. J. and Mitchell, B. C. (1928). The influence of environment on the intelligence, school achievement, and conduct of foster children. *27th Yearbook of the National Society for the Study of Education*, Part I, 103–217.

Fuller, J. L. and Thompson, W. R. (1960). *Behavior Genetics*. John Wiley, New York.

Galton, F. (1869). *Hereditary genius: an inquiry into its laws and consequences*. Macmillan, London (2nd edn., 1892).

Galton, F. (1883). *Inquiries into human faculty and its development*. Macmillan, London.

Girard, A., Bastide, H. and Pourcher, G. (1963). Enquête nationale sur l'entrée en sixième et démocratisation de l'enseignement. *Population* 9–48.

Goddard, H. H. (1917). Mental tests and the immigrant. *Journal of Delinquency* **2**, 243–77.

Goddard, H. H. (1920). *Human efficiency and levels of intelligence*. Princeton University Press, Princeton.

Goodenough, F. L. (1926). Racial differences in the intelligence of school children. *Journal of Experimental Psychology* **9**, 388–97.

Goodenough, F. L. and Harris, D. B. (1950). Studies in the psychology of children's drawings: II, 1928–1949. *Psychological Bulletin* **47**, 369–433.

Gottesman, I. I. (1968). Biogenetics of race and class. In *Social class, race, and psychological development* (eds M. Deutsch, I. Katz and A. R. Jensen), pp. 11–51. Holt, Rinehart, and Winston, New York.

Gould, J. S. (1981). *The mismeasure of man*. Norton and Co., New York and London.

Guterman, S. S. (1980). Social class and IQ revisited: a path analytic study of environmental mediators. Paper presented at the 1980 annual meeting of the American Sociological Association in New York.

Halsey, A. H. (1958). Genetics, social structure and intelligence. *Brit. J. Sociol.* **9**, 15–28.

Halsey, A. H. (ed.) (1977). *Heredity and environment*. Methuen, London.

Halsey, A. H., Heath, A. F. and Ridge, J. M. (1980). *Origins and destinations. Family, class and education in modern Britain*. Clarendon Press, Oxford.

Havighurst, R. J., Gunther, M. K. and Pratt, I. E. (1946). Environment and the Draw-a-Man Test: The performance of Indian children. *Journal of Abnormal and Social Psychology* **41**, 50–63.

Heber, R., Dever, R. and Conry, J. (1968). The influence of environmental and genetic variables on intellectual development. In *Behavioral research in mental retardation* (eds Prehm *et al.*) pp. 1–22. University of Oregon Press, Eugene.

Henmon, V. A. C. and Nelson, M. J. (1942). *The Henmon-Nelson Test of Mental Ability*. Houghton Mifflin, Boston.

Herrnstein, R. J. (1971). IQ. *The Atlantic Monthly* September, 43–64.

Herrnstein, R. J. (1973). *IQ in the meritocracy*. Little, Brown and Co., Boston.

Higgins, J. V., Reed, E. W. and Reed, S. C. (1962). Intelligence and family size: a paradox resolved. *Eugenics Quarterly* **9**, 84–90.

Hirsch, J. (1981). To unfrock the charlatans. *SAGE Race Relation Abstracts* **6**, 1–65.

Hogben, L. (1933). The limits of applicability of correlation technique in human genetics. *Journal of Genetics* **27**, 379–406.

Horn, J. M., Loehlin, J. C. and Willerman, L. (1979). Intellectual resemblance among adoptive and biological relatives: the Texas adoption project. *Behavior Genetics* **9**, 177–201.

INED (1950). Le niveau intellectuel des enfants d'âge scolaire. *Travaux et Documents* Cahier no. 13. PUF, Paris.

INED–INOP (1973). *Enquête nationale sur le niveau intellectuel des enfants d'âge scolaire.* Vol. II. PUF, Paris.

INSEE (1968). *Code no. 2 du recensement de la population de 1968. Code des métiers. Index analytique détaillé et index alphabétique détaillé.* Imprimerie Nationale, Paris.

INSEE (1974). L'enquête formation-qualification professionnelle de 1970. *Collection D.* Vol. 32.

INSEE (1978). *Données sociales. Annexe 1, quelques résultats du recensement de 1975.* Imprimerie Nationale, Paris.

Jacquard, A. (1984). *In praise of difference.* Columbia University Press, New York.

Jencks, C. (1972). *Inequality, a reassessment of the effect of family and schooling in America.* Basic Books, New York and London.

Jensen, A. R. (1969). How much can we boost IQ and scholastic achievement? *Harvard Educational Review* **39**, 1–123.

Jensen, A. R. (1972). *Genetics and education.* Methuen, London.

Jensen, A. R. (1974). Kinship correlations reported by Sir Cyril Burt. *Behavior Genetics* **4**, 1–28.

Jensen, A. R. (1980). *Bias in mental testing.* Methuen, London.

Juel-Nielsen, N. (1965). *Individual and environment. A psychiatric-psychological investigation of monozygotic twins reared apart.* Munksgaard, Copenhagen.

Kamin, L. J. (1973). Heredity, intelligence, politics, and psychology. *Invited address.* Eastern Psychological Association.

Kamin, L. J. (1974). *The science and politics of IQ.* Lawrence Erlbaum Associates, Potomac.

Kamin, L. J. (1977a). Comment on Munsinger's adoption study. *Behavior Genetics* **7**, 403–6.

Kamin, L. J. (1977b). A reply to Munsinger. *Behavior Genetics* **7**, 411–12.

Kaufman, A. S. and Doppelt, J. E. (1976). Analysis of WISC-R Standardization data in terms of the stratification variables. *Child Development* **47**, 165–71.

Kempthorne, O. (1957). *An introduction to genetic statistics.* John Wiley and Sons, New York.

Lawler, J. M. (1978). *IQ, Heritability and Racism.* International Publishers, New York.

Lawrence, E. M. (1931). An investigation into the relation between intelligence and inheritance. *British Journal of Psychology. Monograph Supplements* **16**, 1–80.

Layzer, D. (1974). Heritability analyses of IQ scores: science or numerology? *Science* **183**, 1259–66.

Leahy, A. M. (1935). Nature–nurture and intelligence. *Genetic Psychology Monographs* **17**, 236–308.

Lewontin, R. C. (1970). Race and intelligence. *Bulletin of the Atomic Scientists* March, 2–8.

Lewontin, R. C. (1982). *Human diversity*. Scientific American, Freeman, New York.

Loehlin, J. C., Lindzey, G. and Spuhler, J. N. (1975). *Race differences in intelligence*. W. H. Freeman, San Francisco.

Loehlin, J. C. and Nichols, R. C. (1976). *Heredity, environment and personality*. Unversity of Texas Press, Austin.

Lorenz, K. (1940). Durch Domestikation verursachte Störungen arteigenen Verhaltens. *Zeitschrift für angewandte Psychologie and Charakterkunde* **59**, 2–81.

Mackenzie, B. (1980). Fallacious use of regression effects in the IQ controversy. *Australian Psychologist* **15**, 369–84.

McAskie, M. and Clarke, A. M. (1976). Parent–offspring resemblances in intelligence: theories and evidence. *British Journal of Psychology* **67**, 243–73.

McCall, R. B., Hogarty, P. S. and Hurlburt, N. (1972). Transitions in infant sensorimotor development and the prediction of childhood IQ. *American Psychologist* 728–48.

McCartin, R. A., Dingman, H. F., Meyers, C. E. and Mercer, J. R. (1966). Identification and disposition of the mentally handicapped in the parochial school system. *American Journal of Mental Deficiency* **71**, 201–6.

McKusick, V. A. (1964). *Human genetics*. Prentice Hall, Englewood Cliffs.

Mayhew, H. (1851). *London labor and the London poor*. Harper and Bros., New York.

Miller, G. W. (1970). Factors in school achievement and social class. *Journal of Educational Psychology* **61**, 260–9.

Ministère de l'Education, SEIS (1975). L'échantillon dit 'panel d'élèves', résultat des enquêtes 1973–1974. *Etudes et Documents* No. 32.

Ministère de l'Education, SEIS (1976). L'échantillon dit 'panel d'élèves', principaux résultats de l'enquête 1974–1975. *Etudes et Documents* No. 35.

Ministère de l'Education, SEIS (1978). *Document* No. 4813.

Ministère de l'Education, SEIS (1979a). *Document* No. 4899.

Ministère de l'Education, SEIS (1979b). *Document* No. 4924.

Moshinsky, P. (1939). The correlation between fertility and intelligence within social classes. *Sociological Review* **31**, 144–65.

Muller, H. J. (1966). What genetic course will man steer? In *Proceedings of the third international congress of human genetics* (eds J. F. Crow and J. V. Neel) pp. 521–43. Johns Hopkins Press, Baltimore.

Munsinger, H. (1975a). The adopted child's IQ: a critical review. *Psychological Bulletin* **82**, 623–59.

Munsinger, H. (1975b). Children's resemblance to their biological and adoptive parents in two ethnic groups. *Behavior Genetics* **5**, 239–254.

Munsinger, H. (1977). A reply to Kamin. *Behavior Genetics* **7**, 407–9.

Newman, H. H., Freeman, F. N. and Holzinger, K. J. (1937). *Twins: a study of heredity and environment*. The University of Chicago Press, Chicago.

OECD (1967). *Social objectives in educational planning*. OECD, Paris.

OECD (1971). *Group disparities in educational participation and achievement* **IV**. OECD, Paris.

OECD (1974). *Educational statistics yearbook*. Vol. I. *International tables*. OECD, Paris.

OECD (1975a). *Education, inequality and life chances*. OECD, Paris.

OECD (1975*b*). *Educational statistics yearbook*. Vol. II. *Country tables*. OECD, Paris.

O'Hanlon, G. S. A. (1940). An investigation into the relationship between fertility and intelligence. *British Journal of Educational Psychology* **10**, 196–211.

Papavassiliou, I. T. (1954). Intelligence and family size. *Population Studies* **7**, 222–6.

Paul, S. M. (1980). Sibling resemblance in mental ability: a review. *Behavior Genetics* **10**, 277–90.

Pearson, K. (1902–1903). The law of ancestral heredity. *Biometrika* **2**, 211–236.

Pearson, K. and Moul, M. (1925). The problem of alien immigration into Great Britain, illustrated by an examination of Russian and Polish Jewish children. *Annals of Eugenics* **1**, 5–127.

Penrose, L. S. (1963). *Outline of human genetics* (2nd edn). Wiley and Sons, New York.

Plomin, R. and de Fries, J. C. (1980). Genetics and intelligence: recent data. *Intelligence* **4**, 15–24.

Psychologie (1981). No. 134, p. 5.

Richardson, L. F. (1913). The measurement of mental 'nature' and the study of adopted children. *Eugenics Review* **4**, 391–4.

Roberts, J. A. F., Norman, R. M., and Griffiths, R. (1938). Studies on a child population. III. Intelligence and family size. *Annals of Eugenics* **8**, 178–215.

Roberts, J. A. F. (1941). The negative association between intelligence and fertility. *Human Biology* **13**, 410–12.

Ryan, W. (1971). *Blaming the victim*. Pantheon Books, New York.

Scarr, S. (1971). Race, social class and IQ. *Science* **174**, 1285–95.

Scarr, S. (ed.) (1981). *Race, social class and individual differences in IQ*. Lawrence Erlbaum Associates, Hillsdale, New Jersey.

Scarr, S. and Weinberg, R. A. (1976). IQ test performance of Black children adopted by white families. *American Psychologist* **31**, 726–39.

Scarr, S. and Weinberg, R. A. (1977*a*). Rediscovering old truths, or a word by the wise is sometimes lost. *American Psychologist*, **32**, 681–3.

Scarr, S. and Weinberg, R. A. (1977*b*). Intellectual similarities within families of both adopted and biological children. *Intelligence* **1**, 170–91.

Scarr, S. and Weinberg, R. A. (1978). The influence of 'family background' on intellectual attainment: the unique contribution of adoptive studies to estimating environmental effects. *American Sociological Review* **43**, 674–92.

Schiff, M. (1980). L'échec scolaire n'est pas inscrit dans les chromosomes. *Psychologie* **131**, 51–6.

Schiff, M. (1981). The social waste of academic potential: the IQ hang-up. *6th International Congress of Human Genetics*. (abstract P 15.1).

Schiff, M. (1982*a*). How much can we boost academic achievement? Apparently a lot. *Behavior Genetics* **12**, 354–5 (abstract).

Schiff, M. (1982*b*). *L'intelligence gaspillée; inegalité sociale, injustice scolaire*. Editions du Seuil, Paris.

Schiff, M., Cassou, B. and Feingold, J. (1981*a*). Difficultés d'un recours à la génétique dans l'analyse de certains comportements humains. In *Génétique médicale* (ed. J. Feingold). INSERM/Flammarion Médecine, Paris.

Schiff, M., Duyme, M., Dumaret, A. and Tomkiewicz, S. (1981*b*). *Enfants de* travailleurs manuels adoptés par des cadres: effet d'un changement de catégorie sociale sur le cursus scolaire et les notes de QI. PUF, Paris.

Schiff, M., Duyme, M., Dumaret, A. and Tomkiewicz, S. (1982). How much *could* we boost scholastic achievement and IQ scores: a direct answer from a French adoption study. *Cognition* **12**, 165–96.

Schiff, M., Duyme, M., Dumaret, A., Stewart, J., Tomkiewicz, S. and Feingold, J. (1978). Intellectual status of working-class children adopted early into upper-middle-class families. *Science* **200**, 1503–1504.

Science (1980). News and comment. Identical twins reared apart. *Science* **207**, 1323–8.

Scott, E. M. and Nisbet, J. D. (1955). Intelligence and family size in an adult sample. *Eugenics Review* **46**, 233–5.

Scottish Council for Research in Education (1953). *Social implications of the 1947 Scottish mental survey*. University of London Press, London.

Seashore, H., Wesman, A. and Doppelt, J. (1950). The standardization of the Wechsler intelligence scale for children. *Journal of Consulting Psychology* **14**, 99–110.

Sewell, W. H. and Shah, V. P. (1967). Socioeconomic status, intelligence, and the attainment of higher education. *Sociology of Education* **40**, 1–23.

Sherwood, J. J. and Nataupsky, M. (1968). Predicting the conclusions of negro–white intelligence research from biological characteristics of the investigator. *J. Pers. Soc. Psychol.* **8**, 53–8.

Shields, J. (1962). *Monozygotic twins brought up apart and brought up together*. Oxford University Press, London.

Shuey, A. M. (1958). *The testing of Negro intelligence*. Bell, Lynchburg, Virginia.

Sims, V. M. (1931). The influence of blood relationship and common environment on measured intelligence. *J. Educational Psychol.* **22**, 56–65.

Sinnott, E. W., Dunn, L. C. and Dobzhansky, T. (1950). *Principles of genetics* (4th edn). McGraw Hill, New York.

Skeels, H. M. (1966). Adult status of children with contrasting early life experiences. *Monographs of the Society for Research in Child Development* **31**, No. 3, serial No. 105.

Skeels, H. M. and Skodak, M. (1965). Techniques for a high-yield follow-up study in the field. *Public Health Reports* **80**, 249–57.

Skodak, M. (1950). Mental growth of adopted children in the same family. *Journal of Genetic Psychology* **77**, 3–9.

Skodak, M. and Skeels, H. M. (1949). A final follow-up study of one hundred adopted children. *Journal of Genetic Psychology* **75**, 85–125.

Snygg, D. (1938). The relation between the intelligence of mothers and of their children living in foster homes. *Journal of Genetic Psychology* **52**, 401–6.

Spearman, C. (1914). The heredity of abilities. *Eugenics Review* **6**, 219–37.

Spiess, E. B. (1977). *Genes in populatins*. John Wiley and Sons, New York.

Spuhler, K. P. and Vandenberg, S. G. (1980). Comparison of parent–offspring resemblance for specific cognitive abilities. *Behavior Genetics* **10**, 413–18.

Srb, A., Owen, R. and Edgar, R. (1965). *General genetics* (2nd edn.). W. H. Freeman, San Francisco.

Stern, C. (1973). *Principles of human genetics* (3rd edn). W. H. Freeman, San Francisco.

Stern, W. (1914). *The psychological methods of testing intelligence*. Warwick and York, Baltimore.

Sutton, H. E. (1965). *An Introduction to Human Genetics*. Holt, Rinehart and Winston, New York.

Suzuki, D. T. Griffiths, A. J. F. and Lewontin, R. C. (1981). *An introduction to genetic analaysis*, 2^d edition W. H. Freeman, San Francisco.

Taylor, H. F. (1980). *The IQ game*. Rutgers University Press, New Brunswick, New Jersey.

Terman, L. M. (1916). *The measurement of intelligence*. Houghton Mifflin, Boston.

Terman, L. M. and Merrill, M. A. (1937). *Measuring intelligence*. Houghton Mifflin, Boston.

Terman, L. M., Lyman, G., Ordahl, G. Ordahl, L. E., Galbreath, N., and Talbert, W. (1917). The Stanford revision and extension of the Binet–Simon scale for measuring intelligence. *Educational Psychology Monographs* No. 18.

Thomson, G. (1946). The trend of national intelligence. *Eugenics Review* **38**, 9–18.

Thorndike, E. L. (1916). *Educational psychology: briefer course*. Columbia University Press, New York.

UNESCO (1967). *Conférence des ministres de l'éducation des états membres d'Europe sur l'accès à l'enseignement supérieur*. Vienna, MINEUROP/3.

US Senate, Select Committee on Equal Educational Opportunity (1972). *Environment, intelligence and scholastic achievement. A compilation of testimony*. 77–942 O. US Government Printing Office, Washington D.C.

Vandenberg, S. G. (1971). What do we known today about the inheritance of intelligence and how do we know it? In *Intelligence: genetic and environmental influences* (ed. R. Cancro), pp. 182–218. Grune and Stratton, New York.

Wechsler, D. (1965). *Manuel. Echelle d'intelligence de Wechsler pour enfants (étalonnages français). WISC*. Editions du Centre de Psychologie Appliquée, Paris.

Wechsler, D. (1974). *Manual for the Wechsler intelligence scale for children Revised*. The Psychological Corporation, New York.

Wender, P. H., Rosenthal, D. and Kety, S. S. (1968). A psychiatric assessment of the adoptive parents of schizophrenics. In *The transmission of schizophrenia* (eds D. Rosenthal and S. S. Kety) pp. 235–50. Pergamon Press, Oxford.

Wheeler, L. R. (1942). A comparative study of the intelligence of East Tennessee Mountain children. *Journal of Educational Psychology* **33**, 321–34.

Williams, T. (1975). Family resemblance in abilities: the Wechsler scales. *Behavior Genetics* **5**, 405–9.

Wittinghill, M. (1965). *Human genetics and its foundations*. Reinhold, New York.

de Wolff, P. and Härnqvist, K. (1962). Réserve d'aptitudes: leur importance et leur répartition. In *Aptitude intellectuelle et éducation* (ed. A. H. Halsey). OECD, Paris.

Wright, L. (1969). *Bibliography on human intelligence*. US Department of Health, Education and Welfare, US Government Printing Office, Washington D.C.

Wright, S. (1968). *Evolution and the genetics of populations*. Vol. 1. *Genetic and biometric foundations*. University of Chicago Press, Chicago.

Yerkes, R. M. (1921). Psychological examining in the United States Army. *Memoirs of the National Academy of Science* **15**, 1–890.

Yoakum, C. S. and Yerkes, R. M. (1920). *Army mental tests*. Henry Holt and Co., New York.

Zazzo, R. (1960). *Les jumeaux: le couple et la personne*. PUF, Paris.
Zola, E. (1871). *La fortune des Rougons*, Préface. Librairie internationale, A. Lacroix, Verboeckhoven, Paris.

Name index

Subject index